HOPEWELL CEREMONIAL EARTHWORKS

A grand passage between high walls and deep ditches invites pilgrims into Newark, Ohio's Great Circle Earthworks.

HOPEWELL CEREMONIAL EARTHWORKS

LANDSCAPE MONUMENTS OF THE ANCIENT OHIO VALLEY

JOHN E. HANCOCK

With Marti L. Chaatsmith, Bradley T. Lepper, and Bret J. Ruby

IN ASSOCIATION WITH THE National Museum of the American Indian

Smithsonian Books

WASHINGTON, DC

Published by Smithsonian Books
PO Box 37012, MRC 513
Washington, DC 20013
smithsonianbooks.com

Director: Carolyn Gleason
Senior Editor: Jaime Schwender
Editorial Assistant: Paige Elliott
Digital Imaging Technician: Bill Whitcher

Edited by Joanna Reams
Designed by David Griffin | Moran Griffin, Inc.

This book may be purchased for educational, business, or sales promotional use. For information please write the Special Markets Department at the address or website above.

Library of Congress Cataloging-in-Publication Data available upon request.

Hardcover ISBN: 978-1-58834-812-8

Printed in China
Not at government expense
30 29 28 27 26 1 2 3 4 5

CONTENTS

FOREWORD

The striking, curvilinear design of the National Museum of the American Indian in Washington, DC, stands out from the linear patterns of the National Mall, showcasing a rough-hewn limestone facade and granite walkways that follow the building's curves. In a subtle complement to the building design, specific cosmological references are set into paving stones at the east and south entrances.

The pattern at the east entrance marks the "birth date" of the museum by showing the path and location of the planets that were visible above the horizon on November 28, 1989—the date legislation was signed to create the museum. The spiral moon pattern set into the pavement at the south entrance refers to major lunar standstills—periods of extremes in daily and monthly moonrise and moonset patterns that occur about every nineteen years. Ancestral Puebloan astronomers marked the phenomenon more than a thousand years ago by carving a spiral petroglyph into the rock atop Chaco Canyon's Fajada Butte in present-day New Mexico.

Indigenous peoples were the first astronomers of the Americas, expert observers of the Sun, Moon, and Sky. They documented their experiences in rock carvings, hide paintings, adornment, clothing, art, and the creation of monumental earthworks and ceremonial spaces. The museum celebrates these Indigenous achievements and innovations through its compelling architectural design along with its collections, programs, and scholarship that aim to both engage and educate.

In 1848, the Smithsonian Institution's very first book featured the ancient earthwork-building civilization now called Hopewell, revealing its research on that sophisticated yet little-known culture. The genius of Hopewell archeoastronomy is awe-inspiring; the sacred structures track and align with solar and lunar cycles across time. The museum is proud to support this legacy and encourage preservation and understanding of these important sites, especially for tribal nations as they rediscover the remarkable achievement of their ancestors.

The Hopewell Ceremonial Earthworks are the most recent Indigenous engineering marvels to be named a World Heritage Site among many in the Americas, such as Machu Picchu in Peru and the Qhapaq Ñan Andean Road System, which spans six South American countries. The global recognition for the Hopewell landscape architectural masterpieces underscores the ingenuity and traditional knowledge intrinsic to this ancient culture and its descendent tribal communities..

The Hopewell earthwork builders utilized cutting-edge technologies and managed a vast trading network that reached thousands of miles from their Eastern Woodlands home. Creating enormous, precise geometric earthworks, they developed their skills over time relying on the Indigenous values of reciprocity, respect, and responsibility.

Such values are the keystone of this book. We are honored to partner with the authors of *Hopewell Ceremonial Earthworks* to ensure that this Indigenous-led work reaches the broadest audience possible. The new historical and archaeological knowledge obtained by studying the Hopewell culture and their monuments is significant, and the National Museum of the American Indian is dedicated to sharing these discoveries as part of its mission to educate the broader public about the Indigenous cultures of the Western Hemisphere.

—Cynthia Chavez Lamar (San Felipe Pueblo/Hopi/Tewa/Navajo)

DIRECTOR, SMITHSONIAN'S NATIONAL MUSEUM OF THE AMERICAN INDIAN

The pavement in front of the south entrance of the National Museum of the American Indian in Washington, DC, showcases a spiral moon pattern, referencing major lunar standstills that occur about every nineteen years.

"As Native people, our connections to these and other sites are reflected in a common saying I have heard all my life that 'We walk on the bones of our ancestors' to solemnize our connections to the ones who came before us, as well as to demonstrate our intimate connection to the land."

—JOHN N. LOW
(Pokagon Band of Potawatomi)

Seen from a stone-covered mound in Fort Ancient's North Fort, the winter solstice sunrise appears within one of the site's eighty-four gateways.

PREFACE

In 1848, the Smithsonian Institution published its first book, *Ancient Monuments of the Mississippi Valley,* by two men from Chillicothe, Ohio, named Ephraim Squier and Edwin J. Davis. They had assembled beautiful maps and vistas of scores of earthen mounds and enclosures—most concentrated along the river valleys of southern Ohio—accompanied with careful, often-astonished descriptions of their scope, form, contents, and condition. They did not know who had built them.

When I first saw a copy in the mid-1990s, I had already been teaching Ancient Architecture at the University of Cincinnati for fifteen years, but I had no idea these places existed—indeed, right up the road. Nor did practically anyone I knew, either in my professional architectural history circles or among the public at large. My own astonishment needed to be shared.

So, for more than two decades I cowrote and produced public education and visualization materials about these sites. During that time, I witnessed the gradual growth of mutual respect between archaeologists (who maintained the academic discourse about them) and Indigenous people (who felt ancestral connections to them). After years of participating in collaborative work, I had the privilege of helping to get the Hopewell Ceremonial Earthworks inscribed on the UNESCO World Heritage List in 2023.

World Heritage inscription has now put these amazing places on the global stage—along with Machu Picchu, Stonehenge, the Pyramids, and the Great Wall—as the architectural masterpieces of a sophisticated civilization. In this new role, the Hopewell Ceremonial Earthworks will be giving testimony to the distinctive lifeways and genius of Ohio's Indigenous ancestors, as well as to their own astonishing scope, beauty, and precision. This book aims to provide the visually rich treatment these brilliant landscape monuments need and deserve.

With this purpose in mind, we return to Squier and Davis's nineteenth-century goals of lucidity and visuality, but with some important differences: Besides nearly two centuries of advancing interdisciplinary scholarship, and diversified and improved visualization tools, we also foreground here the sites' Indigenous origins—with themes and ideas from their builders' descendants among today's sovereign tribal nations. In 1848, Squier and Davis were unable to make those connections, or highlight those continuities; today the study and experience of the Hopewell Ceremonial Earthworks is being deeply enriched by them.

Counting its World Heritage Nomination precursor, this book has been decades in the making. Credit and thanks are due to many more people than can be named here except by category: the many participants and supporters of the UNESCO inscription process, notably the several CEOs and superintendents of the Ohio History Connection and Hopewell Culture National Historical Park since 2008, and the leaders who helped drive the process at various stages and in various ways—especially Richard Shiels, Chief Glenna J. Wallace (Eastern Shawnee Tribe of Oklahoma), Hope Taft, Todd Kleismit, and Jennifer Aultman.

For nearly two decades, this book, and the nomination document before it, have depended especially on three people besides myself for much of their primary content: Marti Chaatsmith, who for many years has brought American Indian scholars, leaders, and ideas to the earthworks and whose perspectives infuse the text, and Bret Ruby and Brad Lepper, who as the key site experts from the National Park Service and the Ohio History Connection, respectively, have deep and long-term knowledge of (or have written) the principal historical and archaeological studies of the eight sites featured here.

Throughout 2024, Marti and I led a series of conversations with tribal representatives, adding much to the Indigenous themes and perspectives enriching this text. From that group, we would especially like to thank two careful readers and thoughtful contributors, Joe Stahlman and Logan York, and finally Talon Silverhorn for his beautiful artistry. Other experts reviewing drafts included Jarrod Burks on remote sensing, John Volker on geometry, and Ray Hively on astronomy. Elizabeth Weiser of Ohio State University provided superb editorial assistance on the penultimate draft.

Finally, I wish to thank Carolyn Gleason, Jaime Schwender, and the staff at Smithsonian Books for their clear and expert guidance, and Cynthia Chavez Lamar and the rest of the leadership at the Smithsonian's National Museum of the American Indian for their faith in this team and this project, and for their generous support.

—John E. Hancock

CINCINNATI, OHIO

Massive earthen walls and gateways at Fort Ancient frame passages plunging into steep, forested ravines.

PART I

BACKGROUND

1.

THE HOPEWELL CEREMONIAL EARTHWORKS

"All of us who are Indian are descendants of the mound builders, and their blood runs in our veins."

—DONALD L. FIXICO (Shawnee/Sac and Fox/Muscogee Nation and Seminole)

On September 19, 2023, eight ancient American Indian earthworks in southern Ohio were inscribed on the prestigious UNESCO World Heritage List, establishing their status as cultural treasures of "Outstanding Universal Value." This designation places them among humanity's shared heritage—worthy of protection and celebration by all people and nations. Joining more than 1,200 iconic sites worldwide, the Hopewell Ceremonial Earthworks now stand in the global public imagination as enduring symbols of their creators' extraordinary contributions to human civilization.

The Hopewell Ceremonial Earthworks earned their World Heritage designation by meeting rigorous criteria: First, that they bear exceptional and unique *testimony to a distinctive culture*—in this case, the Indigenous Ohio Valley culture from two millennia ago, now called Hopewell. This criterion is most often used to inscribe ancient sites or those primarily known through archaeological evidence of their builders' traditions and lifeways. But these earthworks also meet a more stringent and rarely applied UNESCO criterion: their geometrical and astronomical precision justify them as *masterpieces of human creative genius*.

The terms of their global significance have been summarized by the World Heritage Committee in its concise Statement of Outstanding Universal Value.

Octagon Earthworks

The two geometric figures of Newark's Octagon Earthworks enclose a total of seventy acres; their astonishing precision is revealed most clearly from the air. The site's main axis and the walls and vertices of its open-cornered octagon align to the major moonrise and moonset positions during a complex, 18.6-year-long cycle.

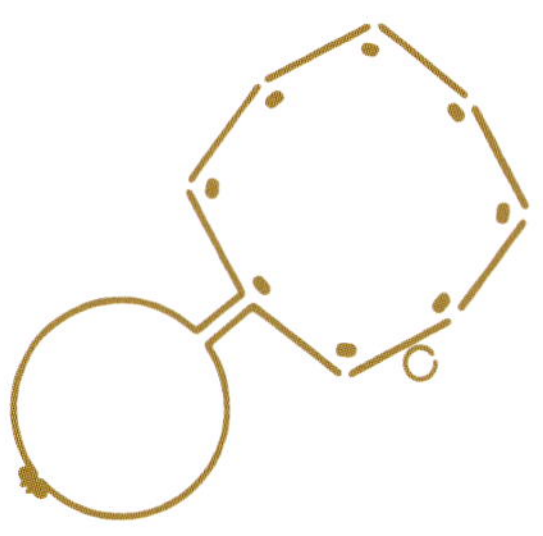

EARTHWORK FUNCTIONS AND SETTINGS

Built as ceremonial gathering places, often involving the burial of ancestral remains, the earthworks feature embankment walls enclosing huge spaces, with carefully positioned and often monumental gateways. They show a remarkable consistency of motifs and dimensions across the region, illustrating the full range of the culture's earthwork types: from landform-based shapes to geometrically precise circles, parallels, squares, and octagons arranged in a variety of combinations. The use of standardized

LEFT

Hopeton Earthworks

This 1840s lithograph of the Hopeton Earthworks near Chillicothe shows its intersecting circle and square. Recent research has revealed a complex construction process—the 1,000-foot-diameter circle was accompanied by a ring of huge timber posts; the square was built up of carefully layered soils in contrasting colors.

OPPOSITE

Great Circle Earthworks

A mile from the Octagon, the Great Circle is the other major surviving feature of what was once the world's largest geometric earthwork complex. Accompanied by its interior ditch, the wall encircles twenty-five acres, rising to sixteen feet where it frames this monumental processional gateway.

measurement units and geometrical principles ties these sites together across the region.

The builders consistently favored hilltop and glacial terrace sites, all located beyond the reach of floods, yet with prominent connections to water—rivers, streams, springs, and constructed ditches and ponds. Besides the earthwork enclosures themselves, these ceremonial landscapes incorporate mounds, water features, and pavements as architectural elements. Substantial stone and timber constructions, both covered and open-air, preceded earthwork construction.

The archaeological record points to cultural practices such as mortuary rites, votive offerings, and calendrical rituals. These sites have revealed some of the finest artistry ever made by the Indigenous peoples of North America. Objects fashioned out of mica, copper, and obsidian—materials brought in from as far away as the Rocky Mountains—display a three-dimensional sculptural complexity and realism exceeding anything that came before. Their vivid depiction of woodland creatures, powerful beings, and cosmological symbols is unprecedented.

Although many other sites were spread across the region (as discussed in chapter 15), this volume focuses on the eight UNESCO-inscribed sites. All are found within the three main clusters of earthwork-building activity in the culture's Ohio heartland—two in Newark (thirty miles east of Columbus), five near Chillicothe (sixty miles southwest from Newark), and one in the southwestern part of the state (thirty miles northeast of Cincinnati). The Hopewell Ceremonial Earthworks are what UNESCO calls a "serial property," meaning that although each site is eligible on its own, the greater Outstanding Universal Value comes from a combination of attributes spread across all eight sites. The order in which they are introduced below, and discussed in the chapters that follow, is geographical—from northeast to southwest. The chronology of their construction is both complicated and as yet undetermined.

MANAGEMENT, EXPERIENCE, INTEGRITY

Three of the sites have been in the care of the Ohio History Connection for a very long time—the Newark Earthworks since the 1930s and Fort Ancient for more than a century. The US National Park Service owns and manages the other five sites in the Chillicothe area as units of the Hopewell Culture National Historical Park, established in 1992. Both agencies maintain management and interpretive plans to ensure the sites' optimal maintenance, protection, and visitation experience. They consult regularly with various stakeholders, including federally recognized tribal nations who are historically associated with Ohio and who represent the many American Indian descendants of the earthwork builders.

The earthworks can be hard to see. They are designed with a subtle architectural language—soft, gentle swells in the earth's surface, extending far into the distance. Their barely perceptible outlines will sometimes appear only in fragments. Some have been subjected to many decades of plowing or lie beneath centuries of forest cover. Compared with Greek temples, Egyptian pyramids, or nearly any other global architectural tradition, these earthworks' conceptual and spatial impacts tend to be elusive.

Yet their brilliance as landscape architectural masterpieces survives through a powerful blend of *archaeological integrity* (lying under the ground to tell the cultural story) and *architectural integrity* (creating vivid spatial experiences). Their architecture benefits from their surviving settings—still predominantly rural or low-density residential areas buffered by parkland. The enclosure walls and mounds retain their integrity—whether as visible, well-preserved or carefully restored architectural forms, or as intact foundations still detected by high-resolution remote sensing methods. Where visible features have faded, those images have informed the architectural plans included in this volume.

The earthworks are not only archaeological sites (scenes of research) and architectural works (enduring monuments), however. They are also places of ongoing Indigenous meaning. Many contemporary American Indians see them as ancestral places, as still-powerful evocations of ceremony and community, resonating with traditional themes surrounding earth, water, land, sky, and time. This volume includes commentary by Indigenous scholars, leaders, and tribal members evoking those connections.

For all people, the earthworks' Outstanding Universal Value is rooted in their self-evident sacredness, as well as in their astonishing forms and their builders' genius. They invite engagement as sacred places with their vast scope, their beauty and precision, and their cosmological functions.

TERMINOLOGY

Each of the three words in the name of the UNESCO-inscribed series (and the title of this book) has a history and specific implications; each deserves some initial explanation.

The modern name of this culture, "Hopewell," derives from Mordecai Cloud Hopewell, the owner of a farm outside Chillicothe, Ohio, where, in the 1890s, archaeologists uncovered the defining characteristics of a cultural tradition so

Mound City

Mound City, lying just across the Scioto River from Hopeton, is the finest surviving necropolis, or burial complex, of the Hopewell culture. A rounded-cornered square encloses an area of seventeen acres and the highest density of mounds of any Hopewell earthwork.

spectacular that it needed to be distinguished from all others before or since. According to the professional archaeological convention of the day (still in use), those cultural characteristics were named after the place where they were first identified. Many American Indians today find it problematic that this ancestral site is named after a non-Native landowner.

We will never know what the earthwork builders called themselves. The sites' managing agencies have consulted with tribal representatives on this question and determined—albeit with some reluctance—that Hopewell is unavoidable for the time being. Communities across eastern North America, speaking diverse and unrelated languages, all contributed to the cultural flourishing now known by that name. Naming the ancestors after one modern descendant tribe could imply that this group was the sole or most important part of that coalition. In this book we use the term but respectfully restrict its use: "Hopewell" here will refer only to a general time period and the set of

UNESCO'S STATEMENT OF OUTSTANDING UNIVERSAL VALUE

The Hopewell Ceremonial Earthworks are a set of eight monumental earthen enclosure complexes built between 2,000 and 1,600 years ago along the central tributaries of the Ohio River in east-central North America. They are the most representative surviving expressions of the Indigenous tradition now referred to as the Hopewell culture. Their scale and complexity are evident in precise geometric figures as well as hilltops sculpted to enclose vast, level plazas. Huge earthen squares, circles, and octagons are executed with a precision of form, technique, and dimension consistently deployed across a wide geographic region. There are alignments with the cycles of the Sun and the far more complex cycles of the Moon. These earthworks served as ceremonial centers, built by dispersed, nonhierarchical groups whose way of life was supported by a mix of foraging and farming. The sites were the center of a continent-wide sphere of influence and interaction and have yielded finely crafted ritual objects fashioned from exotic raw materials obtained from distant places.

Works of Genius. The Hopewell Ceremonial Earthworks are highly complex masterpieces of landscape architecture. They are exceptional among ancient earthworks worldwide not only in their enormous scale and wide geographic distribution, but also in their geometric precision. These features imply high-precision techniques of design and construction and an observational knowledge of complex astronomical cycles that would have required generations to codify. The series includes the finest extant examples of these various principles, shapes, and alignments, both in geometric earthworks and in the preeminent surviving hilltop enclosure. They reflect the pinnacle of Hopewell intellectual, technical, and symbolic achievement.

A Distinctive Culture. The Hopewell Ceremonial Earthworks bear exceptional testimony to the unique characteristics of their builders, who lived in small, dispersed, egalitarian groups, between 1 and 400 CE, among the river valleys of what is now southern and central Ohio. Their economy relied upon a mix of foraging, fishing, farming, and cultivation, yet they gathered periodically to create, manage, and worship within these massive public works. The precision of their carefully composed earthen architecture, and its timber precursors, reflected an elaborate ceremonialism and linked it with the order and rhythms of the cosmos. The earthworks in this series, together with their archaeological remains, offer the finest extant testimony to the nature, scope, and richness of the Hopewell cultural tradition.

OPPOSITE, TOP:

Hopewell Mound Group

A huge, three-lobed mound anchored the Hopewell Mound Group, a large composite earthwork just west of Chillicothe. Its hilltop and geometric shapes enclose 137 acres; its many mounds cover the remains of timber buildings where the most spectacular offerings and regalia known from the Hopewell world were buried.

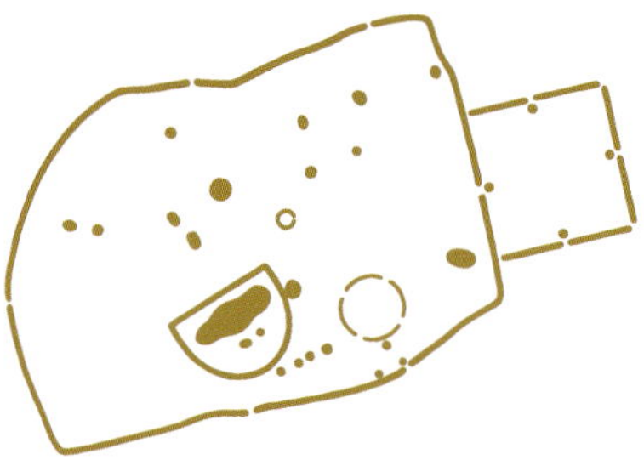

OPPOSITE, BOTTOM:

High Bank Works

South of Mound City, the High Bank Works complement Newark's Octagon with an identically sized circular enclosure linked to a similar octagon; both shapes are clearly shown in this aerial photograph from 1964. Alignments are to key positions of the solar and lunar cycles.

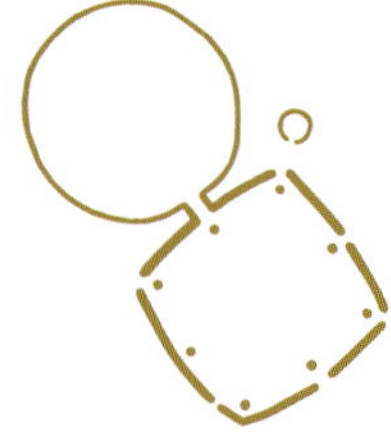

cultural practices that define it, or to the earthworks and other things made by people during that time—but never to the people themselves. There were no "Hopewell people;" there was no "Hopewell tribe."

The ceremonial nature of these places is evident in their vast scope, formal precision, and cosmic alignments. People gathered here for ceremonies. The archaeological record confirms that no one lived inside the enclosures; they were not domestic or urban centers; they were not fortifications. Their extreme architectural scale and elaboration, their connections with the cosmic orders, their embellishment with water and stone, the lavishness of their deposited artistry and material wealth, and the presence of mortal remains of kin and ancestors all point to meaningful public functions—ritualized gatherings that gave structure to the community's understanding of the world and their place in it.

OPPOSITE:

Fort Ancient

The eighty-four earth and stone wall segments at Fort Ancient follow the rims of two connected plateaus high above the Little Miami River, thirty miles upstream from Cincinnati. The largest and most elaborate of the Hopewell hilltop enclosures, at more than 100 acres, it also presents astronomical alignments and many well-preserved water features.

RIGHT:

Seip Earthworks

Fifteen miles southwest of Chillicothe, the Seip Earthworks' largest mound covered the remains of a 6,000-square-foot, timber-framed, ceremonial building. The 100-acre surrounding earthwork combines three geometric figures—a square and two different-sized circles—repeated at four other nearby earthworks.

Colloquially, people tend to refer to these monuments as the mounds, but this is misleading and can seem trivializing. While it's true that mounds are earthworks, not all earthworks are mounds. This distinction matters for three reasons. First, a "mound" implies a self-contained form of piled up earth—a circle, an oval, a conjoined group, or a figure like an animal effigy. By contrast, the term "earthwork" better describes any of the elaborate spatial enclosures and other complex arrangements—which can include mounds—that are the subject of this book. Second, "mound" connotes burial, as was usually the case especially for earlier Adena architecture but is not true of many of the mounds at Hopewell earthworks. Third, when "mounds" is used as the inclusive term for both mounds and enclosures, it can also connote the nineteenth-century convention of calling their architects the Moundbuilders—a name still burdened by the long-discredited racist myth that they were some distant, lost, non-Indian race.

Other terms used throughout this book that might need some clarification include "American Indian," which we use frequently but interchangeably with "Indigenous" or "Native American." All have slightly different nuances in reference, but all are considered acceptable today for referring to the tribal groups of the present continental United States.

Finally, Ohio—the seventeenth state admitted to the Union—took its name from the river that its early American settlers either crossed or floated down. The Ohio River was named, in turn, by the Seneca: *ohi:yo'*, meaning "Beautiful River." The Hopewell earthworks are concentrated along the larger, south-flowing tributaries draining the southern half of today's state of Ohio. Although modern state boundaries are clearly irrelevant to an understanding of the land's ancient inhabitants, the greatest examples of earthworks were in modern Ohio, between Marietta to the east and Cincinnati to the west.

Chief Glenna J. Wallace (Eastern Shawnee Tribe of Oklahoma) and Gerard Baker (Mandan-Hidatsa) pause for reflection during a tour of the Seip Earthworks, 2011.

2.

ANCIENT OHIO TO THE YEAR 1 CE

"The world of the first Americans was richer, greater, more wondrous by far than most of us have ever imagined or than most histories have ever even implied."

—DAVID MCCULLOUGH

The geographic and ecological conditions of this region, and of the settings of these earthworks, are the result of glaciers that covered vast areas of North America in multiple episodes throughout the Pleistocene Epoch, from more than 2 million until about 12,000 years ago. The glaciers flattened the contours of the landscape, and the line where that action ended—over at least three episodes in nearly the same place—is still prominent as a diagonal seam across Ohio, dividing the heavily glaciated Till Plains from the more rugged Appalachian Plateau.

This transition, visible in the abrupt rising of these hilly landscapes, presents itself most strikingly at today's Chillicothe, but it is also evident at Newark and among the deeply carved ravines of the Ohio River's tributaries in southwest Ohio, as at Fort Ancient. The Hopewell Ceremonial Earthworks are concentrated along this boundary, which offered both ideal building sites and ecological abundance.

The advancing glaciers also blocked and reversed the region's ancient rivers. Before the final glaciation, the ancient Teays River system flowed generally northwest across the Ohio region, draining the central Appalachian plateau before heading west toward the Mississippi. These huge rivers—the Teays and its tributaries—deposited deep layers of gravelly soil, which remain in extraordinarily wide valleys like the lower Scioto. The glaciers blocked these valleys, forming huge lakes, which then overflowed and carved new courses—among them today's Ohio River. When the last Wisconsinan glacier retreated northward, the reconfigured topography reversed the drainage in these wide, preglacial valleys, and the smaller, south-flowing rivers that we know today began flowing into the newly cut Ohio River channel.

The new rivers include the Little Miami in southwestern Ohio, which cut the deep gorge below Fort Ancient, and the Muskingum, whose many branches lie in deeply dissected valleys draining hilly southeastern Ohio. Most dramatic is the Scioto, now flowing southward in the wide valley where the giant Teays River once flowed northward. For more than 10,000 years, these wide valleys have accumulated rich soil, laid over the sand and gravel till left behind by the glaciers and the ancient

Marietta's Conus Mound stands within its circular ditch and embankment, today among graves of Revolutionary War veterans.

rivers. Their broad, level terraces are at different elevations—the higher ones created by the larger, ancient rivers, and the lower ones carved by today's rivers.

The upper terraces offered perfect settings for the geometric earthworks—level terrain, high enough to escape flooding, and perfectly drained by their gravel-rich subsoils. Throughout the region, the distinctive combination of large, flat river terraces, and their prominent surrounding plateaus, hills, and ravines, created the prototypical conditions for the monumental earthwork building achievements of the Hopewell culture.

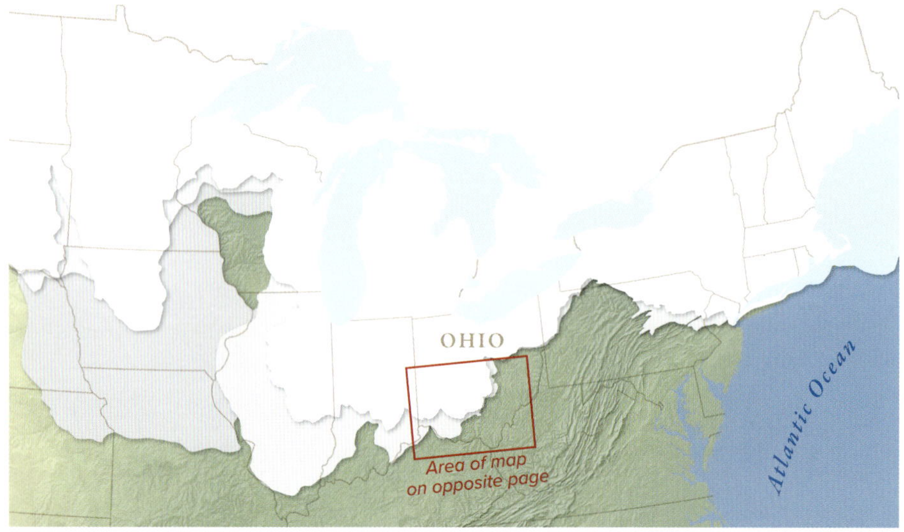

LEFT: The three principal Pleistocene ice sheets reached nearly identical extents over what is now Ohio, all stopping at the diagonal seam that still divides Ohio into flat and hilly terrain.

RIGHT: The distinct boundary zone where the flat glaciated plains meet the more rugged hills of the Appalachian Plateau offered a rich blend of ecologies and ideal sites for the finest of the earthworks, marked here in their respective counties.

OPPOSITE, LEFT: The preglacial Teays River and its tributaries flowed north and west across the region before being blocked, reversed, and rerouted by the advancing glaciers.

OPPOSITE, RIGHT: The shading technique on this 1848 lithograph of the Scioto (Teays) River Valley shows its three terrace levels, formed over eons by both the ancient and modern rivers.

ARRIVAL OF THE ANCESTORS

While much of North America was still covered by glaciers, ancestors of today's American Indians were arriving from Asia, spreading eastward and southward. As the glaciers began retreating, at least 16,000 years ago, people were already in the newly configured landscapes of the Ohio Valley, living in highly mobile bands, gathering plants, and hunting. The distinctive spear points of these Paleoindians, as they are now called, have been found among the bones of long-extinct Ice Age animals like the mastodon. Apart from their spear points and other stone tools, little archaeological evidence of these people has been found.

As the glaciers disappeared and the climate warmed, the tundra- and pine-dominated forests of eastern North America were gradually replaced by the Eastern Woodland ecology of today—hardwood forests threaded by many rivers and streams.

During that transition (what archaeologists call the Archaic period), from about 8000 BCE, people adapted to the changing conditions and began to settle in semipermanent camps, generally near waterways. They made expert use of the food resources in their new environment and began experimenting with small-scale agriculture. By around 900 BCE, these innovations sparked a shift into what is now called the Woodland period, beginning with the Adena culture, when monumental earthen architecture first appeared in the Ohio Valley.

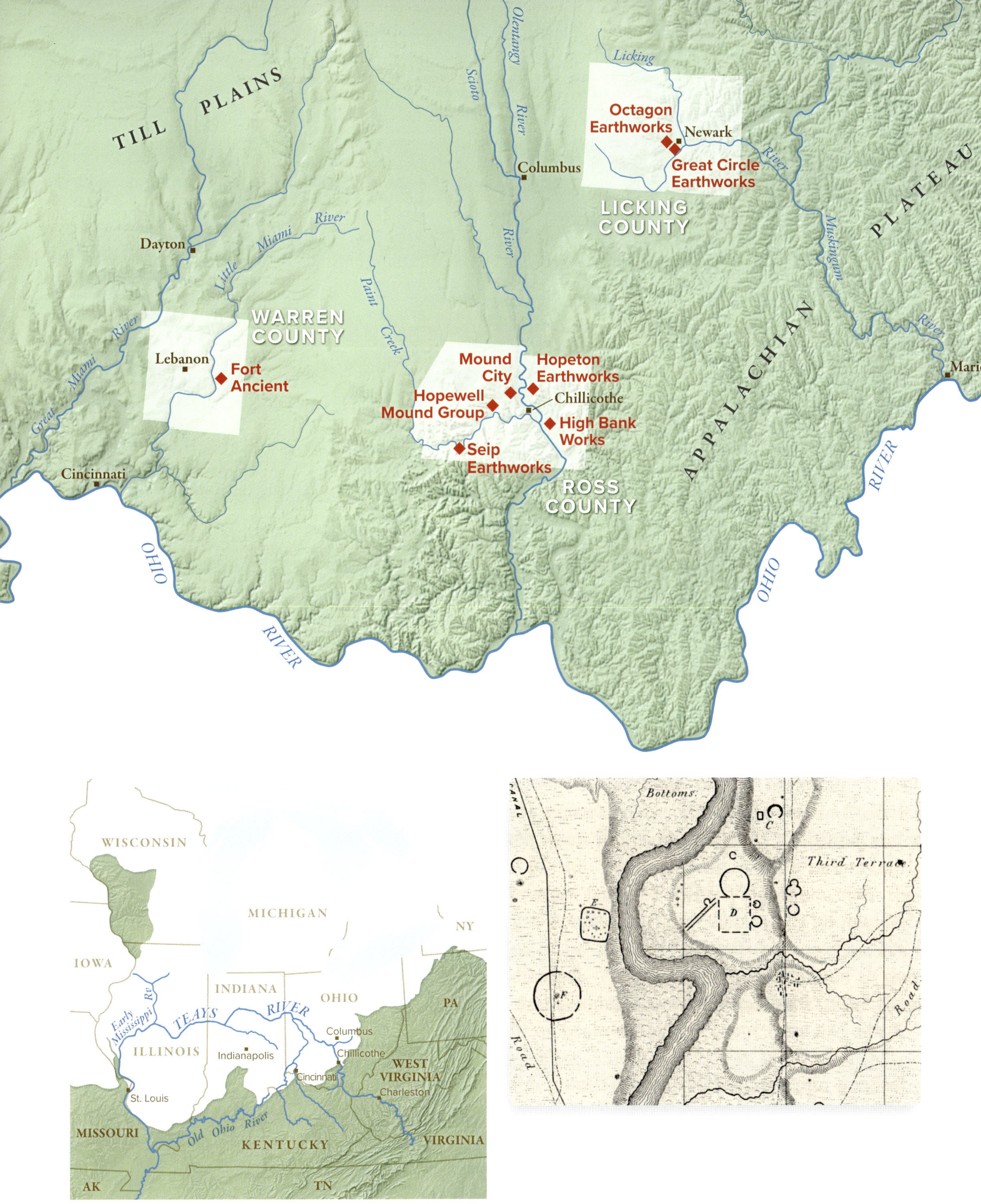

TILL PLAINS
Dayton
Little Miami River
Great Miami River
Lebanon
Fort Ancient
WARREN COUNTY
Cincinnati
OHIO RIVER
Paint Creek
Scioto River
Olentangy River
Columbus
Mound City
Hopeton Earthworks
Chillicothe
Hopewell Mound Group
High Bank Works
Seip Earthworks
ROSS COUNTY
Licking River
Octagon Earthworks
Newark
Great Circle Earthworks
LICKING COUNTY
Muskingum River
Marietta
APPALACHIAN PLATEAU
OHIO RIVER
WISCONSIN
MICHIGAN
NY
IOWA
INDIANA
OHIO
PA
Early Mississippi Rv
TEAYS RIVER
Columbus
ILLINOIS
Indianapolis
Chillicothe
WEST VIRGINIA
Cincinnati
Charleston
St. Louis
MISSOURI
Old Ohio River
KENTUCKY
VIRGINIA
AK
TN
CANAL
Bottoms.
Third Terrace.
C
D
E
F
Road
Road

Ohio's glacial landscapes had created two rich, overlapping ecological zones. The flat Till Plains to the north and west offered deciduous hardwood forests including beech, maple, hickory, oak, and wild black cherry trees, plus extensive wetlands and prairies. The hilly Appalachian Plateau, meanwhile, with its rich soils and sheltered topography, was (and largely still is) covered in one of the most biologically diverse temperate forests on earth, with an unusually rich array of canopy trees, many of them nut-bearing, and understory plants. Fauna in both areas included the same large animals—such as deer, bear, beaver, and wild turkey—along with abundant fish and freshwater mussels. The mound and earthwork builders were nourished by this abundance; the diverse resources of these combined and blended ecologies helped support a remarkable fluorescence of culture.

> *"Indigenous peoples have long-standing oral traditions that emphasize balanced, reciprocal relationships within the multi-species natural world. Stories and traditions reflect vivid, multi-sensory engagement with the world—taking in the sights, sounds, smells, and textures of nature. For example, feeling the wind on our skin, listening to birds sing from the oaks, smelling the fresh air, and seeing the vibrant colors of the landscape throughout the calendar cycle."*
>
> —JOE STAHLMAN (Tuscarora/Pennsylvania Dutch)

ADENA CULTURE

In eastern North America, the Woodland period (ca. 900 BCE to 800 CE) saw the development of agriculture, pottery vessels, more permanent settlements, and greater social and institutional diversity. In the Ohio Valley, these changes characterize the Adena culture, extending to about the year 100 CE. (Adena is the name of an estate near Chillicothe where a 1906 mound excavation uncovered its defining traits; it was the home Thomas Worthington, Ohio's first senator and third governor.)

The first burial mounds in this region display those culturally defining traits, along with pottery making, elaborate ceremonial practices, beautiful artifacts created in exotic materials such as copper and marine shell, and increased plant cultivation—all reflecting a more settled way of life. Substantial earthen architecture speaks of the people's stronger sense of community and commitment to place: monumental mounds, ditches, and small circular enclosures, of which thousands were spread across the region, including far into Kentucky and West Virginia.

William Mills, in his 1911 *Archaeological Atlas of Ohio*, documented and mapped at least 10,000 mounds and earthworks. Most were individual Adena burial mounds on either valley terrace or hilltop sites. Excavations have shown that these mounds often covered the remains of circular timber buildings in which funerary rituals had occurred. A few rose to truly monumental proportions—most dramatically the Grave Creek Mound on a valley terrace of the Ohio River in Moundsville, West Virginia, and the Miamisburg Mound crowning a high hill in Miamisburg, Ohio.

ABOVE: The Miamisburg Mound, the largest Adena-era burial mound in Ohio, stands high on a hilltop in Miamisburg, overlooking the broad valley of the Great Miami River.

RIGHT: The Adena Pipe was found in a mound on Thomas Worthington's Adena estate near Chillicothe in 1906. The preeminent work of Adena culture artistry, it is illustrated here by Talon Silverhorn (Eastern Shawnee).

Some Adena burial mounds were embellished with a surrounding ditch and ring, as impressively illustrated by the Conus Mound in Marietta. Adena architecture also included small, ditched circular enclosures without mounds—earth as spatial enclosure rather than figural object—such as the Mount Horeb Earthwork near Lexington, Kentucky. These are easy to imagine as small-scale prototypes for the Hopewell geometric earthworks that followed, such as Newark's Great Circle.

The archaeological consensus now sees clear continuities between Adena lifeways, ritual practices, and sacred symbolism and those of the Hopewell era, especially in the central Scioto Valley. People of both cultures had wide-ranging interaction or trade networks that brought mica, marine shell, copper, and other exotic materials to the Ohio Valley. And both traditions devoted enormous amounts of time and labor to mound and earthwork construction.

Yet north of the Ohio River, things were about to change.

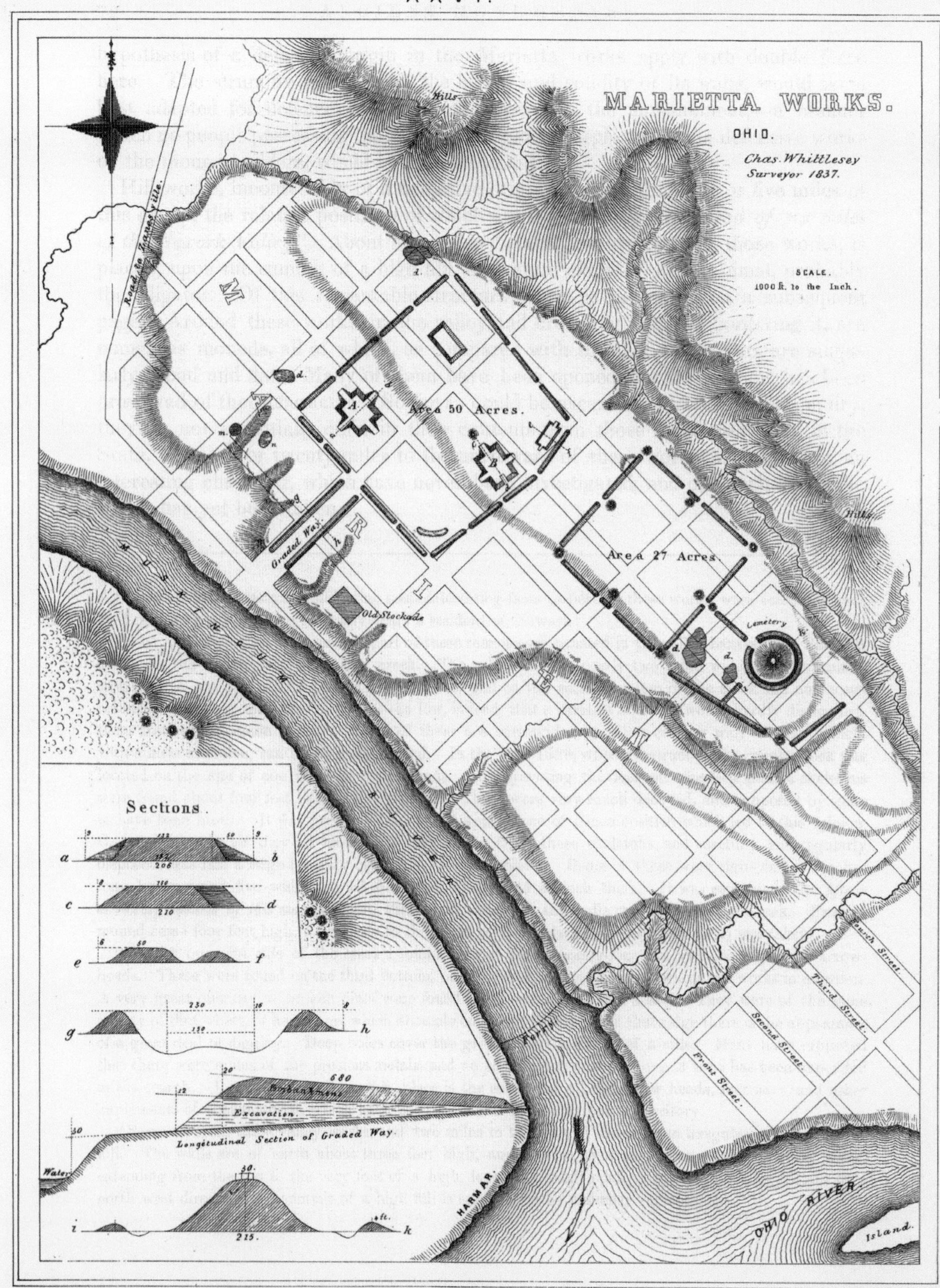
XXVI.
MARIETTA WORKS.
OHIO.
Chas. Whittlesey
Surveyor 1837.
SCALE.
1000 ft. to the Inch.
Hills
Road to Zanesville
Area 50 Acres.
Area 27 Acres.
Graded Way.
Old Stockade
Cemetery
MUSKINGUM RIVER
OHIO RIVER.
Island.
HARMAR.
Ferry
Front Street.
Second Street.
Third Street.
Fourth Street
Sections.
Embankment
Excavation.
Longitudinal Section of Graded Way.
Water
Face P. 73.
Lith. by Sarony & Major

3.

THE HOPEWELL TRADITION AND ITS SUCCESSORS

"The Hopewell Ceremonial Earthworks provide rare connections with truly ancient peoples, 'the Ancestors of the Ancestors.' The Ohio River Valley is the birthplace of so many cultural innovations and sacred iconography that influence even tribes today."

—AMERICA MEREDITH (Cherokee Nation)

After about the year 1 CE, and rather abruptly, people in the central Scioto Valley began to express a far greater level of sophistication and precision in earthwork design. Unlike Adena mounds, these new Hopewell earthworks were fewer but far larger and more complex, serving as places of ceremony and burial for people assembling from far greater distances. The Hopewell culture's sphere of influence expanded greatly, with visitors bringing huge quantities of exotic raw materials into the Ohio Valley to be used in regalia and rituals. New types of large, rectangular shrine buildings enclosed clay fire basins or altars. These distinctively Hopewell practices flourished for about four centuries in the Scioto, Miami, and Muskingum valleys north of the Ohio River, while Adena traditions continued in regions south and east of the Ohio for another two centuries.

The region's ecological richness helped nourish this dramatic cultural flourishing but does not fully explain it. The sudden, remarkable achievements in southern Ohio may also have been driven by a significant human factor—a memory of ancestral accomplishments such as an exceptionally charismatic leader, or a widely noted event. Within a century, the sheer density of elaborate monuments across this region set it apart from all others and helped propel the rapid spread of distinctive new ceremonial ideas, forms, and practices throughout much of the continent.

These new ideas were not limited to a single group of people but instead became an influential movement, spreading to many regions of eastern North America. Across the vast, continent-wide distances that archaeologists call the Hopewell Interaction Sphere, mound burials show distinctive and easily recognizable hallmarks of the close communication and shared beliefs that arose

At Marietta, Ohio, Hopewell architects built a huge, geometric complex that engulfed a preexisting Adena mound and ring (right center).

A large mound in the center of the Seip Earthworks covers the remains of a complex timber-framed shrine building; it contained many tombs and precious offerings.

at this time. For this reason, it is misleading to think of Hopewell as a "culture," as this implies a degree of overall unity that doesn't fit the archeological record. It seems more akin to a religious movement, like Islam or Roman Catholicism in our time, through which new or refreshed cosmological and spiritual ideas, symbols, and practices come to be adopted by groups with otherwise widely differing ways of life.

MONUMENTAL ARCHITECTURE

Across the Ohio Hopewell heartland, the scale, precision, and complexity of Hopewell monumental architecture increased suddenly and dramatically, reflecting unprecedented knowledge and ambition. While Adena circles and mounds had been a focus of local community life, Hopewell earthworks gathered more diverse and distant groups from across the region and beyond. The construction process alone required huge gatherings: The minimum number of workers needed to build an enormous earthwork in a short period of time was much larger than the best estimates of the local resident populations.

All that earth-building—the carefully mounded layers of earth visible today—followed the construction, use, and dismantling of often huge and elaborate timber shrine buildings where the burials and ceremonies had taken place. Within their earthwork sites, and among the remains of these buildings, the people left their beloved kin and respected leaders together with elaborate arrays of material wealth and beautifully crafted works of artistry and regalia.

Most of these huge landscape projects were concentrated in what is now southern and central Ohio in three regional clusters—along the Great and

THE QUESTION OF RELIGION

Traditional American Indian ideas of the sacred are different from most connotations of today's Western, monotheistic religions, and almost certainly more like those of the Hopewell era. So, describing the earthwork builders' spiritual conceptions of the world and their place in it as a religion can be misleading. The word "religion," with its implicit Western reference to authorities that lie beyond the present world, does not align easily with current Native American languages or traditional beliefs. In most Indigenous views, everything given to human experience in the natural world is spiritually significant and has a spark of life—animals, plants, clouds, rocks, hills, rivers, Sun, Moon.

The widespread American Indian cosmological model of the three-tiered universe—the inhabited Earth between the Beneath World and the Above World—does not separate the lived environment from those other domains or their creatures and spirits. Instead, it connects them across liminal boundaries that are crossed regularly in both directions. The unified spirituality of all things leads to ideals of respect and reciprocity, as all these interrelated domains must be maintained. Mystery, harmony, love, and beauty become integral aspects of life to be shared within the lived world in ceremony and in community. "Worldview" or "cosmology" may be a better way to describe this kind of understanding.

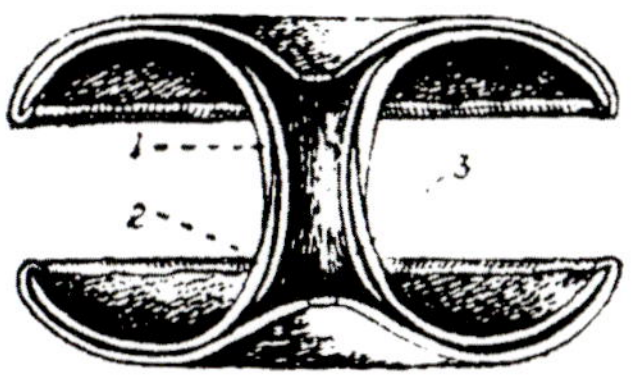

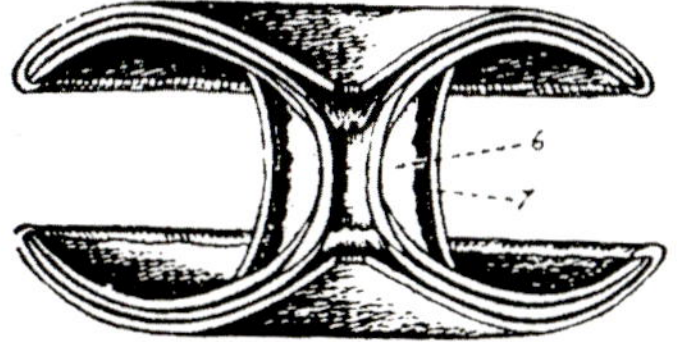

ABOVE, LEFT: In an unpublished 1892 manuscript, Charles C. Willoughby illustrated the complex, multicomponent manufacture of copper earspools from the Hopewell Mound Group.

ABOVE, RIGHT: In this digital sculpture by Talon Silverhorn (Eastern Shawnee), a pair of newly completed copper earspools lie on a stone workbench with some extra sheet copper and the tools of their manufacture—hammer stones and antler punches.

Little Miami rivers in the west, among the Muskingum's upper tributaries in the north, and along the Scioto and Paint valleys in the south-central part of the state. Nineteenth-century reports documented at least nine hilltop "forts" and thirty-seven geometric enclosures of substantial size or complexity that are now known to be Hopewell in origin. Several of these sites illustrate the breadth and regional variations of Hopewell architecture (described in chapter 15).

INFLUENCE AND INTERACTION

The archaeological record reveals that Hopewell forms and ideas were shared and adapted as far away as Illinois, the Lower Mississippi Valley, the Gulf Coast, the southern Appalachian Mountains, and Ontario. They took hold among distinct communities who otherwise had differing languages and customs. Identical designs for log-lined tombs have been found in Illinois and Louisiana. Pottery with similar bird decorations was made in Ohio, Illinois, and Mississippi. Comparable metal-jacketed panpipes were in use from Florida and Arkansas to Wisconsin, Michigan, and Ontario.

Most striking was the widespread use of the characteristically Hopewell bi-cymbal earspools; their complicated manufacture required shared, specialized knowledge as well as copper from faraway Lake Superior or the southern Appalachians. Their distinctive use in burials (held in the hands, as well as placed on the ears) demonstrates shared beliefs across the Hopewell world about the meanings and uses of visual symbols and regalia.

People made long-distance expeditions to bring the exotic materials to be crafted and then placed in the mounds—mica from the Smoky Mountains, copper from Lake Superior, obsidian from Yellowstone, marine shells from the Gulf of Mexico, and more. This was not trade; these valuable materials accumulated at the Ohio ceremonial centers without a corresponding return of goods to their places of origin. Venturers from Ohio imported them as tokens of their long-distance spiritual quests to powerful, faraway places; pilgrims brought others as offerings. Most of these exotic materials arrived in a raw state, to be fashioned at the earthwork sites into works of exquisite artistry for use, and ultimately for sacrifice, in the ceremonies.

SETTLEMENT AND COMMUNITY

Together with a few other examples from around the world, Hopewell studies have helped dispel the belief—common among anthropologists until recently—that great public works could be created only by urban societies with powerful rulers. Current research indicates that Hopewell social organization and project leadership occurred among otherwise dispersed groups of egalitarian forager-farmers. No cities have been found, not even villages—and barely one hundred or so of their small farming hamlets. One important example in the central Scioto Valley core—a site called Brown's Bottom, south of Chillicothe—comprises just a few (perhaps three) large, multifamily houses or clan lodges surrounded by open work areas, outdoor cooking areas with earth ovens, and places for refuse disposal. Efforts to better understand the scope and extent of Hopewell domestic life are a primary focus of current research.

Houses varied in size, shape, and construction but were built on a framework either of vertical posts set in the ground with a framed-out roof, or of pliable saplings bent over and tied into a dome or vault. Many displayed the distinctive Hopewell plan—a rectangle with rounded corners. The walls were likely covered by bark sheets or woven mats, and some may have been wattle and daub (mud plastered over twigs woven between the posts). Roofs were covered

TRADITIONS OF TRAVEL

The faraway origins of materials such as mica, copper, and obsidian suggest long-distance travel and sophisticated route networks—both waterways and overland trails—into territories far beyond the reach of recognized kinships or shared languages. Among the historical Ohio tribes, stories persist today of individuals setting out on long trips on foot, along well-trodden routes, to what is now Georgia, or Arkansas, or even farther—journeys of many days or even months. These stories reflect a tradition of long-distance quests likely stretching back to spiritual journeys to and from the Hopewell Ceremonial Earthworks. The ancient trails would have remained in more-or-less continuous use, carrying many of the same goods among many of the same destinations as in the Hopewell era.

This long-distance travel would have required systems to facilitate communication and diplomacy, and protocols for moving safely through other tribal territories, as well as knowledge of the routes, their vistas and landmarks, places to get food or tools, or to meet local guides and interpreters. The Lewis and Clark Expedition demonstrates the feasibility of such journeys: Their way was paved by multilingual Indigenous guides and gift-giving, and they didn't "discover" anything. They were shown places by American Indian guides who knew exactly where they were going, what they would see, whom they would meet, and what gift-giving protocols to follow.

A three-inch-tall copper face fashioned in sheet copper, and resembling this digital sculpture by artist Talon Silverhorn, was found beneath the large mound at the Seip Earthworks.

with woven mats, bark sheets, or thatch. Ample room for storage would have been found among the rafters. Inside, built-in benches lined the perimeter for sleeping, seating, and storage.

The most striking characteristic of some of these Hopewell houses is their size. The houses at Brown's Bottom ranged from one to two thousand square feet and had multiple hearths for cooking and heating, suggesting that multifamily intergenerational groups of about twenty people lived together under one roof over an extended period. They buried their dead—including a pet dog in one instance—just outside. These large dwellings are in marked contrast to the small hamlets documented at other places, such as the Murphy sites west of the Newark Earthworks.

Research in the Paint and Scioto valleys has suggested that small clusters of these households were dispersed along the floodplains and terraces, organized by lineages and clans into community territories extending for several miles. Larger affiliations brought these local communities together into alliances that were symbolized in part by burying their honored dead together in the shared ritual spaces at earthwork sites. The variety of those honorific burials reflects the relatively egalitarian structure of Hopewell leadership.

PLANTS AND ANIMALS

The people living in these settlements went beyond hunting, fishing, and gathering and became committed to farming. In addition to benefiting from the region's abundant wild resources, they made important advances in agriculture, such as dramatically increasing the clearing of forests for the cultivation of

Talon Silverhorn's image of a domestic interior draws on evidence from excavations at Brown's Bottom near Chillicothe.

crops. The many oil- and protein-rich seed plants of the Eastern Agricultural Complex were cultivated over time, selected for desirable features, and tended in large gardens. Domesticated crops included acorn and crookneck squashes, sunflowers, sumpweed, erect knotweed, and goosefoot. Maygrass and little barley, although not domesticated, were abundant and were grown outside their wild range.

The landscapes surrounding the earthworks were skillfully cultivated ecosystems, not wilderness. To create their gardens and fields, the people opened large clearings in the forest, using seasonal burns and tree girdling. Burning encouraged the trees to produce more acorns and other nuts and fostered berry-producing edge plants and other fresh growth that attracted deer and other game animals. Rotating crops in these clearings and then periodically abandoning them ensured the replenishment of the soil. This commitment to agriculture required community organization and responsibility, as at least some of the people needed to stay put for the growing and harvesting seasons, while others probably made seasonal rounds.

The people managed a web of intimate relationships with myriad plants and animals. Besides their crops, the Hopewell diet was quite diverse. While some were tending crops, selecting seeds, and burning off new fields, others were hunting, fishing, and gathering wild plants including several varieties of nuts. White-tailed deer was the most important animal food, followed by the smaller mammals, freshwater mussels, fish, turtles, and birds such as turkey, ducks, and geese. The main hunting gear was the *atlatl* (spear-thrower) and flint-tipped darts. (The bow and arrow were not adopted for at least another two centuries.) Expert skills were required for both crafting and successfully deploying these hunting tools, as well as traps, snares, nets, and weirs.

FOOD AND DRESS

They processed their seed crops by winnowing, milling, and grinding them into grits or flour, then boiled them in pottery vessels for serving as gruels or stews. Many foods were cooked in earth ovens: Rocks were heated in pits, then sealed together with leaf-wrapped bundles of meat or tubers for slow cooking over hours or days. People likely enriched their diet with jerky and pemmican, breads, herb-flavored water, and tree saps and syrups. Fruits and berries included grapes, honey locust, pawpaw, hackberries, elderberries, and mulberries, plentiful in the bottomland forests and in the managed areas surrounding houses, earthworks, and cleared fields.

Feeding thousands of people during earthwork construction projects and celebratory gatherings—over several days or weeks—would have required monumental logistical operations, with highly organized planning, delegation, and production systems. A cluster of huge earth ovens at the Hopewell Mound Group may illustrate an example of high-volume meal preparations.

Small clay figurines found at the Turner Earthworks show how both men and women bundled their hair into buns and sometimes partly shaved their heads. Women wore wrapped skirts or shawls; men wore loincloths, cloaks, or robes. Tattoos and body painting were probably common. They made clothing and footwear from tanned hides and woven or twined cloth. Textiles (some

A COLORFUL, SENSORY WORLD

"People of the Hopewell world were surrounded by the colors, sounds, textures, and patterns of life in all its forms. Plants, flowers, birds, butterflies, and other animals suggest a palette for Woodland life, inspiring clothing, ornaments, and items for gifting. Water features at the earthworks would have attracted migrating birds and animals, plus frogs, salamanders, and other liminal creatures, creating unique landscapes and soundscapes. Their gardens too would have been full of creatures, sun, shadow, and sound.

Their artistry reflects this beauty, just as their beliefs and actions held respect for the natural world. And all this was reflected in Hopewell iconography, the making of essential items for use in their daily and ceremonial lives, and for survival. These items reflect the people and their world, and with the earthworks and burial mounds they represent acts of commitment to family, relatives, community, and ancestors, through connections to the land, nature, and the Sky."

—MARTI CHAATSMITH

preserved by having been buried next to copper) were woven using yarns spun from plant fibers and rabbit hair, alone or in combination. Some yarns were exceptionally fine and woven into cloth resembling homespun linen. Dyes made with locally sourced pigments added colorful patterns inspired by nature or abstract geometries reminiscent of the earthworks. Accessories and decorations included freshwater pearls, animal teeth and claws, and shells.

These beautifully dressed and coiffed people, expert in many arts, lived rich daily lives in productive, well-organized small communities, secure in both the natural bounty of the environment and the fruits of their own agrarian labors, hunting prowess, culinary techniques, and craft skills. Having mastered the foundational needs for living, they were able to develop an elaborate spiritual life and underwrite astonishing investments of time, care, wisdom, and labor in earthwork design and construction. The earthworks, in turn, provided communal centers where the dispersed communities could gather from far and near for ceremonies, festivals, and feasts. Shared food, labor, and ritual sealed alliances among people, plants, and animals—ensuring respect, restoration, and renewal. The huge enclosures established a vision of order, aligning the human world with the cyclical rhythms of the cosmos.

THE FORESTS RETURN

By about 400 CE, forests were beginning to reclaim the earthworks. The ceremonial gatherings were occurring less frequently by then, and no new earthworks were being built. Archaeobotanical evidence suggests that, over the following centuries, the interplay of erosion and deposition of organic matter would have maintained the earthwork forms at very nearly their original size, although scarred somewhat by the repeated action of fallen, decaying, and uprooted trees. Indigenous peoples who lived in the region during the

OPPOSITE: In this digital portrait by artist Talon Silverhorn, a Hopewell-era hunter is setting out on a cold, clear, autumn morning. His hair, accessories, and clothing are based on representations found at the Turner Earthworks and other sites.

BELOW: Clay figurines from the Turner Earthworks (sketched here by Charles C. Willoughby in 1922) show how the people dressed and wore their hair.

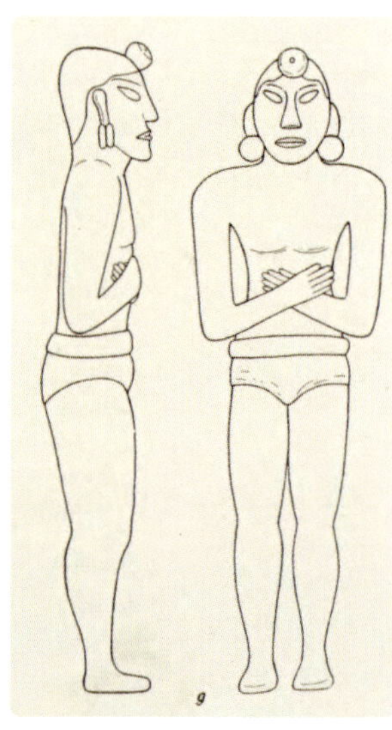

intervening centuries would have known these places, having grown up among them, and it is likely that they viewed them as ancestral sites, treating them with respect, reverence, and even awe.

Evidence shows biological and cultural continuity of American Indian groups from Hopewell times to at least the mid-600s CE. The people seem not to have moved away or died off; they simply stopped building monumental earthworks or conducting the types of ceremonies associated with them. Instead, they built small stone mounds to serve as local community cemeteries. Pottery making, hunting, gathering, and farming activities continued with little change, but the focus of ritual life was shifting from the ceremonial centers to larger settlements. People gathered instead in small village plazas, where community life revolved around their outdoor kitchens and other shared facilities. Large earth ovens suggest a communal economy. New technologies also emerged by the late 600s, perhaps most notably the bow and arrow, whose rapid-fire capabilities, versatility, and ease of use gave it many advantages over the atlatl.

Some Native settlements continued to be located in and around the earlier ceremonial centers into the tenth century, with new burials sometimes placed into the centuries-old mounds and earthworks. The antiquity and spiritual power of these huge monuments would have been obvious, even beneath the regrown forests, and the new burials may have been attempts to reactivate or harness that power, or to rekindle the old ways in a spiritual revival.

A model in the SunWatch Museum near Dayton illustrates the concentric plan of the meticulously studied Fort Ancient culture village there, inhabited from about 1000 to 1450.

By around 900 CE, cultural change was sweeping across eastern North America, associated with the widespread adoption of maize (corn) agriculture and a more settled village life. What is known today as Mississippian culture was a great, regional civilization centered around the middle Mississippi Valley (Missouri and Illinois). At its peak between 1000 and 1200 CE, it produced a series of large urban centers with massive pyramidal mounds—most notably Cahokia, just east of what is now Saint Louis. These highly structured, ruler-controlled, maize-dominated agricultural economies could feed concentrated populations numbering in the tens of thousands.

THE FORT ANCIENT CULTURE

In the Ohio Valley as elsewhere, changes came quickly under the influence of this cultural transition. By about 1100 CE, Ohio's forests were being more widely cleared to accommodate corn's intensive, large-scale cultivation. Life in this region shifted further toward larger settlements and a more stable, village-based way of life. These changes have been named the "Fort Ancient" culture because one such settlement was found within the much older Hopewell-era walls of the Fort Ancient Earthworks. They were substantial villages with concentric rings of usually rectangular, thatched-roof houses surrounding an open central plaza and enclosed by a fence or stockade and sometimes a low, ditched embankment.

In this era, no large cities appeared in Ohio (the nearest was at Angel Mounds in southwestern Indiana), and although the people depended on maize agriculture, they did so here without a central, hierarchically controlled economy. Some Fort Ancient villages, however, did have privileged leaders who lived in larger, Mississippian-style houses and who had more meat in their diet

than other villagers. Some of these leaders may well have come from Cahokia, bringing with them even more cultural changes.

Residents of such towns probably built Ohio's two major effigy mounds—the Great Serpent in Adams County and the so-called Alligator Mound near Newark—both of which reflect traditional Mississippian iconography imported into an Adena-Hopewell landscape. Mississippian serpent motifs are especially prevalent in Ohio on copper jewelry, rock art, and Mississippian-style pipes from this period. Throughout much of the Eastern Woodlands, belief in the Great Horned Serpent or the Underwater Panther as the main spirits of the Beneath World continued well into the Contact Period.

By the 1500s, the people living in these Fort Ancient settlements were almost certainly the historic Miami and Shawnee tribes, who were already acquiring European goods such as glass and brass beads. These new items illustrate Indigenous people's cultural persistence and early interactions through the time of contact. They incorporated the new, exotic items into their daily and ceremonial lives with great creativity, as decorations for their homes, jewelry and clothing accessories, and other personal belongings.

But along with those beads came waves of new infectious diseases, which swept through the Ohio Valley and beyond, followed soon after by wars and migrations largely driven by European rivalries and expansions.

Robert Dafford's Portsmouth, Ohio, floodwall mural depicts Lower Shawnee Town, a large Indigenous settlement at that location in the 1700s.

4.

MODERN OHIO

"Will we not soon be driven from our respective countries and the graves of our ancestors? Will not the bones of our dead be plowed up, and their graves be turned into fields? Shall we give up our homes, our country, bequeathed to us by the Great Spirit, the graves of our dead, and everything that is dear and sacred to us, without a struggle? I know you will cry with me: Never! Never!"

—TECUMSEH (Shawnee)

Within a few decades following the arrival of Columbus in 1492, the impacts of European contact were being felt in the Ohio Valley, long before the advent of any permanent colonial settlements. New infectious diseases swept through the Native populations, who had no immunity to them. Virulent plagues including smallpox, bubonic plague, and measles spread rapidly across the continent from village to village along traditional trade routes, wiping out between 70 and 95 percent of North America's Indigenous population. By 1550, those remaining in the Ohio Valley, whose settlements had been dispersed along the various tributary valleys, coalesced into larger towns within the main corridor of the Ohio River and were using European goods such as brass and copper kettles and iron nails and axes.

The devastating epidemics were followed by long waves of a cooling climate (from the 1500s to 1700s) called the Little Ice Age and a series of conflicts between 1640 and 1701 involving tribal alliances and the new colonial powers on the continent. Known as the Beaver Wars, these were mainly incursions into Ohio lands by an allied group of northeastern tribes named the Haudenosaunee (pronounced Hoh-deh-no-SHOW-nee, and called the "Iroquois Confederacy" by the French), with their English and Dutch allies. They came from what is now northern New York State in repeated skirmishes against the tribes then living in Ohio, who were allied with the French. At stake was the supply and control of the lucrative trade in beaver pelts.

By 1700, the success of these incursions, and the threat of more violence, had largely depopulated the Ohio country and displaced the surviving groups to refuges largely outside the region. A period of rapid change followed,

An 1840s lithograph from Ephraim Squier and Edwin Davis's *Ancient Monuments of the Mississippi Valley* imagines the earthwork complex at Marietta just after the settlers had cleared the forest.

made more chaotic by the further spread of European trade goods, including firearms, and the pressures of encroaching colonial expansion in the east and south. This turmoil subsided into a rebalancing of power, and that stability enabled some Indigenous groups, like the Shawnee, Miami, and Ottawa, to return to their earlier homelands. At the same time, others who had been pushed westward by colonial settlement—notably the Lenape (Delaware)—were welcomed into the area.

For a while, Ohio was a place where these various Indigenous groups could regroup, recover, and form new alliances. They established farms, growing corn, beans, squash, and pumpkins. They built large towns, which also attracted French and British traders and negotiators. But this period of relative peace was short-lived. Already by 1730, settlers had been crossing the Appalachian Mountains into the Ohio Valley and occupying American Indian lands, and new conflicts, more epidemics, forced acculturation, and finally removal would follow.

Through all these transitions, the earthwork sites lay quietly under long-reestablished forests. The impacts of so much death, warfare, disruption, migration, and displacement may help explain why, by the time of Euro-American contacts in the Ohio region, there seemed to be no knowledge of the ancient earth-building traditions, or the meanings of their enigmatic forms. Either that knowledge had been lost, or the Indigenous peoples living in the area were unwilling to share it.

DISPLACEMENT, WAR, REMOVAL

In the 1763 Treaty of Paris, France transferred its claim on the Ohio region to Great Britain, and it became part of what the British intended as an "Indian Reserve" stretching from the Appalachian Mountains to the Mississippi River. But despite this restriction, European settlement began and then greatly increased following the American Revolutionary War (1776–83), when Britain ceded its claim on the region to the newly established United States of America. The new nation immediately opened to settlement what was then known as the Northwest Territory, much of it through what were called "military districts"—meaning that, in the absence of cash, the new government gave land grants as payment to veterans for their service in the war.

The earliest colonial settlements began as fortifications, notably Marietta and Cincinnati (both in 1788). As the towns began to grow, new settlers were quick to build among the major earthwork complexes there. These were ideal town sites, with good access to water and superb

INDIGENOUS KNOWLEDGE OF THE EARTHWORKS

Native people had to be familiar with the earthworks, as their way of life entailed a complete mastery of their environment. Indeed, the prominence of this ancient architecture, spread across commanding sites like high hilltops and major river confluences, would have been hard to miss. The archaeologist Warren King Moorehead, who grew up near Fort Ancient, told this story:

"Mr. North of Old Town . . . used to relate to interested boys stories of adventure with Indians handed down by his father, who had heard them from the lips of Simon Kenton . . . . One of these mentioned that Kenton—who spoke Shawano well—said the Indians had no tradition of the builders of Fort Ancient, but that they visited the place enroute to the Ohio and did homage to the spirits of its makers."

—WARREN KING MOOREHEAD

Jean and Joyotopaul Chaudhuri, in their book *Sacred Path: The Way of the Muscogee Creek*, describe that tribe's oral traditions telling of their ancestors' spring and fall pilgrimages to "special mounds" to the north. How far north is not specified, but as their homelands encompassed much of the southeastern United States, Ohio may have been their destination. Some of those ancestors may have carried mica from its sources in the southern Appalachians.

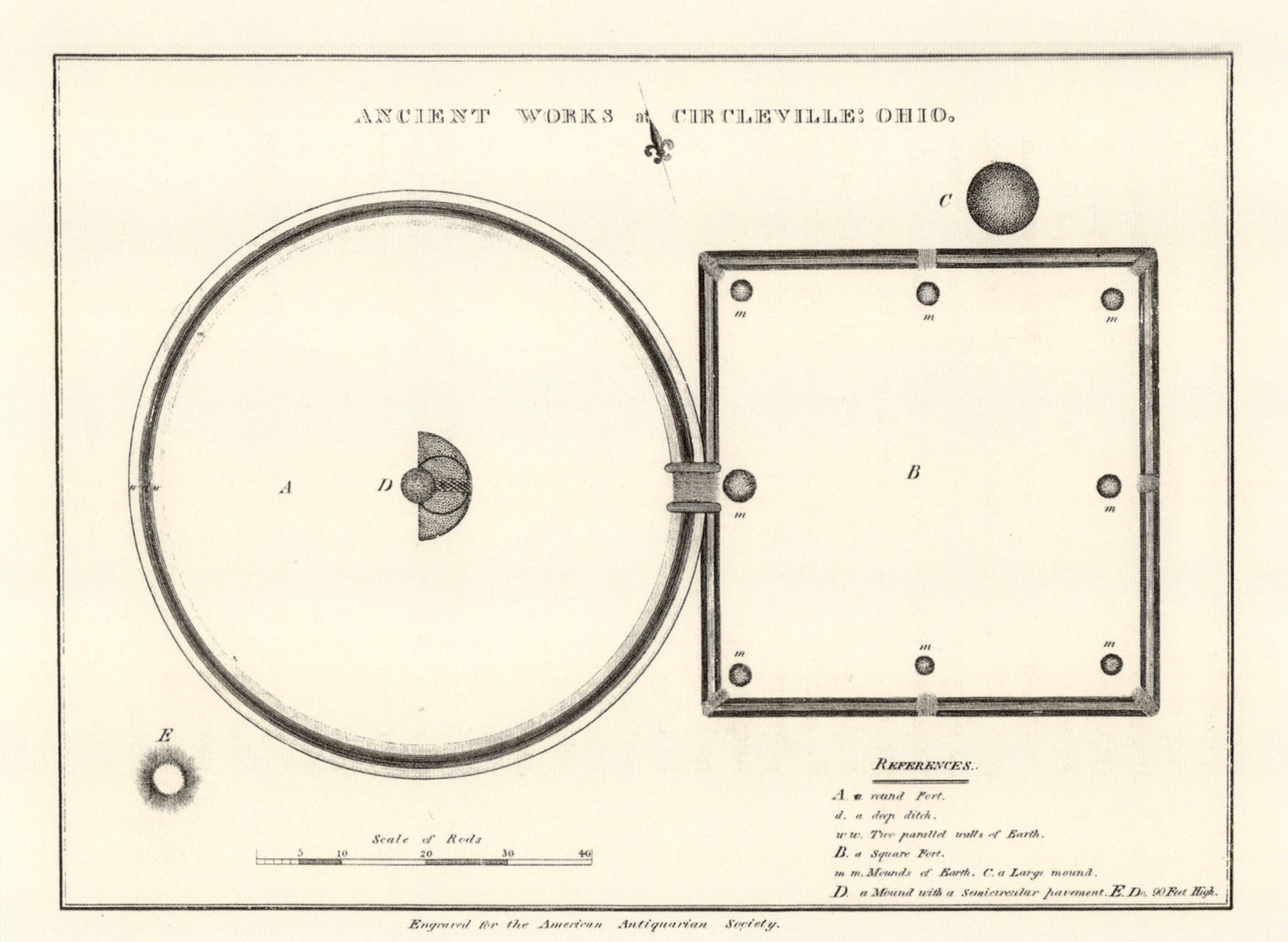

agricultural lands. The next twenty years saw the rapid establishment of most major towns in the region. The forests came down quickly for farmland, firewood, and lumber, and were nearly gone by the mid-1800s. As many of the earthwork sites went into agricultural use, their walls began to degrade.

Despite some initial optimism that the settlers and the Natives could coexist in peace, the situation deteriorated quickly, sparking much conflict and eventually prompting the Northwest Indian War, a series of military campaigns the US government fought for a decade against a confederation of fifteen tribes including the Miami, Wyandotte, and Shawnee. The tribes won significant victories in defense of their homelands and their way of life, but these conflicts finally ended with the US victory at the Battle of Fallen Timbers in 1795. The Treaty of Greenville followed, extinguishing American Indian land claims throughout southern Ohio.

By 1800, settlers were arriving in ever-larger numbers in the Muskingum, Scioto, and Miami River valleys, establishing towns, clearing forests, and planting large farms for wheat, corn, and livestock. Towns and road networks (and soon after, canals) transformed the landscape and further degraded

OPPOSITE: The earliest antiquarian to record the earthworks systematically, in 1820, was Circleville postmaster Caleb Atwater, who included the double ring and square in his own town.

ABOVE: The earliest surveyors of Ohio's earthworks found most of them shrouded in deep forests, no doubt complicating their measurement procedures.

the earthworks. These forces accelerated rapidly, culminating in the Indian Removal Act of 1830. The US and Wyandotte Tribe treaty of 1842 required the last of the Native population to give up their lands in Ohio and to be removed to "Indian Territory" west of the Mississippi River—what later became the state of Oklahoma.

The new settlement towns in Ohio grew rapidly throughout the 1800s. By the end of the century, they had developed an increasing commitment to industry as well as agriculture. Canals in the early part of the century, and railroads from the 1840s onward, fostered the rapid development of commercial and transportation corridors in the major valleys. Populations boomed. Of the major Hopewell earthwork complexes that were documented throughout the nineteenth century, most of those in the path of the growing cities and towns did not survive (at Cincinnati and Circleville, for example) or did so only in fragments (at Marietta and Portsmouth). At Chillicothe, though, only Works East was entirely destroyed; the other major geometric earthworks there stood well beyond the periphery of the growing town. At Newark, far-sighted citizens successfully preserved the most spectacular features of the original, four-square-mile complex.

EARTHWORK ENCOUNTERS

European encounters with the earthworks were being documented as early as the 1770s. François-René, vicomte de Chateaubriand, referred in his 1801 *Discussion historique sur les ruines trouvées au bord de l'Ohio* to the "extraordinary monuments [that] have been discovered on the banks of the Muskingum, Miami, Wabash, Ohio, and especially the Scioto rivers." The first Europeans in the Ohio Valley were impressed by the earthworks but baffled about their origins. With no definitive explanations from the people they found among them—and most European newcomers being inherently skeptical that Indigenous ancestors could have built anything so large, intricate, and precise—some very strange attribution myths arose.

The first systematic account appeared in 1820, when Circleville postmaster Caleb Atwater documented them in his "Description of Antiquities Discovered

In the early 1900s, visitors to Fort Ancient found the interior still largely cleared of trees from its days as pastureland, and the access roads remained unpaved.

in the State of Ohio and Other Western States." Published as a 160-page report in the first volume of the *Transactions and Collections of the American Antiquarian Society,* Atwater's work mapped and described sites throughout the Ohio Valley region, including the Hopewell Mound Group, Seip Earthworks, Fort Ancient, and the Newark Earthworks. Atwater assumed that the earthworks had been built as defensive structures and advanced a theory (begun by others) that the builders were related to the Hindus of India.

Throughout the nineteenth century, the earthworks and "Moundbuilders" of Ohio fascinated explorers, scholars, and the general public, fostering spirited national controversies. Gradually the idea that the earthworks were forts became doubtful; nor did the growing evidence suggest that anyone other than ancient American Indians could have built them. Yet widespread theories persisted that they must have been built by people from another continent—Egyptians, or Israelites, or a Welsh tribe, or the Vikings. Under the name of various "Myths of the Moundbuilders," these notions confused the study and appreciation of the earthworks even as much good documentation work was being done. This confusion continued well into the twentieth century and persists even today.

Meanwhile, the founders of the United States knew and admired the Ohio earthworks. Thomas Jefferson read Atwater's report and wrote to the president of the American Antiquarian Society to congratulate them on this important publication. He expressed his hope that "the monuments of the character and condition of the people who preceded us in the occupation of this great country will be rescued from oblivion before they will have entirely disappeared." George Washington, having surveyed lands in the Ohio Valley himself, also argued for their preservation. Jefferson's secretary of the Treasury was Albert Gallatin, another eager scholar of ancient America and among the first to credit these works to American Indians.

EARLY INVESTIGATIONS

Public interest in the earthworks peaked by the mid-1800s, when two men from Chillicothe—Ephraim Squier, a newspaper editor, and Dr. Edwin Davis, a physician—set out to survey the earthworks of the entire Mississippi and Ohio river system. Supported by Gallatin, their magisterial volume, *Ancient Monuments of the Mississippi Valley,* documented hundreds of sites, and it became the first publication of the newly founded Smithsonian Institution in 1848. Today, their elegant, measured drawings are the best guides we have for many of the sites that have vanished. The principal goal of their work was to answer one question: Who built the mounds and earthworks? Was it American Indians, or some other people? Although they were not yet able to reach the correct answer, theirs was an early application of scientific principles of observation and reasoning to the unwritten past, and thus a pioneering work of archaeology.

In the work of Atwater, Squier and Davis, and many others over the following decades, the Hopewell Ceremonial Earthworks remained the major focus through the development of American scientific archaeology. These publications were among the first to open the eyes of Euro-Americans, and

XVI.

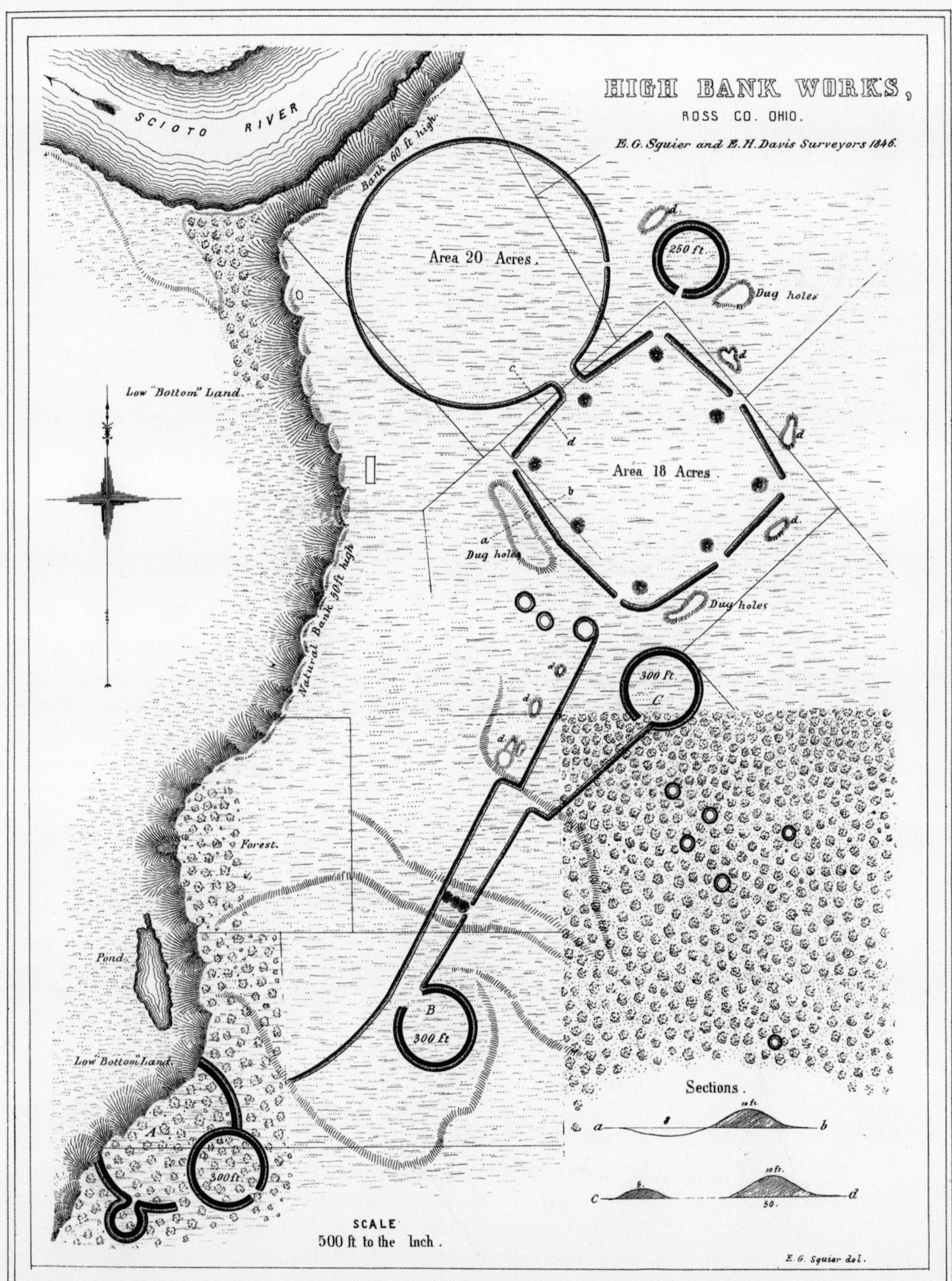

Face P. 50.

Lith. of Sarony & Major N. York.

CURIOSITY AND GREED

As the first settlers began clearing forests and plowing fields, artifacts turned up in the soil—flint points, axe heads, and other tools. The sheer quantity made it clear that the land had been inhabited for a very long time. As burial mounds started to be destroyed (standing in the way of streets or larger fields), more precious objects came to light among the exposed graves. Other mounds were targeted by treasure hunters, and a tragic tradition of looting and selling was born. Enthusiastic antiquarians like Squier and Davis, and more after them, also dug into the mounds, though not for treasure but for answers.

Their studies were commissioned by scientific institutions with genuine curiosity about the past. The grandeur of the earthworks and what was being found in them inspired an urgent desire to solve the "Moundbuilder Question": Who had built these magnificent monuments? These investigations were done without the consent of the Native descendants of the people whose remains and valued possessions were being exhumed in the process. For the first few decades of this work, it was not yet clear to the investigators that these were American Indian ancestors. But by the turn of the twentieth century, that had become generally settled science—although excavation work continued until the late 1900s, when greater respect for tribal views began in earnest.

scholars worldwide, to the long and rich Indigenous history of the country. The work of Squier and Davis in particular was an archaeological milestone, revealing that some earthwork complexes were associated with mortuary activities and contained elaborate and beautiful objects made from exotic materials. Forty years later, in 1889, Cyrus Thomas, also of the Smithsonian, described and surveyed the major remnants of the Newark Earthworks, Hopeton Earthworks, and High Bank Works, improving on the accuracy of previous measurements. Thomas's work was, like Squier and Davis's, specifically commissioned to determine whether the earthworks were built by American Indian ancestors. His 800-page *Report on the Mound Explorations of the Bureau of Ethnology* reviewed all the evidence, consulted with many experts, and confirmed the Indigenous origins of the earthworks, which have been settled science ever since.

The increasingly scientific methods of archaeology were also reflected in the work of Frederic Ward Putnam, curator of the Peabody Museum of Archaeology and Ethnology at Harvard University and sometimes referred to as the father of American archaeology. In the 1880s, Putnam traveled to Ohio to investigate at Serpent Mound and the now-lost Turner Earthworks on the Little Miami. He vigorously encouraged publicity, funding, preservation, and further studies of American antiquity. Hoping to showcase the brilliance of Ancient America at the 1893 World's Columbian Exposition in Chicago, Putnam retained an eager young Warren King Moorehead (just twenty-five at the time), who headed for the mound-covered farm just west of Chillicothe belonging to Mordecai Cloud Hopewell.

Squier and Davis's plan of the High Bank Works included wall sections and a variety of outlying works to the southwest that were still detectable in the 1840s.

The site's importance was known from Squier and Davis's work of half a century earlier. The dazzling, prodigious results of Moorehead's work at what would later become known as the Hopewell Mound Group made the Chicago exhibits a huge success. They established the distinctive and brilliant characteristics of the culture, and, following the archaeological convention of naming cultures after the place where their defining evidence was first identified, the concept of "Hopewell" was born. The exhibit also did much to establish American antiquity as a topic of widespread and lasting importance, meriting further investigation.

A recent aerial photo shows Mound City's restored mounds, forested perimeter, and proximity to the Scioto River.

DESTRUCTION AND PRESERVATION

Though the canals were gradually abandoned between the 1890s and the 1930s, increases in the number of automobiles, roads, and highways continued to spur the expansion of towns and suburbs. Both Newark and Chillicothe grew rapidly during the middle decades of the twentieth century. Newark's two protected earthworks became surrounded by modest, early-to-mid-twentieth century houses, which have remained largely unchanged to the present. By the last quarter of the century, Chillicothe's growth was threatening Hopeton and the Hopewell Mound Group. Fort Ancient, High Bank, and Seip were far enough from urban development to remain largely unaffected, though the latter two continued to be severely compromised by farming. Mound City, meanwhile, occupied the center of a large tract of federal land, given over in this period to prison grounds from which it could be easily shielded.

The Ohio State Archaeological and Historical Society (OSAHS), as the Ohio History Connection was called until 1954, managed Fort Ancient beginning in 1890 after it was acquired as Ohio's first state park. In Newark, successful local efforts and a series of recreational and military uses managed to preserve the Great Circle and Octagon Earthworks, and they were transferred to the OSAHS in 1933. Mound City became federal property in 1917 and, following its brief use as a military camp, was managed by the OSAHS and then the National Park Service starting in 1946. When Hopewell Culture National Historical Park was established in 1992, Mound City was joined by Hopeton Earthworks, Hopewell Mound Group, and High Bank Works, along with Seip Earthworks, which had been an Ohio state memorial since 1927.

The absence of tribes from Ohio since their final removal in the 1840s, and the impact of assimilation in the century that followed, resulted in limited tribal involvement with the sites and current owners until recently. It was not until the 1960s that tribes began to secure recognition of self-determination and coalesce movements to raise awareness of long-held treaty rights. Following the 1990 passage of the Native American Graves Protection and Repatriation Act (NAGPRA), both the National Park Service and the Ohio History Connection began to engage with the tribal nations who have historical connections with this region, now mainly based in Oklahoma and other states.

A contentious past has given way in the twenty-first century to positive working relationships and intentional processes for American Indian participation in the interpretation and stewardship of the sites and the treatment and disposition of archaeological collections. (This process is detailed further in chapters 13 and 14.) As Native descendants are returning to the earthworks today, their deep connections are being recovered and expressed. Many Indigenous ways and ideas remain entwined with those of the ancient ancestors; the earthworks express continuing perspectives of the natural world and current worldviews connecting water, Earth, and Sky.

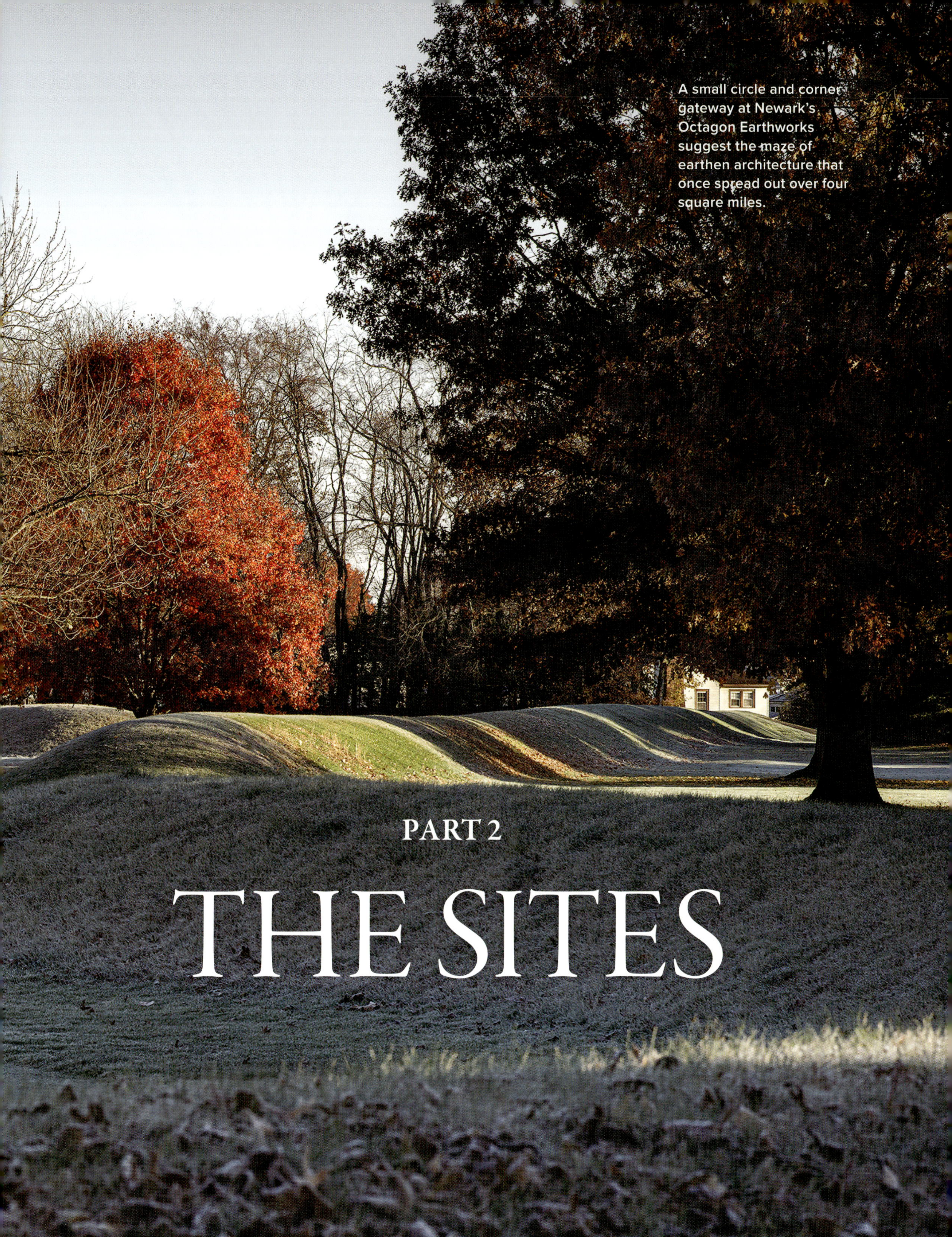

A small circle and corner gateway at Newark's Octagon Earthworks suggest the maze of earthen architecture that once spread out over four square miles.

PART 2

THE SITES

The southern wall of Newark's Octagon is seen here looking east; its southeastern gateway and gateway mound are on the left, and the small circle is to the right.

5.

NEWARK'S OCTAGON EARTHWORKS

"The people who built these mounds were brilliant. Their genius lies in combining complexity and simplicity simultaneously. Their mathematical and astronomical complexities challenge our mental capacity while simultaneously their simple [forms] evoke a calming, soothing, and in some instances a spiritual effect."

—CHIEF GLENNA J. WALLACE (Eastern Shawnee Tribe of Oklahoma)

Newark's Octagon and Great Circle Earthworks are the principal remaining pieces of what was once the largest geometric earthwork complex in the world. Long, wide, walled roadways connected them to two other geometric figures and to the surrounding waterways. This remarkably harmonized composition—what archaeologist Brad Lepper calls "a giant ritual machine"—covered four square miles across a broad, roughly triangular high glacial terrace. Most of this grand complex was lost to the growth of the town, but today the Octagon and Great Circle each stand impressively in parklike settings with mature trees buffering much of their perimeters. Their histories and significance require first an introduction to the entire Newark Earthworks ensemble, and a brief history of how these two pieces survived as its best-preserved components.

The setting is a broad valley about twenty-five miles east of Columbus, and fifty-five miles northeast from the Hopewell concentrations around Chillicothe. Here Raccoon Creek and the South Fork of the Licking River unite to become the Licking River, which flows eastward into the Muskingum, which in turn enters the Ohio at modern Marietta. When completed, the earthworks sprawled across an elevated terrace, about thirty feet above the floodplain of these three rivers and surrounded by low sandstone hills. The site is also the nearest large, level landscape to the Flint Ridge quarries, which yielded the distinctive, rainbow-colored stone that had already been famous across North America for at least 10,000 years. Points and artistry crafted in Flint Ridge flint were a Hopewell-era signature.

The mature oak and hickory forests of ancient Ohio were interrupted by large prairie openings, occurring both naturally and with maintenance by humans. Pollen analyses have shown that the Great Circle, for example,

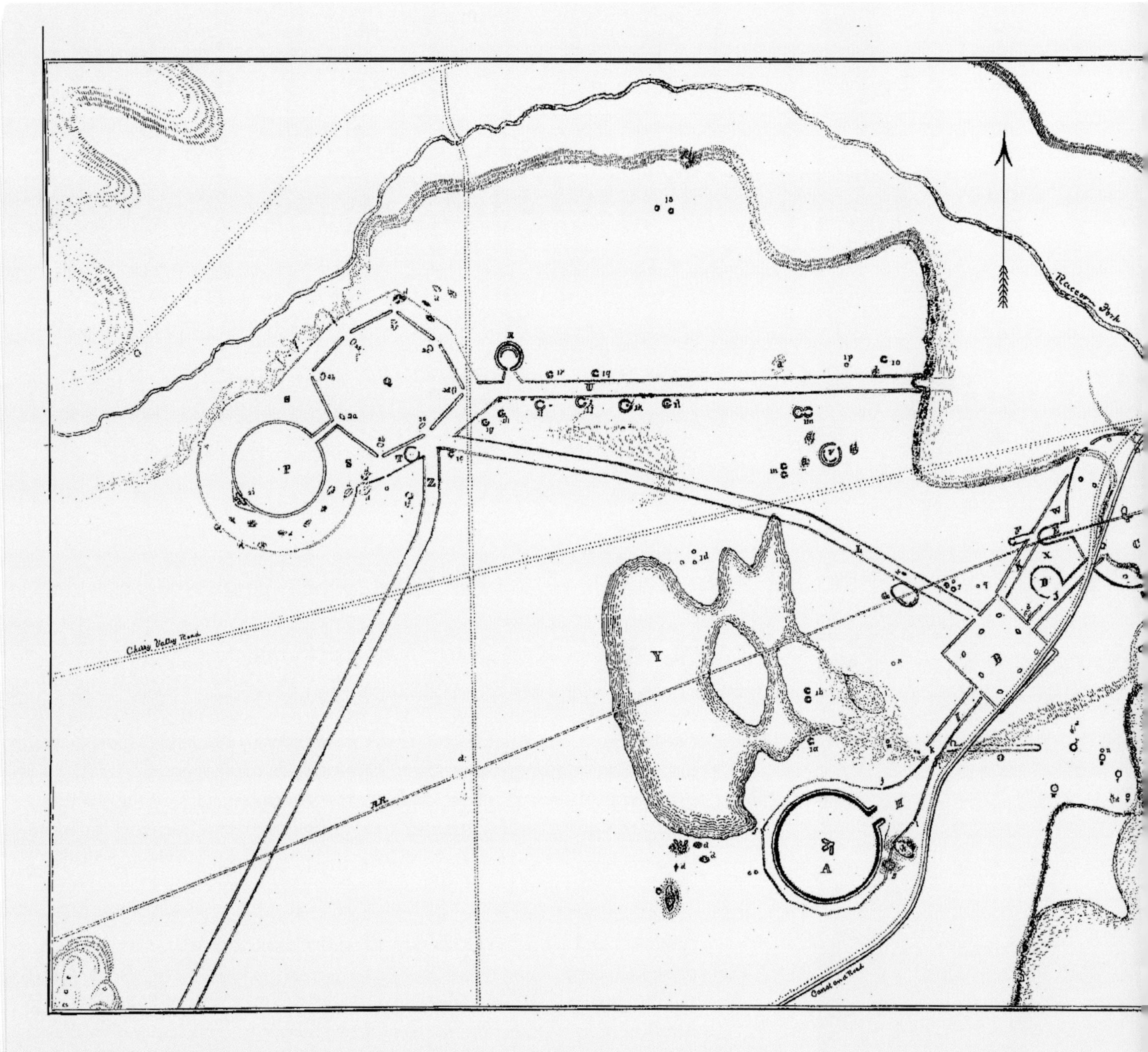

was constructed over a long-established grassland with scattered oak trees. Prior to the earthworks, the Newark area had been a well-developed prairie for hundreds and perhaps thousands of years. The earthwork builders maintained and enlarged it to help increase the density of game animals, to open clear views of the nearby horizons, and to plan and construct their monuments.

Waterways surround this broad terrace on three sides, and a low area—once a large marshy lake—occupies its center. The geometric elements of the complex hugged the perimeter of this terrace, and earthen walls framed

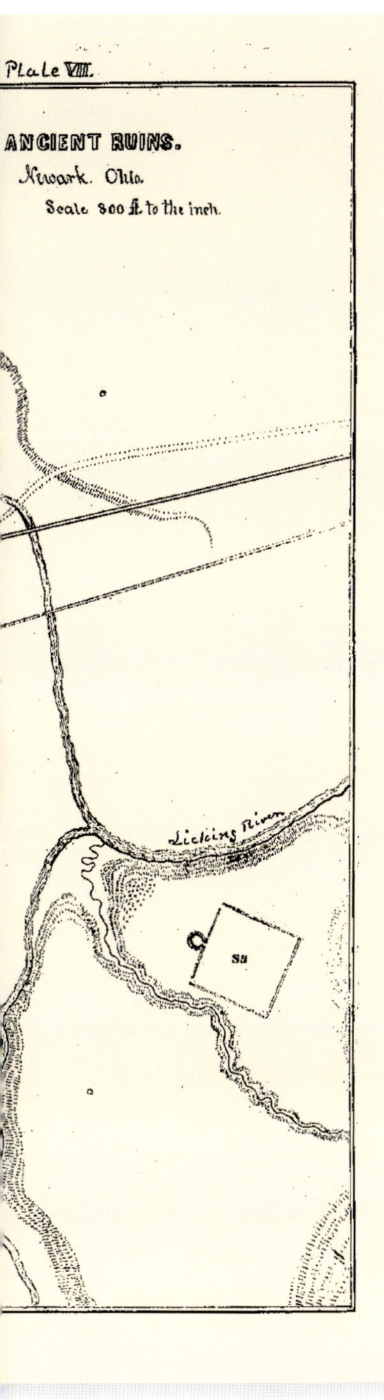

James and Charles Salisbury created the Newark Earthworks' most accurate map in 1862. Today, the Octagon Earthworks (upper left) and the Great Circle (center bottom) are the only major features remaining.

roadways connecting them to each other and to the surrounding scarps. Low earthen lines also formed a complete, continuous perimeter around the entire complex, leaving only three points where visitors could enter without climbing over walls.

Each entrance gave access to a parallel-walled ceremonial avenue from one of the three surrounding waterways, suggesting that visitors may have arrived mainly by river transport and purified themselves with river waters before entering the earthworks. Inside the complex, the wide, parallel-walled roadways directed their movement from one enclosure to another.

CONSTRUCTION, SCOPE, COMPONENTS

Newark's high glacial outwash terrace provided an ideal site for earthwork building—level ground with well-drained soil, far above the reach of floods. The local prairie landscape simplified the task of tree removal. Still, the entire complex required the builders to excavate, move, and redeposit nearly 7 million cubic feet of soil. For digging, they used pointed sticks, shell hoes, and hoes or picks made with a deer shoulder blade attached to a wooden handle.

They hauled the soil in baskets from various locations, depending on the type needed for each feature of the design. At three twenty-pound baskets per cubic foot, that would have been more than 20 million hand-carried loads. Leaders directed the deposition and sculpting of this soil into vast, precise shapes. It was not sourced or dumped randomly but carefully chosen and placed for particular effects. One source was a steep terrace bluff where the Octagon Earthworks overlook Raccoon Creek; mining soil there would have been quite easy by simply pulling it off the face of the hillside into the baskets and then carrying it up a short embankment.

Walls barely three feet high defined the avenues linking the five large geometric figures, averaging 180 feet apart. Their spatial effect was subtle, yet still suggestive of ritual processions. Small remnants of these walls remain near the southern edge of the Octagon. From that same location, another set of parallels once extended in a straight course to the south-southwest. Nineteenth-century surveyors traced these walls for six miles. They appear in 2023 aerial laser (LiDAR—"light detection and ranging") data as far as eight miles out and were visible for seventeen miles in 1930s aerial reconnaissance. Now known as the Great Hopewell Road, their arrow-straight course points exactly toward the cluster of similar earthworks at modern Chillicothe.

Only one of ancient Newark's components was connected directly by these avenues to all the others: an essentially perfect, 932-foot-square enclosure more than a mile east of the Octagon. Eight small mounds stood inside each of its four corners and the midpoints of its four sides, as is typical of other Hopewell squares. The Wright Earthworks preserve a remnant of one of its sides, together with a short segment of an adjacent wall—part of the passage heading north toward the complex's elliptical burial area.

The people of Ancient Newark buried their honored dead in what is now called the Cherry Valley Ellipse. It does not survive today, but it contained at least eleven mounds, a small circular enclosure, and a flat-topped platform mound. It was ancient Newark's cemetery—the functional, ceremonial equivalent of Mound City in the Chillicothe area. None of the mounds in Newark's ellipse were ever studied by archaeologists, so little is known of the ancestral or ritual remains or any ceremonial deposits that may have been left beneath them. An early report described one of the mounds as having fourteen burials, laid out with an estimated "fifteen to twenty bushels of mica sheets." Any such materials or artifacts from the burials in the ellipse are now lost, with one notable exception: From the large, irregularly shaped mound in the center came the extraordinary figurine called the Shaman of Newark.

A UNIFIED CONCEPTION

The major components of the Newark Earthworks complex were interrelated in complex ways. The diameter of the Octagon's connected circle is 1,054 feet—a dimension shared at many other Hopewell earthworks and now referred to as the Observatory Circle diameter (OCD). The area of the Great Circle is equal to that of a square with a length of one OCD on each side. The center of the Great Circle is six OCDs from the center of the Observatory Circle. Six OCDs also separated the centers of the Octagon and the Wright Square. The perimeter of the Wright Square was equal to the circumference of the Great Circle. The area of the Wright Square was equal to the area of the Observatory Circle. These astonishing relationships were laid out without mathematical abstractions like pi or square roots (chapter 11 discusses how this may have been accomplished).

This integral unity also involved alignments to the 18.6-year lunar cycle. The center points of the Great Circle and the Observatory Circle (six OCDs apart) define an alignment to the maximum southern moonrise. An equivalent

THE SHAMAN OF NEWARK

The only significant work of Hopewell artistry known from the Newark Earthworks is the figurine now known as the Shaman of Newark, depicting a religious practitioner wearing a bearskin. The bear's head rests on the figure's head, and its claws cover the hands. The figure wears the characteristic Hopewell-style earspools. A long-haired human head, adorned with matching earspools, rests in the lap—perhaps being prepared for burning or burial, or for use in a divination ritual. The figure seems to be in the act of transforming into an animal spirit: The raised left hand beside the head seems to be either lowering the mask down over the face or lifting it off. The object has no way to stand on its own; it needed to be held in the hands, and the moment of transformation could be enacted simply by tilting it up or down.

Bears have long been important in American Indian tradition and shamanic ritual, thought to be especially attuned to the ways of healing—the handing down of medical knowledge or the gathering of medicinal plants. Paintings of nineteenth-century Indigenous ceremonies depict leaders in full bear regalia much like the Newark Shaman's. Bear teeth (including those from Rocky Mountain grizzlies) are among the exotic artifacts often found in Hopewell graves, sometimes studded with pearls.

alignment between the centers of the Octagon and the now-vanished Wright Square pointed to the minimum southern moonrise.

> *"Ancient Newark's intricate precision and unity might suggest it was conceived in advance by a singular remarkable intellect—or team. Although based on astronomical and geometrical knowledge that would have taken generations to codify, this unified masterwork could have been executed within a single generation—a perfected synthesis of ideas already developed, mainly in the Scioto and Paint Valleys. Data on the sequence and dating of Hopewell earthworks, and Newark in particular, is still limited, so much more evidence will be needed to test this hypothesis."*
>
> —BRAD LEPPER

The only artifact known to have come from the mounds in the Cherry Valley Ellipse is the bearskin-wearing figure known as the Shaman of Newark, now with the Ohio History Connection and illustrated here by Talon Silverhorn (Eastern Shawnee).

DESTRUCTION, INVESTIGATION, PRESERVATION

When the Hopewell era ended and Newark's human-cultivated prairie was no longer maintained, the forests returned. Yet the huge and precise earthen forms would have been obvious to later American Indian groups, and from about the eighth to the tenth century, they did attract some small-scale ceremonies such as interments. When the early settlers arrived, they found huge numbers of mature black cherry trees filling Newark's broad terrace and the surrounding valleys—perhaps proliferated by people enjoying cherries at ancient feasts—and inspiring the "Cherry Valley" name now used throughout the area.

Before 1800, the lands of Licking County were surveyed and partitioned as compensation for veterans of the American Revolutionary War (part of the US Military District), putting the largely reforested earthworks into the hands of speculators and settlers. Parts of ancient Newark's square and ellipse were destroyed as early as the 1820s by the construction of the Ohio and Erie Canal; at least one of the burial mounds was taken down to make way for one of its locks. The completed canal provided an artery for further development into the 1830s, and the rest of the Cherry Valley Ellipse and its mounded tombs disappeared quickly as Newark grew around and over them. The building of the Central Ohio Railroad in the 1840s accelerated this process, and the site of the ellipse became a center of industrial activity.

The Smithsonian's *Ancient Monuments of the Mississippi Valley* featured the Newark Earthworks prominently, with a map of the complex based on a survey by Charles Whittlesey initiated in 1836; it shows the canal passing through the earthworks, as well as the road (modern Newark's West Main Street) running between the major enclosures and cutting through two sets of parallel walls. When this map was published in 1848, Squier and Davis noted that the "ancient lines can now be traced only at intervals, among gardens and outhouses. . . . A few years hence, the residents upon the spot will be compelled to resort to this map, to ascertain the character of the works which occupied the very ground upon which they stand."

Later, David Wyrick's 1860 map showed more of the site under cultivation and the Central Ohio Railroad slicing through the burial mound cluster. The largest and most central of the mounds was cut in half, and others provided soil for the railroad embankment. Two years later, James and Charles Salisbury's

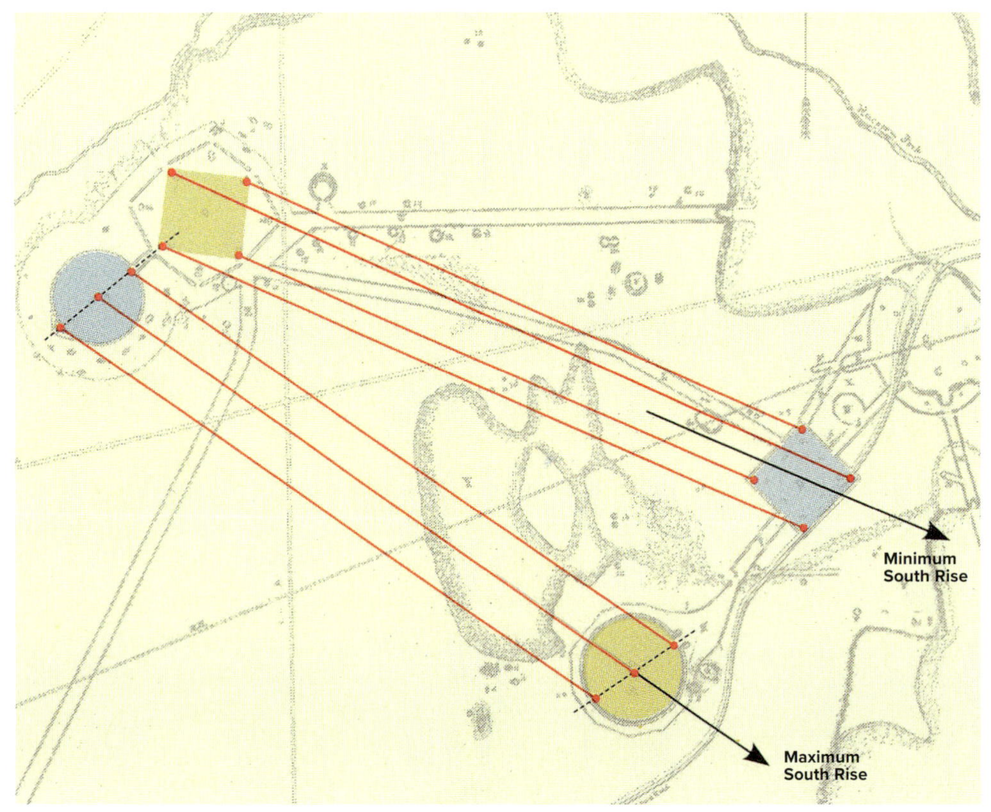
Minimum
South Rise
Maximum
South Rise

careful survey could be based only on flattened remnants of mounds and scattered traces of the outer perimeter and parallel walls. By that time, only the Great Circle and the Octagon Earthworks remained largely intact.

When these nineteenth-century maps are compared to aerial photographs today, two things become clear. First, the Salisbury map is by far the most accurate; it registers almost perfectly on top of the modern images. Second, for large parts of the Newark Earthworks, Squier and Davis were correct when they warned that much would disappear. Yet they were overly pessimistic. A few far-sighted citizens of Newark worked to preserve parts of this wonder of the ancient world, finding surprising ways to incorporate the most spectacular of its remnants into the contemporary landscape. The three surviving pieces of the Newark Earthworks were recognized collectively as a National Historic Landmark in 1964. The application described them as among "the best remaining evidence for the masterful construction of large geometric structures by the Hopewell."

OPPOSITE, TOP: The wide Observatory Mound rises over the Octagon Earthworks' circular enclosure wall, and marks the beginning of the site's long, central, lunar-aligned axis.

OPPOSITE, BOTTOM: Overlaying the Salisbury map indicates the corresponding area relationships (blue, yellow) of the original Newark Earthworks complex, including the Wright Square. The circle and square at lower right also had equal perimeters. Centerpoints on the principal figures define alignments to the minimum and maximum southern moonrises. The centers of each set of related figures were also six OCDs apart.

OCTAGON EARTHWORKS SETTING

The original four-square-mile extent of the Newark complex is now traversed by the gridded streets and houses of the modern town; this was the main area of its growth through the nineteenth and early twentieth centuries. But just beyond Thirtieth Street, on perfectly level ground, a few of the long, straight walls of the Octagon Earthworks rise, improbably, next to narrow residential lanes, backyards, and buffering tree lines. The walls extend—with astonishing, uncanny precision—near oblong mounds and a small circle.

Beyond these first impressions, the Octagon Earthworks spread far across to the northwestern edge of the level site, completing their geometries near the steep escarpments overlooking Raccoon Creek. The immediate surroundings provide a calm and quiet setting. The land is a public preserve, owned by the Ohio History Connection since 1933. It was leased to a private golf club from 1911 through 2024, which maintained it in good condition. Site restoration work and full public access began in 2025.

SITE FEATURES

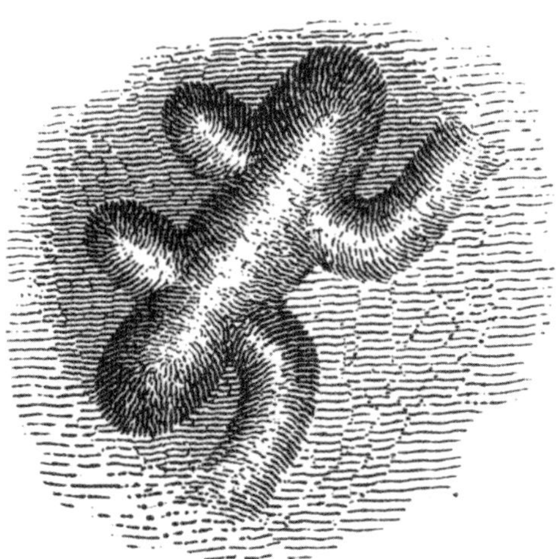

ABOVE: A detail from Squier and Davis's drawing of the Observatory Mound shows how it lies across the former gateway into the Observatory Circle.

The Octagon Earthworks comprise two geometric enclosures: a large circle and an even larger octagon, connected by an avenue formed by short parallel walls. The walls of the circle, called the Observatory Circle, are between three and six feet high, maintaining level crests as the ground undulates somewhat beneath or outside them. The circle's diameter is 1,054 feet, yielding an area of twenty acres. Directly opposite the parallel-walled avenue, along the southwestern rim of the circle, the two halves of the circular wall turn outward in parallel extensions, suggesting a former gateway.

A large earth and stone platform mound covers those parallel extensions. Called the Observatory Mound, it stands twelve feet high—eight feet higher than the adjacent embankment—over a 66-by-160-foot base. It marks the start of the Octagon Earthworks' principal axis, through the parallel walls of the avenue, across the Octagon, toward the Moon's northernmost rise point on the distant horizon.

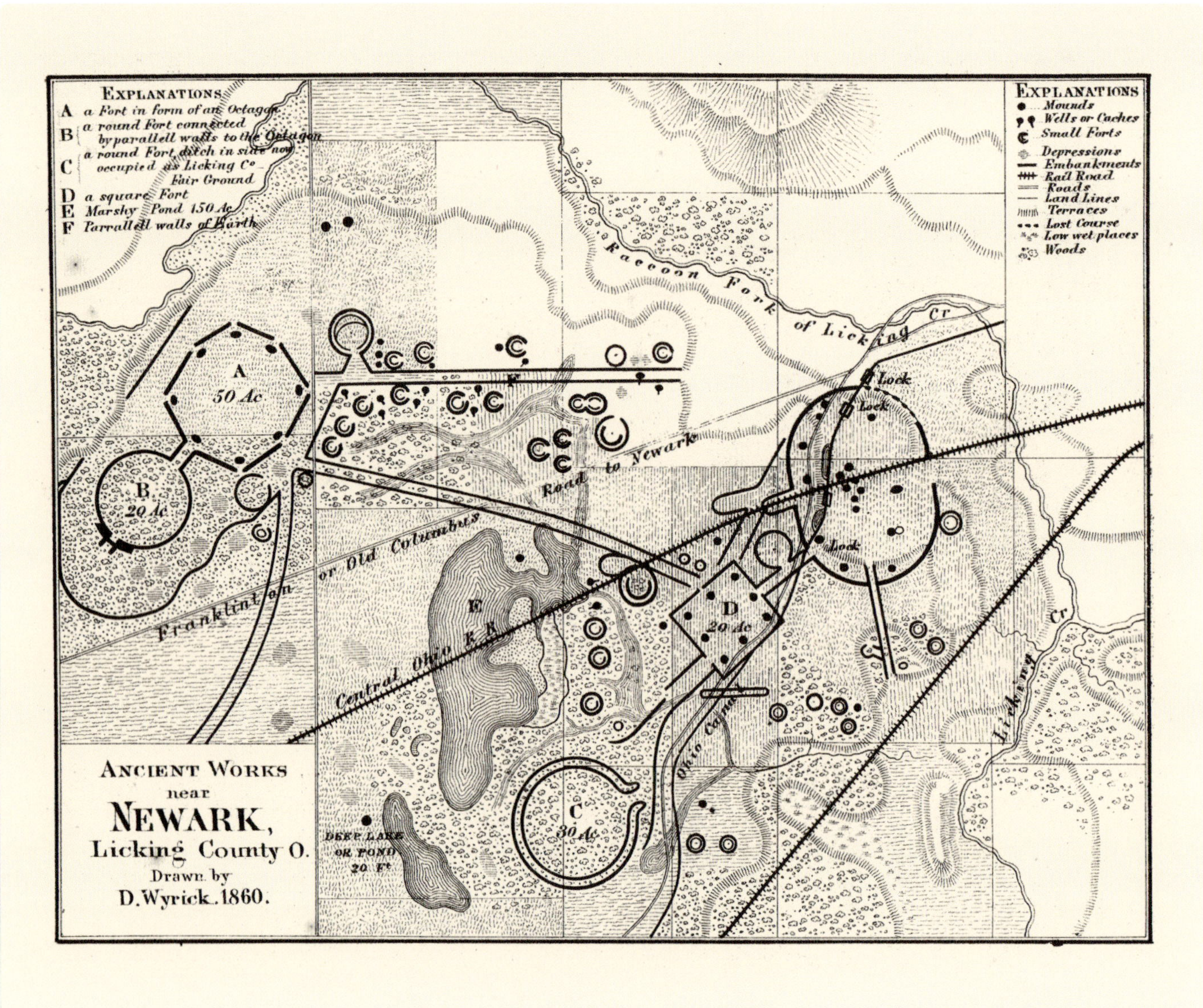

David Wyrick's map of the Newark Earthworks shows the extent of forest clearance across the area by 1860; also compare to the Salisbury map on pages 60–61.

The avenue connecting the Observatory Circle to the Octagon is ninety feet wide and 300 feet long. At just under six feet high, its walls form a continuous angle and level crest with the two adjacent walls of the Octagon. The six remaining walls of the Octagon are nearly identical in height and in their 550-foot length, and together they enclose an area of forty-one acres. The seven remaining corners of the Octagon open through gateways, varying slightly in width. All eight gateways are accompanied by oblong platform mounds standing just inside them—somewhat wider than their corresponding openings, and somewhat higher than the enclosing walls.

CONSTRUCTION AND GEOMETRY

Little is known so far about the construction processes used to build the Octagon Earthworks. Their precise forms, however, indicate the use of a standardized system of measurement and a distinct and highly refined

The Octagon's uncanny precision is apparent inside the perfectly linear, swelling forms of its eight walls (here the southernmost); their heights match typical adult eye level, creating a perfect artificial horizon.

vocabulary of earthwork figures, profiles, and sizes. These may well have been developed over years of experimentation at other sites, especially in the Scioto Valley, before being applied with such consummate perfection here at Newark.

The Octagon Earthworks exhibit an astonishing formal precision and dimensional unity. The Observatory Circle is within two feet of the ideal circumference of a perfect circle with its 1,054-foot diameter. The distance from the Observatory Mound to the center of the Octagon, along the site's principal axis, is twice the Observatory Circle's diameter. The sides of an imaginary square, inscribed diagonally inside the Octagon and connecting its primary axial and cross-axial gateways, have this same dimension. From each of the four corners of this inscribed square, the three opposite octagon gateways are all equally distant (at 1,490 feet, the diagonal of the inscribed square). This same square, if rotated forty-five degrees, would mark the centers of the mounds standing inside the Octagon's other four gateways.

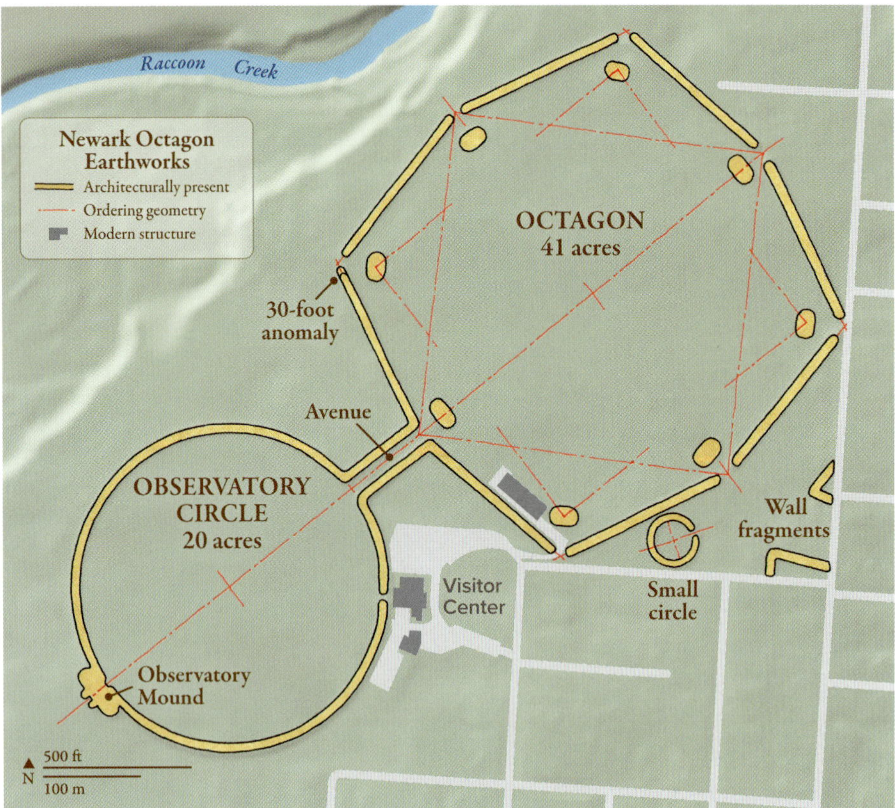

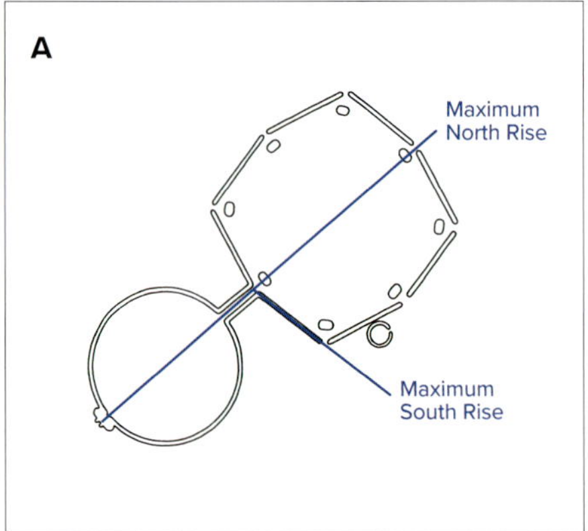

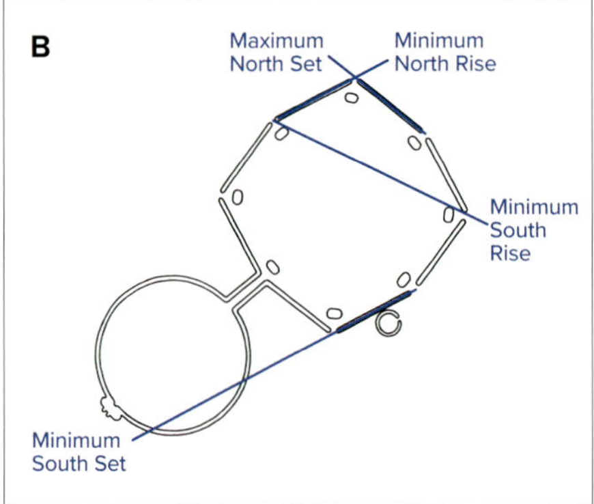

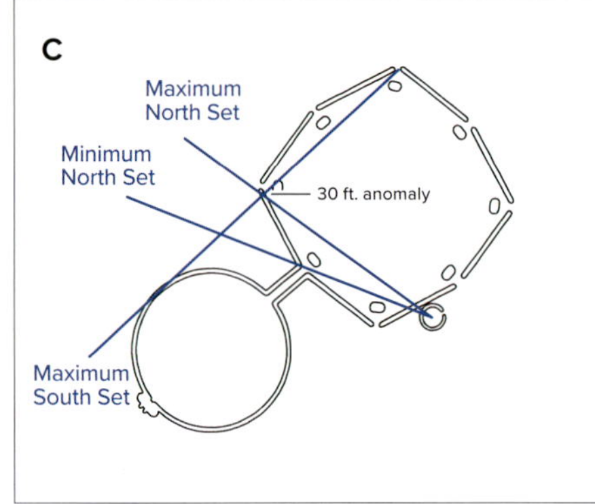

This length, the OCD (1,054 feet or 321 meters), is evidently the multiple of a standard—though now unknown—unit of Hopewell measurement used across the region. Circles at two other now-lost earthworks in the Scioto valley—Circleville and Seal Township—shared this same diameter, as do features at most other sites in this series.

ALIGNMENTS TO THE MOON

Alignments to all eight of the Moon's key positions are encoded in the architecture of Newark's Octagon Earthworks. The site's principal walls, axes, and corners mark six of them. The most prominent alignment, along the site's principal axis, is to the maximum northern moonrise—observable over several consecutive months every 18.6 years. Viewed from the Observatory Mound, this moonrise will appear along the centerline of the parallel-walled avenue and above the far gateway of the Octagon. The maximum southern moonrise aligns along the southwestern wall of the Octagon, viewed from the corner where it joins the avenue [diagram A]. Three more lunar standstills align with the Octagon's northern and southern walls, while the last of these six alignments is the minimum southern rise, appearing above the eastern gateway when viewed from the northwestern apex [diagram B].

One more lunar standstill position involves a strange feature of the design [diagram C]. Nineteenth-century surveyors recorded the Octagon's west-southwestern wall (the one adjoining the avenue) as thirty feet shorter than its symmetrically placed counterpart—the only exception to the earthwork's otherwise perfect symmetry. This apparent anomaly was "corrected" during minor restorations in the early 1900s, but the original point where this wall ended seems to have mattered: The Moon's maximum south set aligns from the northern apex, across this point, and tangent with the Observatory Circle.

The thirty-foot anomaly also figures in alignments from the center of the small circle just outside the Octagon's southern perimeter. From there, the shortened wall was a marker, from one end to the other, of the full range of lunar positions: the maximum northern moonrise across its far end, and the minimum northern across the near corner where it meets the avenue [diagram C]. Had that wall been its "proper" length, these alignments would have been absent.

The encoding of the Octagon's lunar alignments would have required a system of temporary markers, such as timber posts, set and reset to test and record key foresight and back-sight positions over generations of careful observation, before the investment of labor in building the walls. An 1815 site map by Robert Walsh indicated a "cavity" beside each of the Octagon's gateway mounds; a later excavation at one of those locations revealed evidence of a timber post—possibly placed to mark or test alignments.

MODERN HISTORY

The Squier and Davis map showed parts of the Octagon Earthworks cleared for farming by the 1840s. In 1888, William H. Holmes resurveyed the site for the US Bureau of Ethnology and determined that, although the northern portions of the Octagon Earthworks were in cultivation, they still were "quite distinct," and that "most of the south half is yet in the original forest and has never been injured by the plow."

Both the Octagon Earthworks and the Great Circle remain well preserved because local citizens found ways to adapt them to military and entertainment

THE MOON'S MOVEMENTS

The Moon's patterns of movement in the sky are much more rapid and complicated than those of the Sun. The sunrise swings between its maximum (solstice) positions each year—from northeast to southeast and back again. But the moonrise does so each month, and the angle between its extreme positions is not fixed; it changes continuously, increasing slowly over a period of 9.3 years, and then diminishing again over another 9.3 years.

This pattern yields four points along the horizon where the Moon's rising position appears to pause and reverse direction: the *maximum* northern and southern rises, when the monthly oscillation angle is at its widest, every 18.6 years, and the *minimum* northern and southern rises, 9.3 years later, when that oscillating angle is at its narrowest. Four corresponding moonset positions occur on the western horizon, making a total of eight "lunar standstills" throughout what is referred to as the long lunar cycle. This complicated pattern, explained more fully in chapter 9, would have taken generations to understand because of its long period of repetition.

At the climax of its generation-long cycle, the Moon rises stealthily above the Octagon Earthworks' parallel-walled avenue, its bright form and angled path initially filtered by trees.

functions. Just four years after Holmes's survey, a group of civic-minded individuals proposed purchasing the land and presenting it to the state of Ohio for use by the state militia (now the National Guard). The militia occupied the site, called Camp McKinley, between 1893 and 1908. During the summers, as many as 3,500 soldiers camped inside the circle. They mounted cannons on the walls, likely contributing to the popular misconception that the earthworks were ancient fortifications. The troops also worked to restore the damage done to the walls prior to their arrival. In the process, they lengthened the wall that was thirty feet "too short"; of course, its function within the lunar alignment scheme was not yet known.

ABOVE: A National Guard encampment, circa 1895, was the first use of the Octagon site after its preservation was assured by becoming state property.

OPPOSITE: During its use as a military camp, the avenue and Octagon had been cleared of trees, here seen in 1911 prior to the golf club's tree planting program.

By 1908, the state militia had outgrown the site and moved to another location, returning the property to the City of Newark. Many in the community wanted the site to become a city park, but a group of prominent business leaders proposed instead to turn it into a golf course and country club. The city had no funds to develop and maintain the property as a park, and the club's advocates agreed to keep the grounds open to the public. The site was leased to the "Moundbuilders Country Club" in 1910, which built its clubhouse straddling the Observatory Circle. In 1933, the Licking County commissioners transferred ownership to the Ohio State Archaeological and Historical Society (now the Ohio History Connection), which continued the lease arrangement with the country club through 2024.

Because of its history of use as a golf course, the site has seen few archaeological investigations and yielded no known Hopewell-era artifacts. In 1994, Ohio History Connection archaeologists excavated near the southern corner of the Octagon and found the remains of one of Robert Walsh's "cavity" features; its pit and three-inch central posthole gave radiocarbon dates of 260 and 400 CE respectively. That excavation demonstrated that the site has considerable archaeological integrity and significant potential for future research.

AUTHENTICITY AND EXPERIENCE

"I think that the accomplishment at Newark is great for a number of reasons. Of course, the physical scale and precision of it is a great accomplishment. But the fact that this structure simultaneously encodes geometrical and astronomical information is an astounding and highly motivating discovery for any society that makes it. Even today, modern physicists are motivated in a sense by the same kind of dual desire: that is, the desire, the passion, in fact, to find a correspondence between mathematical symmetry and natural phenomena. That is a very powerful discovery, and I think that we're dealing with something like that here."

—RAY HIVELY

Newark's Octagon Earthworks are a geometrical and astronomical tour de force, a perfect synthesis of mathematical order and cosmic complexity, all made visible here with unparalleled formal majesty. With its exceptional combination of immensity and precision, and its excellent state of preservation, this site offers the finest presentation of Hopewell architectural genius. The perfectly linear walls, elegantly screened gateways, and eye-level horizons display the builders' still-unknown techniques of precision measurement on such a vast scale.

This perfectly formed geometry, by also aligning with all eight lunar standstills, reveals the builders' profound astronomical understanding. That its forms, functions, and principles correspond with those of the High Bank Works, fifty-eight miles away, shows that their technical and ritual knowledge was widely shared. The scope and precision of the Octagon Earthworks are a testament both to the society's technical genius and to their ceremonial and cosmic vision.

EXPERIENCING THE MOONRISE, 2005

"Nipahuma, our mother who goes by night, the first mother, the mother of all mothers, nurtured her children, and then when her purpose was complete, she returned to the spirit world; but before she left she told first man and woman that she would never forget them. She continues to watch over us at night as the Moon. The children promised to remember Grandmother Moon whenever she appeared in the sky."

—HITAKONANU'LAXK/TREE BEARD (Lenape)

The Octagon Earthworks and their sister site, High Bank Works near Chillicothe, were designed to mark the Moon's key rising and setting positions throughout the long, 18.6-year cycle. Moon watching and the intervals of time it measures were clearly of immense importance to these people. We are used to observing the Moon's phases—how it seems to come and go through a monthly routine, prominent in the night sky for part of that time and then disappearing for a while. For all ancient cultures, the patterns of the Moon's appearance and positions—more complex, mysterious, and surprising than the Sun's—gave it special meanings and special roles in their cosmology.

Like many modern American Indian tribes, Newark's builders probably used the Moon's monthly phases to structure a seasonal calendar. But the earthworks show us they were also interested in the Moon's other habits—and its much, much longer time cycles. The Octagon's lunar alignments were unknown to modern scholars or visitors until the 1970s, when they were rediscovered by accident. Professors Ray Hively and Robert Horn of Earlham College in Richmond, Indiana, first came to measure the site in 1974, in a spirit of near-complete skepticism.

They wanted to show their students, in a new course on the history of cosmology, that it would be possible to find solar alignments in virtually any complex, well-documented structure. Their goal was to discredit the practice of over-eager "alignment hunting" inspired by the Stonehenge controversies at the time. After a thorough survey of the site, they were astonished to find no solar alignments. What they did find was even more astonishing: there among the Octagon's walls and gateways were all eight of the far more complicated and obscure lunar positions.

They first published their findings in the 1980s, and plans were soon underway for gatherings where this ancient phenomenon could be witnessed for the first time in nearly two millennia. Astronomy data pinpointed the several consecutive months in late 2005 and early 2006 when the nearly full moon would rise over the site's main axis. Posters were printed and invitations sent. For those who were there, it was a powerful experience as, despite unpredictable weather, the ancient architecture displayed its uncanny accuracy.

"We were looking at getting to be the first people in 1,600 years to go and watch something happen in a place and in a way that it was originally intended. And, after anticipating that moment for over fifteen years by then, it still made the hair on the back of my neck go up to actually see the Moon rise, right on axis, and at the appointed time. It made me stop and think about how we don't normally watch moonrises. We know when the sun rises; it gives clear notice of its coming. The moonrise, though, is a completely different beast, it sneaks up on you, and you don't know it's happening. But even if you do know, even then when it happens, it's just, 'ohhh.' And so there we stood, on the central alignment, and looked along where those walls said to us, whispered across the centuries, 'There it will happen.' And when it did, it was just one of the most memorable moments of my life."

—JEFF GILL

"A hundred American Indian Studies professors were attending their national conference at Ohio State University. We took them out that evening after dark. It had been raining and had stopped. We got to the site and there was this mist: you couldn't see the walls of the earthworks let alone the Moon. But we had brought a Lakota spiritual leader, and Native singers from around the state, who led us in. We walked into the center of the Octagon. The Native leader sang and prayed. We stood there in the mist unable to see anything at all for about a half an hour. We observed the Moon lifting into the sky as predicted by the earthen architecture. It was occluded by clouds at first, then burst out in shiny glory. And as we walked

Over several consecutive months every 18.6 years, the moonrise position returns to its northernmost position on the eastern horizon, where it aligns with the central axis of the Octagon Earthworks.

back, I saw fifty-year-old college professors with tears running down their faces. It was a tremendously moving experience."

—RICHARD SHIELS

"It was night; a kind of wet, foggy dew was happening. It had been a rainy, cloudy day and evening, but just when the Moon was to rise, it seemed to break. And there she was. There she came to visit. I could smell people burning sage. I could smell sweet grass. I could hear low chanting, and it transported me for that moment. I could feel the power of that place."

—CHRISTINE BALLENGEE-MORRIS

Although the lunar phase cycle does not align perfectly with the solar year or the seasons, many North American Indigenous cultures (like others globally) have long favored the Moon as a marker of time. These Native calendars are structured on the Moon's 29.5-day interval of waxing and waning, with twelve of these lunar months then reconciled to the solar year by adding a periodic thirteenth "leap month." With these calendars, the turning of nature's seasons through a full year is marked by the "Moons;" the traditions name each one after what is going on around them in their ecological environment, dividing the year into patterns of life and work. The names differ greatly from one tribe to another, though they typically evoke seasonal tasks (Harvest Moon) or what is appearing in nature (Blackberry Moon, Frost on Grass Moon). Ceremonies for the seasons and community tasks reflect the belief that the Moon is tied to both spiritual life (as a giver of wisdom, guidance, or protection, for example) and practical matters, such as the movement or behavior of the animals.

"The Moon is a woman; we identify her as 'she.' One of the Canadian sisters has taught me that when our people go, our females, and that Moon is full, they're dancing around the Moon. And that's when we have our ceremony, and we talk to them, and we send them our prayers, so they can take them on to the Creator. Every time I see the full Moon, I think about, you know, our ancestors, my mother and all of them, dancing around the Moon. And that's a good thought, a good thought."

—LINDA S. POOLAW (Kiowa/Delaware, 1942–2025)

The ditches of the Great Circle's monumental gateway create a wide, sharply defined entrance platform.

6.

GREAT CIRCLE EARTHWORKS

"These places . . . embody the spirit and the record of their significance to our ancestors, which makes them significant to us today. They are a cultural and ancestral inheritance belonging to all the Indigenous descendants of their builders."

—STACEY HALFMOON (Caddo Nation)

Just over a mile from the Octagon, near the southeastern edge of Newark's large terrace, stands the Great Circle—the other major surviving component of the original complex. Its huge earthen ring rises in a peaceful park at the southern boundary of the city of Newark, where it meets the neighboring town of Heath. The South Fork of the Licking River flows nearby to the east, with steep wooded hills rising not far beyond. Small houses along tree-lined streets surround the site on three sides.

The principal access is off a busy highway, yet the mood shifts quickly to the quiet park setting, buffered and sheltered by mature trees. From the park's main entrance path, the high wall rises prominently on the left, growing into a powerfully monumental gateway whose huge, ditched embankments define an axis into the heart of the circle and out, past a small museum, to the northeastern horizon. Parkland to the north and east contains other remnant earthworks.

CIRCULAR WALL AND DITCH

The most immediately impressive feature of the Great Circle Earthworks is its grand entrance—a monumental pair of parallel embankments, their crests 200 feet apart. They rise to a height of sixteen feet above the exterior ground level and are accompanied on their interiors by sculpted ditches of equal depth, whose rims sharply define an entrance platform sixty feet wide and 165 feet long. Processions would have crossed the platform, framed by the high walls, into the interior, where the huge circular space opens out into the far distance and a low, swelling form rises in the center. With a diameter of almost 1,200 feet, and enclosing twenty-five acres, this is the largest surviving geometric enclosure built by the Hopewell culture. It could accommodate multitudes.

The height of the perimeter wall varies from its tallest at the gateway down to just five feet along its southwestern rim. The ditch follows along

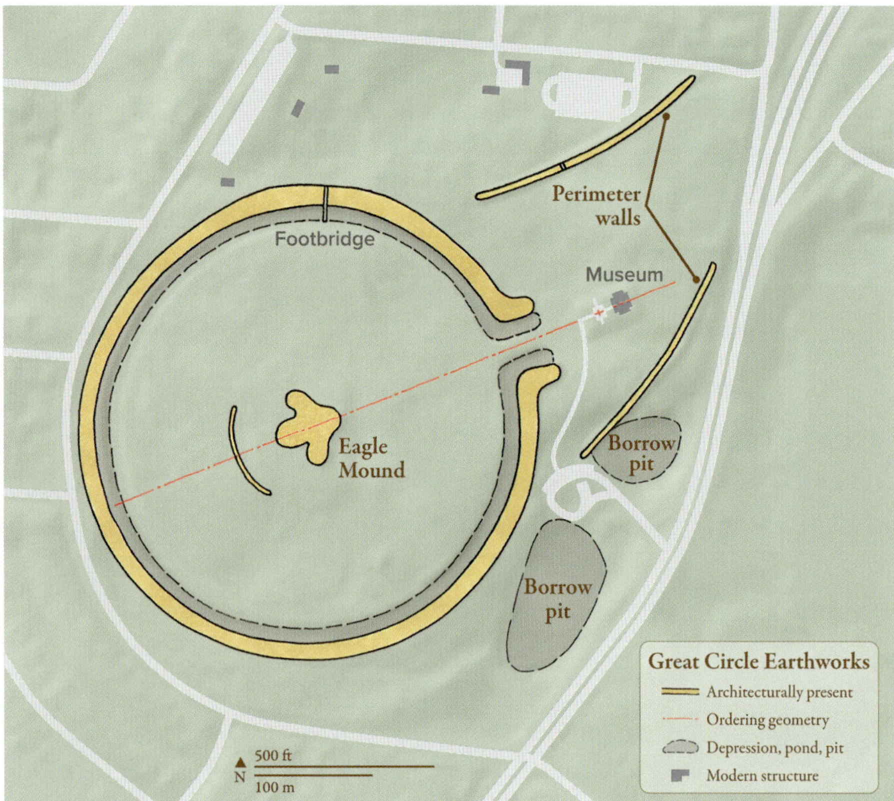

the inner edge of the wall, its depth equal to the height of its adjacent wall, creating a continuous surface that amplifies the scale and impact of the enclosure. The builders combined contrasting soil colors within the wall, using a yellowish hue for the interior face, strikingly different from the brown soils of the wall's exterior. They lined the ditch with clay and stone to help it retain water.

Several features suggest that the Great Circle might have been the earliest among the geometric earthworks treated in this series—a transitional work on the way to the full Hopewell achievement. First, it resembles a typical Adena earthen ring, complete with interior ditch and eastern gateway, although the scale difference here is a dramatic innovation. Second, the geometry is a bit imperfect; the circle's northern rim is faintly segmented. Third, the wall was built on an unprepared prairie surface rather than after careful removal of the topsoil, which was the later and near-universal Hopewell practice. Finally, it lacks two features present in all the others: the standard measurement OCD and alignments to principal solar or lunar standstills. Still, if the Great Circle does mark a beginning, a point of design departure, then the innovation here in terms of spatial impact and monumentality is breathtaking.

CONSTRUCTION

In 1992, an excavation through the Great Circle embankment wall uncovered the original soil surface and the sequence of the wall's construction. Pollen and other evidence showed the site to have been an open prairie surrounded by an oak and hickory forest. The excavators encountered a small mound beneath the wall, suggesting that a ring of mounds may have stood in a circle, marking out the perimeter as a first step in the construction. The builders then excavated the inner ditch, using its dark colored soil to overlay and connect the mound series beneath a continuous embankment. Finally, they took yellow gravelly soil from the deep pit just east of the enclosure and laid it up along the wall's interior. We can't know whether the community intended the contrasting soils to be visible (at least when they were fresh), or whether they had a symbolic or other purpose, effective even when obscured by vegetation.

They engineered the inner ditch to hold water, as it still did when Caleb Atwater found it "half filled" during his visit in 1820. An 1887 OSAHS investigation found the ditch lined with "fine gravel and cobble stone" and with a stone pavement along its inner edge. Besides providing much of the soil for the wall, this ditch would have created a dramatic water feature—its reflective surface presenting an image for the celebrants of Sky and Earth floating upon the watery Beneath World of American Indian belief.

OPPOSITE, RIGHT: The contiguous surface of the Great Circle's interior ditch and embankment wall is at its most impressive at the monumental gateway, diminishing gradually toward the far perimeter.

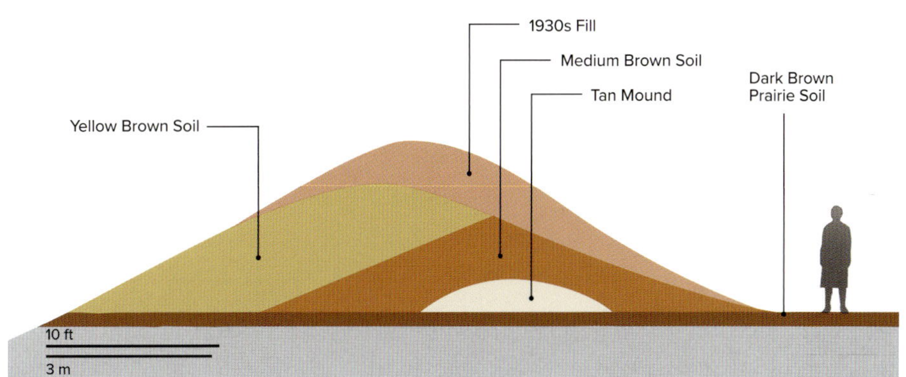

RIGHT: A cross section of the Great Circle wall shows soil types of contrasting color—yellow facing into the circle, and brown on the exterior—similar to other earthworks such as Hopeton.

EAGLE MOUND

The broad, undulating Eagle Mound, named for its symmetrical, winged shape, rises in the center of the Great Circle. Restored in the 1930s to the dimensions recorded by Squier and Davis ninety years before, its central section is six feet high; its other three lobes are somewhat lower. Head to tail, it measures just over 150 feet, with a wingspan of 200 feet. At some distance behind this mound, a long, low crescent remains from the time of the mound's restoration, based on the records of Squier and Davis, although no evidence has confirmed it as a feature of the original design.

Eagle Mound was excavated in 1928 by the OSAHS's Emerson Greenman, revealing the posthole pattern of a ninety-eight-by-twenty-three-foot, timber-framed building with screen walls (or lines of posts) extending from it like two wings. At the center of this structure was a large, shallow rectangular basin lined with fire-hardened clay. Though it seemed similar to the crematory basins found in other Hopewell mounds, there were no traces of human remains in the sand that filled it. As at other sites, when people were finished using this structure, they dismantled or burned it and covered its floor with earth to form the mound.

The scope and precision of the Great Circle are, as with most Hopewell earthworks, especially evident in an aerial view.

Very few Hopewell-era artifacts have been found at the Great Circle. Greenman found two copper ornaments—a beaver and a crescent—and many small scraps of cut mica on the floor of the Eagle Mound building. Otherwise, only a grooved axe and a copper celt come from the interior of the circle. Most other artifacts recovered from the area are associated with the entertainment venues that occupied the site in the nineteenth and early twentieth centuries.

GEOMETRY

The Great Circle is a key element in the Newark complex's harmonized circles and squares. Its perimeter matched that of the Wright Square, and its area equals that of the OCD-sided square inscribed in the Octagon. Chapter 11 explains further how the interlocking properties of squares and circles apparently fascinated the Hopewell architects. The center of the Great Circle is six OCDs from the center of the Octagon's Observatory Circle, and that line points to the maximum southern moonrise.

The Great Circle's northeasterly orientation is striking, with its winged central mound like an arrow aimed outward through the grand entrance. That axial alignment, however, does not mark any of the major lunar or solar standstills. Instead, at sixty-nine degrees east of north, it points to the spring cross-quarter sunrise on May 5, the date midway between the spring equinox and the summer solstice—still understood by gardeners as the ideal time for planting.

More of ancient Newark's unifying geometry—the continuous perimeter that once encircled the entire complex—has been restored in the parkland north and east of the Great Circle. Two segments roughly 500 feet long converge

SPIRIT BARRIER

In his 1997 book *An Archaeology of the Soul*, Robert Hall describes the belief among some tribes that water serves as a barrier protecting the living from the movement of the souls of the dead or other supernatural manifestations that could not pass through or over water. Either separately or together, water and circular geometry contribute to the magical effect. One could substitute ashes for water, and walking in a circle around a person could silence them. Part of the water's effectiveness may have been its reflective surface; taboos about mirrors—that they can capture a spirit or soul—are widespread across many global cultures.

The Great Circle, with its clay-lined ditch intact, presented a monumental expression of this power of circularity and water. During dry seasons, water-associated materials like clay or river stones still made the symbolic point. At Fort Ancient, a water barrier is doubled: a string of ponds follows along inside the walls, while constructed ditches complete a riverine boundary outside. Mound City has eight clay-lined pits positioned outside its enclosure wall. Although the Great Circle and Fort Ancient had no major funerary functions or burials inside, other motives may have required control over the movement of the spirits.

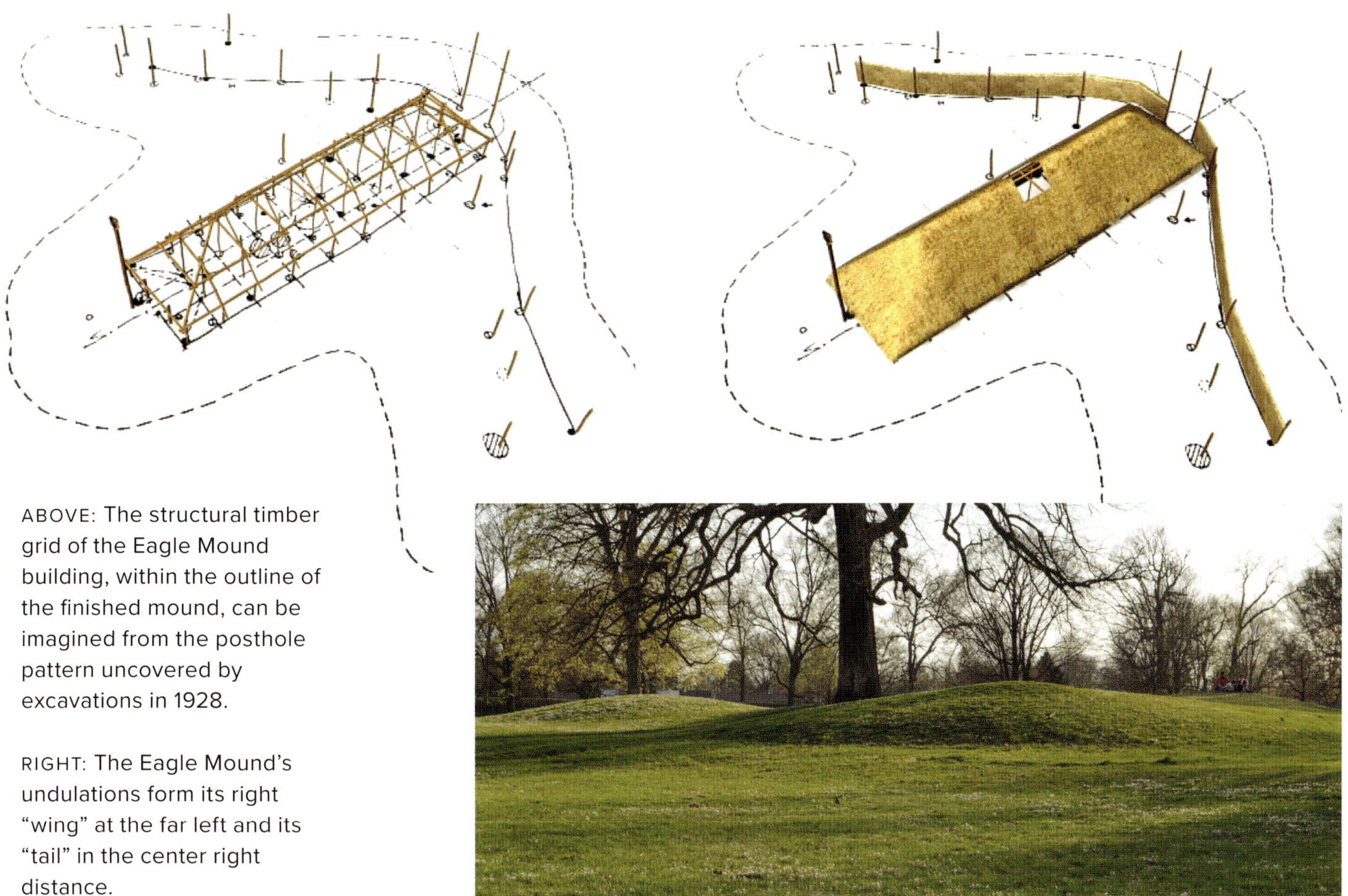

ABOVE: The structural timber grid of the Eagle Mound building, within the outline of the finished mound, can be imagined from the posthole pattern uncovered by excavations in 1928.

RIGHT: The Eagle Mound's undulations form its right "wing" at the far left and its "tail" in the center right distance.

toward the northeast, where they once defined a broad passage toward the square more than a quarter mile away. In 1992, an excavation located their preserved foundations, confirming that the locations of these restorations, done sixty years earlier, are correct.

Two large pits dominate the area to the southeast of the Great Circle, adjacent to the current parking area and the highway; the one to the north is the more pronounced today. They were likely borrow pits—sources of the yellowish soil used to form the interior face of the earthwork.

MODERN HISTORY

Following the end of the Hopewell era around 400 CE, forests reclaimed the site. No evidence of intervening use or occupation by later Indigenous people has been found. The earliest record of Euro-American contact with the Great Circle dates from 1800, when a Cherry Valley pioneer named Catherine Stadden reported that her husband Isaac had "found an old fort in the woods while hunting deer." They returned together on horseback for a tour. Soon after, the earthwork was preserved in its untouched condition, thanks to the efforts of one Nathan Seymour, its first owner. Seymour did not allow the interior of the enclosure to be plowed, nor did he cut the old growth trees within the encircling wall and ditch.

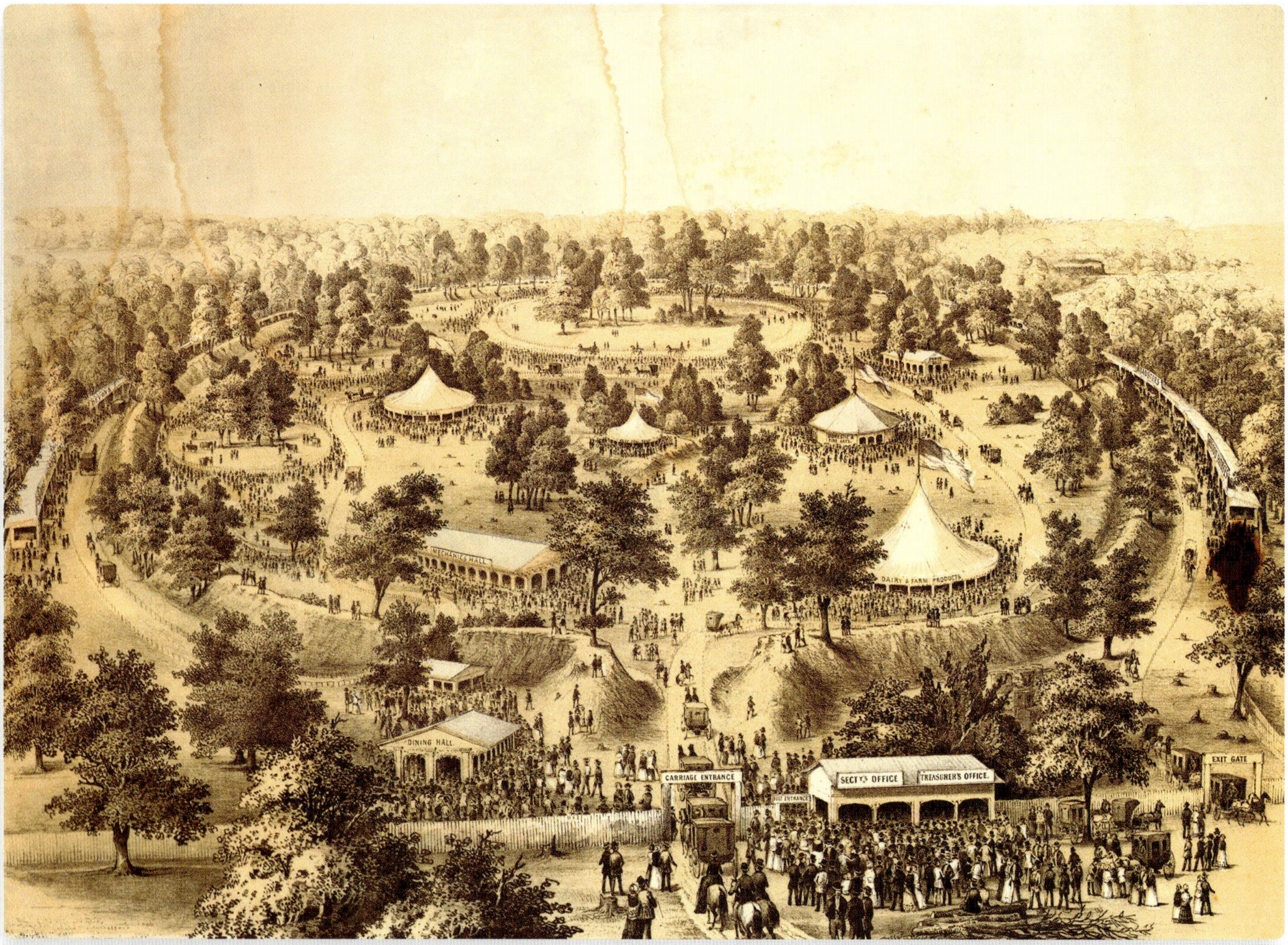

206,994
Historic Mound, Idlewilde Park,
Newark, Ohio

In 1854, the Great Circle became the Licking County Fairgrounds, whose half-mile-long horse racing track, grandstand, livestock buildings, and other attractions remained in use until 1933. In October 1861, the fair was suspended while the Great Circle served as Camp John Sherman, where the Seventy-sixth Ohio Volunteer Infantry Regiment trained for the US Civil War. In 1884, Buffalo Bill's Wild West Show came to the fairgrounds. With thousands of Licking County residents sitting on the earthen embankments, Buffalo Bill himself and his whole crew rode in and out of the grand gateway. He said it was the most amazing place he ever did the show.

James Lingafelter, a local banker, established a summer resort on the site in 1898. Called Idlewilde Park, it became central Ohio's premiere amusement park throughout the next decade. Attractions included a Ferris wheel, a "switchback railroad" (roller coaster), a casino, a theater, bowling alleys, shooting galleries, a dance pavilion, a billiard hall, four ponds with boating and swimming (one of which was the large borrow pit outside the earthwork), and a "European" hotel and restaurant. Even with all these facilities, Idlewilde Park's promoters declared that its "crowning glory" was the "mysterious Old Fort" itself.

In 1931, fifteen members of the Meskwaki Nation (then called "Tama Indians") visited Newark as part of the King Brothers' Wild West Rodeo. They camped at the Great Circle fairgrounds, setting up their tepees near the horse barns. The local newspaper reported an interview with Chief John Buffalo, who expressed the group's surprise and excitement upon seeing the earthworks and who correctly surmised their antiquity ("many thousands of Moons old") and the tools and methods of their construction. According to the report, Chief Buffalo intended to have "photographs made of the mounds with his Indians grouped on them to send back to his folks on the western reservation."

OPPOSITE, TOP: A nineteenth-century engraving shows the Great Circle as the site of the Ohio State Fair in 1854.

OPPOSITE, BOTTOM: The Great Circle's monumental gateway was a principal attraction of Idlewilde Park in the early 1900s.

RESTORATION AND MANAGEMENT

In 1933, the county commissioners deeded the Great Circle over to the OSAHS. The same year, work began under Greenman's direction to restore the walls where they had been worn down by fairgoers, restore the Eagle Mound following his excavations, and prepare for the removal of the fairground buildings. The site had sustained modest damage during its use as a fairground and amusement park, less to the earthwork than to the land around it. In 1934, the Civilian Conservation Corps (the US government's Depression-era work program, the CCC) began a three-year program to complete the restorations. The work was meticulous and mainly informed by the descriptions given by Squier and Davis in the late 1840s.

The structures remaining today from the CCC period are the superintendent's stone-clad house and a picnic shelter near the northwest corner of the property, along with a stone bridge and steps over the northern section of the Great Circle ditch and embankment. In 1971, the Ohio History Connection built the small museum outside the Great Circle's gateway and installed a bronze orientation model of the entire Newark Earthworks complex out front.

The archaeological investigations in and near the Great Circle, though few, have added important knowledge about Hopewell architecture, specifically timber ceremonial buildings, the coloration and application

ABOVE, LEFT: In the 1930s, a stone footbridge replaced this wooden ramp that once connected the Great Circle's fairground-era horse barns to its interior racetrack.

ABOVE, RIGHT: Visitors often sit and rest on the softly elevated crest of the restored Eagle Mound, centering themselves within the Great Circle's magnificent space.

of soils in the circular wall, the water-retaining methods used in its interior ditch, and the nature of the environment at the time the earthwork was built.

AUTHENTICITY AND EXPERIENCE

The Great Circle's spatial grandeur begins with its immense earthen gateway—the most dramatic architectural feature of any surviving Hopewell earthwork. One can imagine the grand processions crossing its broad platform, between high walls and deep ditches. Inside, the huge circular enclosure presents Hopewell spatiality at its finest—perception-stretching distances, defined within a clear geometric order, and not shrouded by forests or compromised by degradation. The wall's enclosing form is enhanced by the continuous slope into its once-watery interior ditch.

From any position, the constructed horizon directs our focus toward the gentle undulations of Eagle Mound, where visitors are often inspired to pause or rest, in quiet reflection. Newark's Great Circle is an archetypal sacred space, an image of cosmic monumentality. Its huge, level, green disc seems to float, its soft-formed perimeter creating a world apart. Its gently swelling central focus and its majestic shade trees evoke a serene, meditative mood.

WE ARE STILL HERE

"I was giving a group of Eastern Shawnee tribal members a tour of the Great Circle, which ended at Eagle Mound. Most of the group wandered off to enjoy the rest of the site, but tribal elder Brett Barnes remained. Though confined at the time to an electric scooter, he struggled to stand up, saying he felt the need to say something. I waited to hear what it was, but his words were not directed at me. Gazing intently at Eagle Mound, he spoke quietly in the Shawnee language for a minute or two. Assuming he was praying, I was embarrassed not to have given him more privacy. But he explained that it wasn't a prayer—he was speaking to the ancestors. I asked if he could share what he had said. He replied that he told them, 'We are still here.'

I was overwhelmed by that simple declaration. Despite the long separations of time and distance, Barnes could feel the immanence of his ancestors within the Great Circle, and he felt compelled to reassure them that Indigenous descendants were still here. World Heritage inscription requires a site to have authenticity, which in part is judged by the 'spirit and feeling' of the place. Barnes' experience at the Great Circle is surely a powerful testimonial to the enduring spirit and feeling of the place."

—BRAD LEPPER

COSMOLOGY

"For Native Peoples—past and present—the Earth is a being, personified. She provides us with the life-sustaining energies to thrive and survive on her fertile soils. In our relationship with her and her many offspring—waters, vascular plants, trees, mammals, fish, birds, clays, and rocks—we understand the sacrifices of their energies for our needs. As a result, we give thanks and offerings of gifts in acknowledgement."

—JOE STAHLMAN (Tuscarora/Pennsylvania Dutch)

Newark's Great Circle is a cosmic spatial experience—with its earthen ring and watery ditch, its green disc and winged icon, its majestic axis. These features suggest long-standing American Indian cosmological beliefs—traditions intimately connected to the natural world, the riverine landscapes, and the creatures of the forest. American Indian beliefs maintain a respectful kinship with all these things. When water is part of an earthwork's design, or when small woodland creatures adorn the bowls of ceremonial smoking pipes, those connections are apparent.

A cosmological model known across the continent is the three-layered universe. The Sky is the Above World, the Earth we live on is in the middle, and the Beneath World is a watery domain. These worlds are connected by a vertical line—an axis mundi—and the Earth World is divided into four quarters. Different tribes had their own variations, but this basic understanding was shared throughout the Eastern Woodlands at least since the Mississippian era and probably long before. In some accounts, the Earth World is a synthetic combination of all three realms.

We live on the Earth World along with four-legged animals, plants, stones, soil, and so on. This world is a disk floating on the water—the Beneath World—and is surmounted by the celestial dome of the Above World. Many creation stories tell of the land—the Earth—being formed from a bit of mud, brought up out of the water by an animal (muskrat, crawfish, water beetle, duck; it varies by tribe). In Haudenosaunee and Ojibway accounts, the primordial mud is placed on a turtle's back, where it grows to become the Earth—"Turtle Island."

The Sun inhabits the Above World in the daytime Sky, one aspect of a creative deity providing life-sustaining warmth and sacred fire for the Earth World and its inhabitants. So too, the Thunderers inhabit the day Sky, wielding thunder, lightning, and storms. The Beneath World is manifested as the starry night Sky, dominated by the Milky Way (the "Path of Souls" after death in many beliefs) and inhabited by the Moon, one aspect of a creative female deity associated with birth or rebirth, fertility, and vegetative growth in the Earth World. Most Eastern Woodland peoples see the Moon as a reflection or manifestation of an Earth Mother or Grandmother associated with the Beneath World, the land of the dead.

The Above and Beneath Worlds are in dualistic opposition—day and night, Sky and water, Sun and Moon. Humans use prayer and ritual to maintain these oppositions in a proper balance. The axis mundi linking the three realms can be represented in art and ceremony by a living tree, or by a wooden post rooted in the Beneath World and rising into the Sky. A rising column of smoke also connects the Earth World, and the gathered community, to the spirits of the Above World. Cremation fires send the deceased's spirit skyward; ceremonial pipe smoking carries prayers to the divine powers above.

Each of these layers has its associated animals and spirit powers: the Thunderbirds of the Above World are engaged in a mythic struggle (or balance) with the Beneath World's Underwater Panthers—powerful beings with attributes of both panthers and snakes. In various accounts, they may have serpent scales but also horns or legs. The Great Serpent and Underwater Panther are probably different aspects or versions of the same mythical being. For the Haudenosaunee, serpents have a role in consuming the dead (bodily decomposition is in effect a "digestion") and transporting their souls to the land of the ancestors over the Milky Way. The opening of a grave, ossuary, cave, tree trunk, or whirlpool—all points of contact with the Beneath World—was figuratively the open mouth of the Great Serpent.

Connections are also represented by the liminal animals. Those who can travel between one realm and another or are at home in more than one, like birds or beavers, are particularly powerful and appear frequently in Hopewell artistry. Ducks and roseate spoonbills, for example, who know the air, the land, and the water equally well, are featured often, as on a double-headed

A lone tree can serve as an axis-mundi, a symbolic connection of the Earth World with the Above World—home of the Sun and the Thunderers—and with the Beneath World.

smoking pipe from Hopewell Mound Group, or the Duck Pot from Mound City.

The Beneath World can be accessed through caves or rock shelters or evoked in the presence of water—in springs, rivers, pools, or waterfalls. Just as there are liminal animals who can travel between one realm and another, liminal places in the landscape can serve as thresholds between the worlds. Most important, the essential features of such places of encounter can also be constructed features of ritual spaces, such as the reflective ponds and watery ditches at the earthwork sites.

The world is also understood as quartered by the four directions. The cardinal points—east, north, west, and south—receive honor through prayers, often addressed to the winds and other associated spirit powers. Hopewell geometry reflects this four-part quartering of the universe, as in an elegant copper circle from the Hopewell Mound Group, or the large post circle at the same site, where four entrances mark its division into quadrants.

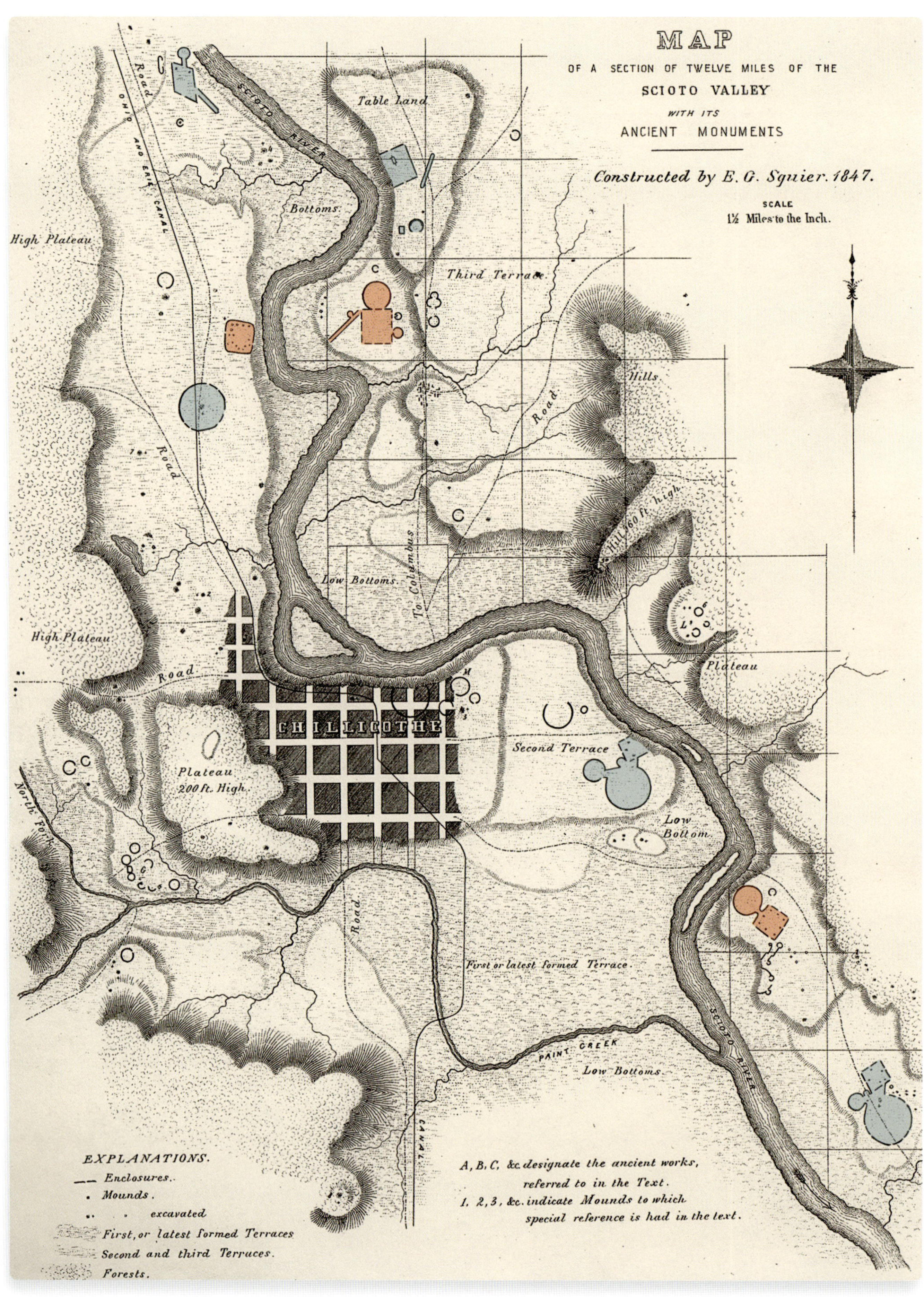
MAP
OF A SECTION OF TWELVE MILES OF THE
SCIOTO VALLEY
WITH ITS
ANCIENT MONUMENTS
Constructed by E. G. Squier. 1847.
SCALE
1½ Miles to the Inch.
Table Land
Scioto River
Ohio and Erie Canal
Road
Bottoms
High Plateau
Third Terrace
Hills
Road
Hill 360 ft. high
Low Bottoms
To Columbus
High Plateau
Road
Plateau
CHILLICOTHE
Second Terrace
Plateau
200 ft. High
North Fork
Low Bottom
Road
First or latest formed Terrace
Paint Creek
Low Bottoms
Scioto River
Canal
EXPLANATIONS.
Enclosures.
Mounds.
excavated
First, or latest formed Terraces
Second and third Terraces.
Forests.
A, B, C, &c. designate the ancient works, referred to in the Text.
1, 2, 3, &c. indicate Mounds to which special reference is had in the text.

7.

HOPETON EARTHWORKS

"Soil was the palette from which they chose to paint their interpretation and understanding of the world. These places, whether they are places of worship or tools to measure the creation, should be treated as altars. Altars to either the mysteries or to the cosmos."

—CHIEF BENJAMIN BARNES (Shawnee Tribe)

Mound City and the Hopeton Earthworks lie directly across the Scioto River from each other, about three miles north of Chillicothe. Both occupy the high, wide terraces formed when outwash from the last glaciation filled the ancient Teays River Valley. Several other large geometric earthwork complexes were once spaced more-or-less evenly along this dramatic, twelve-mile section of the valley. Hopeton lies within a large horseshoe bend of the river, overlooking the Scioto's floodplain below and in turn overlooked by a third terrace above. A long footpath rises from a parking area, skirts the edge of a vast open meadow, and then climbs to the upper terrace. From this elevated position, a breathtaking view opens out over the monument and the wide valley panorama beyond.

From most vantage points, visitors are isolated from the noise and intrusions of the modern world, as native grasslands, croplands, and riparian vegetation—as well as the sprawling monumentality of the earthworks themselves—dominate the landscape. The ruins of the square's southeastern corner and western wall are visible as two wide, gentle humps in an old farm road, and the square's northwestern corner rises to much of its original height. All the major geometric elements stand out today in the national park's differential mowing scheme, which leaves uncut native grasses and wildflowers to outline the precise shapes. The huge geometric figures spreading across this broad riverine landscape offer an especially vivid image of the vastness of Hopewell spatiality.

Squier and Davis's 1847 map of the Chillicothe area shows several Hopewell geometric earthworks along the Scioto and its tributaries. Hopeton and Mound City stand across from each other near the top; High Bank Works is at the lower right (all shown here in red).

SITE FEATURES

The architecture of the Hopeton Earthworks is dominated by two large geometric enclosures—an irregular square with rounded corners and a slight

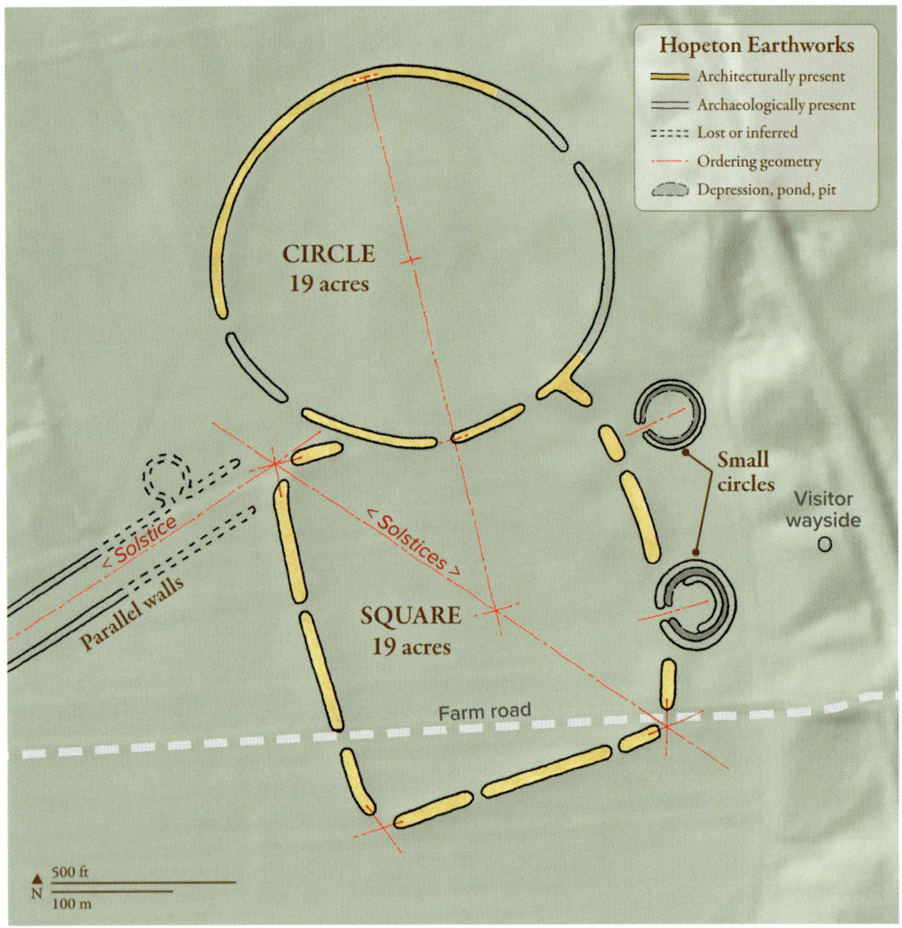

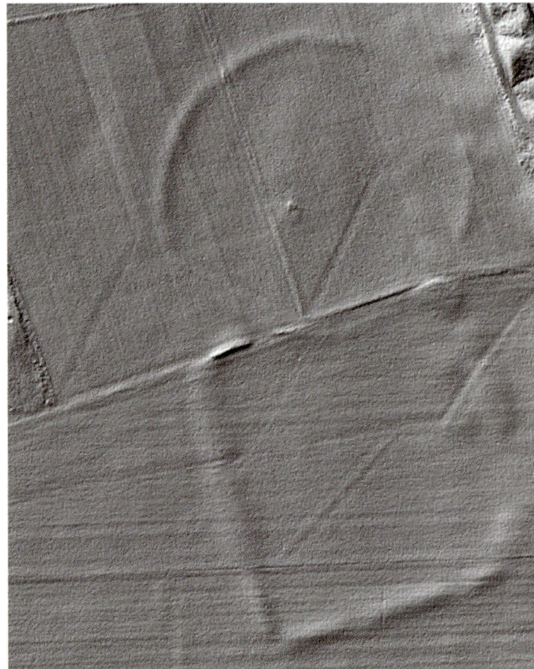

outward curvature in its northeastern face, and a more nearly perfect circle slightly overlapping it. These two figures have essentially equal areas and together encompass thirty-eight acres. Faint traces remain of three ancillary earthworks—a pair of parallel linear embankments originally stretching for nearly 2,400 feet toward the Scioto River, and two small circular ditch-and-bank enclosures, 200 and 250 feet in diameter, each with a gateway facing into the northeastern side of the square.

The "square" at Hopeton is actually an irregular rectangle with overall dimensions of 890 by 950 feet, composed of eleven distinct segments. In the mid-nineteenth century, its walls measured nearly twelve feet high and fifty feet wide at their base. Their broad, level summits could, in the words of Squier and Davis, "admit the passage of a coach." Although much reduced by plowing today, these walls can still be readily traced on the ground. A portion in the southeast corner retains more than six feet of relief, its soil spread out to an approximate width of seventy-five feet. A section at the northwest corner retains a very distinct form, because throughout decades of farm use it was preserved in a fence line. The square's northwest to southeast diagonal aligns with both the summer solstice sunset and the winter solstice sunrise.

The adjacent large circle is more nearly perfect than the square, yet it is actually an ellipse with an average diameter of approximately one OCD. Its wall is composed of clay and averaged five feet high and thirty feet wide in the mid-nineteenth century. The western and northern sections can be traced on the ground today, though not easily. The magnetic signature of a narrow ditch follows the outer edge of the circle, and LiDAR images show most of its original shape. Magnetic surveys in 2016–17, in cooperation with the National Park Service and the *Deutsches Archäologisches Institut*, revealed the precise foundations of the walls, plus a series of regularly spaced, three-foot-diameter postholes ringing the circle's interior—the apparent traces of a monumental woodhenge.

Hopeton's circle-and-square combination resembles Mound City and its nearby but now invisible Shriver Circle (which Squier and Davis illustrated together in their publication). Positioning the equal-area circle and square together at Hopeton suggests a possible origin of the novel idea to bring into harmony what had previously been separate spatial symbols—a step toward later applications elsewhere showing greater geometric precision.

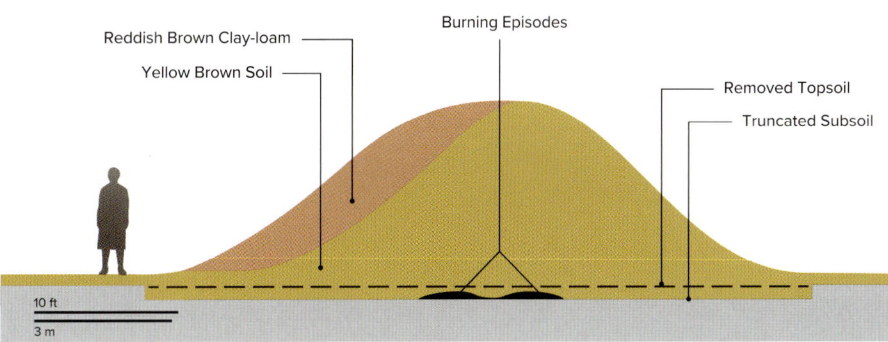

OPPOSITE, RIGHT: A LiDAR image of the Hopeton Earthworks shows the current surface expression of the walls.

ABOVE: A 2002 excavation through the wall of Hopeton's square revealed its distinct soil colors; the dark reddish soil in the foreground is the base of the wall's original exterior slope.

RIGHT: A cross section of one of the Hopeton square's eleven segments indicates its construction sequence and soil placements; the lower left portion corresponds to what is visible in the trench photo.

CONSTRUCTION PROCESS

Investigations by archaeologists Bret Ruby and Mark Lynott between 1996 and 2008 have made Hopeton perhaps the best-dated of the Hopewell earthworks. More than thirty radiocarbon dates from within the earthwork walls indicate that most construction probably occurred between the years 1 and 250 CE. Evidence indicates that the walls were built in stages using soils with distinct colors and textures for each phase, but any pauses between construction episodes were too short for vegetation and organic soils to develop.

Wall building involved a complex sequence of steps. First, the topsoil was stripped off along the wall's footprint to create a uniform surface. The builders kindled small fires on this prepared ground and, while they were still burning, laid down dark organic soil and sometimes sprinkled mica flakes. They built up the wall in a specific cross-sectional pattern, maintaining distinct boundaries between two homogeneous soil types. Most often, yellowish silt loam came first, forming the core and the interior aspect of the wall. Then reddish sandy loam was laid up along the exterior.

At Hopeton's large circle, this meticulous process of wall construction was either preceded or followed by the erection of a series of monumental timber posts set at twenty-foot intervals along the inside edge of the embankment, creating a gigantic woodhenge. To erect each post, they set it into a

In 2016, Hopewell Culture National Historical Park began an interpretive planting and mowing program at the Hopeton Earthworks, bringing its partially ruined earthen walls into clear view.

straight-sided pit to a depth of four feet, well below the frost line. When the posts were later removed, they backfilled the holes with soil. The diameter and depth of the postholes indicate that these were massive, dressed timbers at least the size of telephone poles—up to eighteen inches in diameter and at least twelve to sixteen feet tall.

The two smaller circles east of the square open their gateways into gaps in the square's slightly curving northeastern wall. Both had ditches following their interior rims, while the southern one also had another arc of earth along the inside of its ditch.

Though their topographic presence has faded from view since the 1800s, Hopeton's parallel walls persisted in aerial photographs until the 1960s and left faint traces in magnetic data as late as 2017. Spaced 150 feet apart and less than three feet tall, their path began near the northwestern corner of the square and extended toward the southwest for nearly half a mile to the edge of the second terrace. Their southeasterly orientation frames a view of the winter solstice sunset, seen from the same point as the sunrise on the same day across two corners of the square.

MODERN HISTORY

The terrace surrounding the Hopeton site saw intermittent periods of occupation after 400 CE, and some Indigenous peoples may have reused or altered portions of the earthwork a few centuries later, around 1000. There is no evidence of the site's occupation after 1500. The region's native hardwood forests reclaimed the landscape during the final centuries before Euro-American colonization.

EARTH, SOIL

"The Hopewell earthworks are piles of dirt in the same way that the Parthenon is a pile of rocks."

—BRAD LEPPER

"Building with earth was purposeful. Stone could have been used but to many Native peoples of North America, earth may have been more appropriate because earth was likely the most sacred material for the Native builders. We the Potawatomi call it Kumde Kwe—'Mother Earth.' We have a family relationship and bond with the earth. We celebrate it."

—JOHN N. LOW (Pokagon Band of Potawatomi)

The earthwork builders were genius soil engineers. Building all their durable monuments out of soil—the Earth—one basket load at a time, it was clearly a lot more than just dirt for them. They understood the properties of different soil types: good for drainage, or to hold water, or to maintain different slopes. They often layered it in different colors or mixed it with sand or gravel. Sometimes they burned it to make it red. They had to travel far from the construction site to get the best types for certain uses. But they also valued the soil for more than just its physical properties. It was the Earth itself, and full of meaning—it gives life, it consumes the dead; it is part of the reciprocal unity of the sacred world. And formed into complex earthworks, it marked their understanding of the heavens, of their community, and of their territory.

RIGHT: Squier and Davis's plan of the Hopeton Earthworks includes cross sections of the major walls and shows several smaller earthworks in the vicinity.

BELOW: Magnetometry data at Hopeton's large circle show its exterior ditch (the dark line) and the regularly spaced postholes of a giant woodhenge along its interior edge.

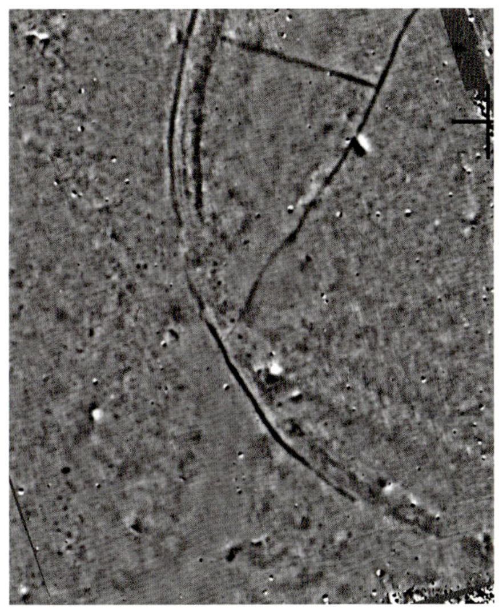

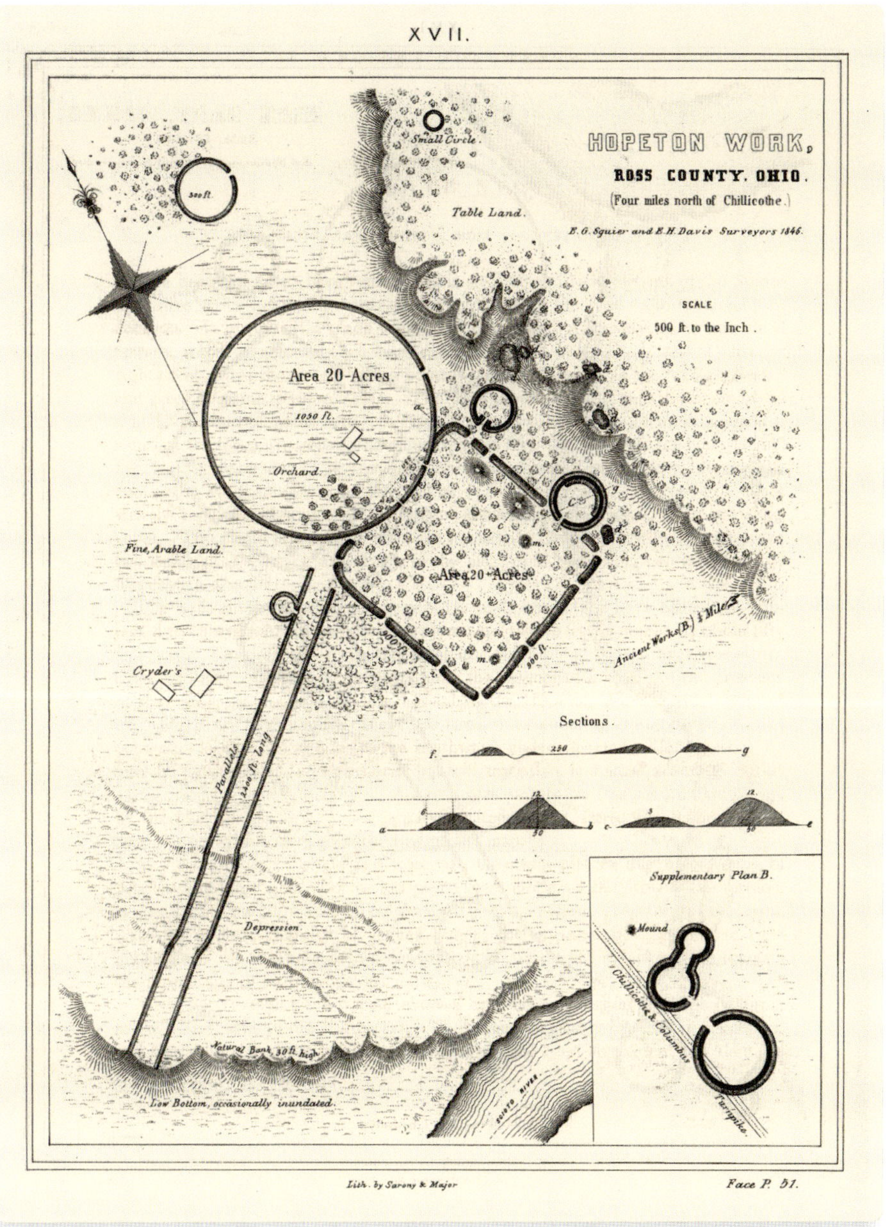

Hopeton was among the first Hopewell earthworks brought to the attention of a wide audience. A map appeared in 1809 in *The Port Folio*, a monthly review published in Philadelphia, naming Thomas Worthington as the landowner, who had received these lands as payment for his service surveying the Virginia Military District. From the early 1800s, a cluster of structures known as the Cryder Farm stood west of the earthworks, of which only a sandstone house foundation remains.

When Squier and Davis documented the site in the late 1840s, it had been under the plow for only three or four decades, but most of the walls were already spread out into lower and wider profiles. Besides the Cryder farm, their map shows two other structures and an orchard within the large circle; its enclosing wall was by then "much reduced of late years by the plough, [though] still about five feet in average height."

In 1889, after four more decades of annual plowing, Hopeton Earthworks, along with High Bank Works, were surveyed by Cyrus Thomas. In "The Circular, Square, and Octagonal Earthworks of Ohio," he noted that the large circle and square were still visible and could be "readily traced. In fact, the lowest point of the square is yet five feet high. The circle is more worn, the western half averaging about two feet high." The greater accuracy of Thomas's survey clarified that the "square" is in fact an irregular polygon with no perfectly straight walls or right angles, and that the large circle is slightly oblong.

PRESERVATION AND RESEARCH

Still in private hands and actively farmed, the earthworks suffered from the widespread adoption of the diesel tractor after World War II, which was far more damaging than the horse-drawn plows of the previous century and a half. Both the National Park Service and the Ohio History Connection began planning for the acquisition of the site in the late 1950s. Efforts accelerated quickly after a landowner subdivided the property in 1961 for residential development and bulldozed one of the square's walls. A collaborative preservation effort led to the site's listing as a National Historic Landmark in 1964, although the earthworks remained in private hands and farming continued.

Housing developments and gravel mining in the area over the next two decades prompted protective action. In 1980, the US Congress passed legislation to authorize the addition of the Hopeton Earthworks to the existing Mound City Group National Monument, though without funds to purchase the land, private ownership and cultivation continued for another ten years. By the time farming ended on the site, much of the earthen architecture still stood at about one-third of its original height. The National Park Service acquired the site in 1990, with later purchases adding nearby buffer areas with nonmound archaeological resources and a corridor connecting the earthworks to the Scioto River.

Since 1994, Hopeton has seen the most intensive and sustained field investigations of all the works in this series. The National Park Service's long-term study used both remote sensing technologies and targeted excavations. Magnetic surveys from 2001 to 2005 covered almost seventy acres, clearly delineating the primary earthwork walls and guiding Mark Lynott's detailed investigations of wall construction.

A decade later, the park's joint investigations with the *Deutsches Archäologisches Institut* gathered more than 280 acres of magnetometry data at Hopeton, revealing the postholes of the colossal woodhenge. With more radiocarbon dates than any other Ohio Hopewell site, and with so much known to be intact in the ground, Hopeton will continue to play a significant role in the widening understanding of earthwork construction sequences and methods.

Hopeton is a nonmortuary site, so excavations there have mainly revealed earthwork construction and cooking features. The wide range of artifacts, gathered from strategic surface collection and excavation, are mostly fragments of craftwork and the debris of domestic or feasting activity. They include knives, bladelets, and plant and animal remains, mainly from specialized activity areas near the earthworks but not inside them.

OPPOSITE: Chief Glenna J. Wallace of the Eastern Shawnee Tribe of Oklahoma, with then-Superintendent Dean Alexander and park archaeologist Bret Ruby (middle), celebrated the dedication of new visitor amenities at the Hopeton Earthworks.

ABOVE: The Hopeton Earthworks spread across the landscape beneath the park's stone-rimmed visitor wayside, with the square (left), a small circle (left foreground), and the large circle (far right).

AUTHENTICITY AND EXPERIENCE

The view over the Hopeton Earthworks from the high terrace vividly presents the vastness of Hopewell landscape space—huge geometric figures and tree-lined riverbanks set within a nearly pristine view of the wide valley beyond. Viewed from among the remains of the walls, now marked by differential mowing, their outlines are augmented in many locations by visible topographic relief. At close range, the human, earthwork, and landscape scales reveal their nearly incomprehensible contrasts and show the astonishing commitment necessary to build such massive walls—up to twelve feet high—with individual basket loads and in such carefully contrasting patterns.

Hopeton's contrast with the relative spatial intimacy of Mound City, just across the river, is striking. Yet together they occupy the very center of the Hopewell heartland. Unlike Mound City, with which it was likely a ritual pair, Hopeton presents no evidence of mortuary activity, yet the scope and elaboration of its construction speak of reverent expertise in building with earth, its huge woodhenge reveals timber architecture of immense scope, and its solstice alignments match principles linking Sky knowledge to architecture at other Hopewell sites.

REMOTE SENSING

Many images in this book come from new archaeological methods collectively referred to as "geophysics"—various technologies that can reveal what is beneath the ground without digging. Magnetometry, ground penetrating radar, and other remote sensing tools like LiDAR have transformed earthwork archaeology, both as ways of studying already known sites and as tools for finding previously unrecorded ones. They can enable better targeted research excavations or even make excavation unnecessary.

Throughout the 1800s, the study of earthworks was limited to what could be seen and surveyed, and then to what was considered worth excavating—the latter usually motivated by a search for valuable artifacts and therefore limited to mounds. In 1848, Squier and Davis recorded eighty-eight earthworks in Ohio; six decades later William Mills located more than 500 (and more than 10,000 mounds) in his *Archaeological Atlas of Ohio*. Many earthworks that survive from their surveys—along with many more that have never been known at all—are now detectable only by these new methods, and yet these technologies reveal them in startling detail.

In the early-to-mid-twentieth century, the new medium of aerial photography could capture the still-visible traces of many earthworks. An ambitious pilot named Dache Reeves created a huge set of photos in the 1930s, capturing many sites for the last time before they were erased by increasingly mechanized agriculture. The US government has since maintained a regular program of aerial photography, in which faint traces of earthworks frequently appear, depending on the soil moisture conditions on any given day or year. Previously unknown earthworks even show up occasionally on standard internet satellite imagery; the ease of searching those has helped identify sites for new geophysical surveys.

The technology known as LiDAR—light detection and ranging—shoots laser light from an airplane and times its reflection to produce three-dimensional models of the ground surface. Software can filter out trees and buildings, exaggerate the relief, and add colored layers or shading so that otherwise-invisible forms appear. Digital photogrammetry, a technique by which multiple aerial photographs are combined, can also create three-dimensional topographic models.

Another technique, ground penetrating radar, sends electromagnetic energy pulses into the ground while reflection patterns detect subsurface features by variations in material, density, or electrical properties. The resulting radargram can pinpoint features at many levels, such as graves, cisterns, pits, and soil layers. Similarly, electrical resistivity tomography uses direct current to detect variations in the composition or moisture-retaining capacity of subsurface soils.

The geophysical technology most frequently illustrated in this volume is magnetometry. The images—often as stunningly compelling as the best aerial photos—are produced by data points measuring variations in the earth's magnetic field. Sensors collect the data and, with each point registered to a GPS location, produce an accurate map. By mounting several interconnected sensors on a combined rig, archaeologists can cover large areas. Topsoil is more magnetic than clay or gravelly subsoil, so ditches, pits, and postholes appear dark because more topsoil has been either placed or eroded into them. The precise margins of original embankment walls appear slightly lighter, because the specific soil types the builders placed there have different magnetic signatures. Heat-altered sediments also stand out in magnetic data,

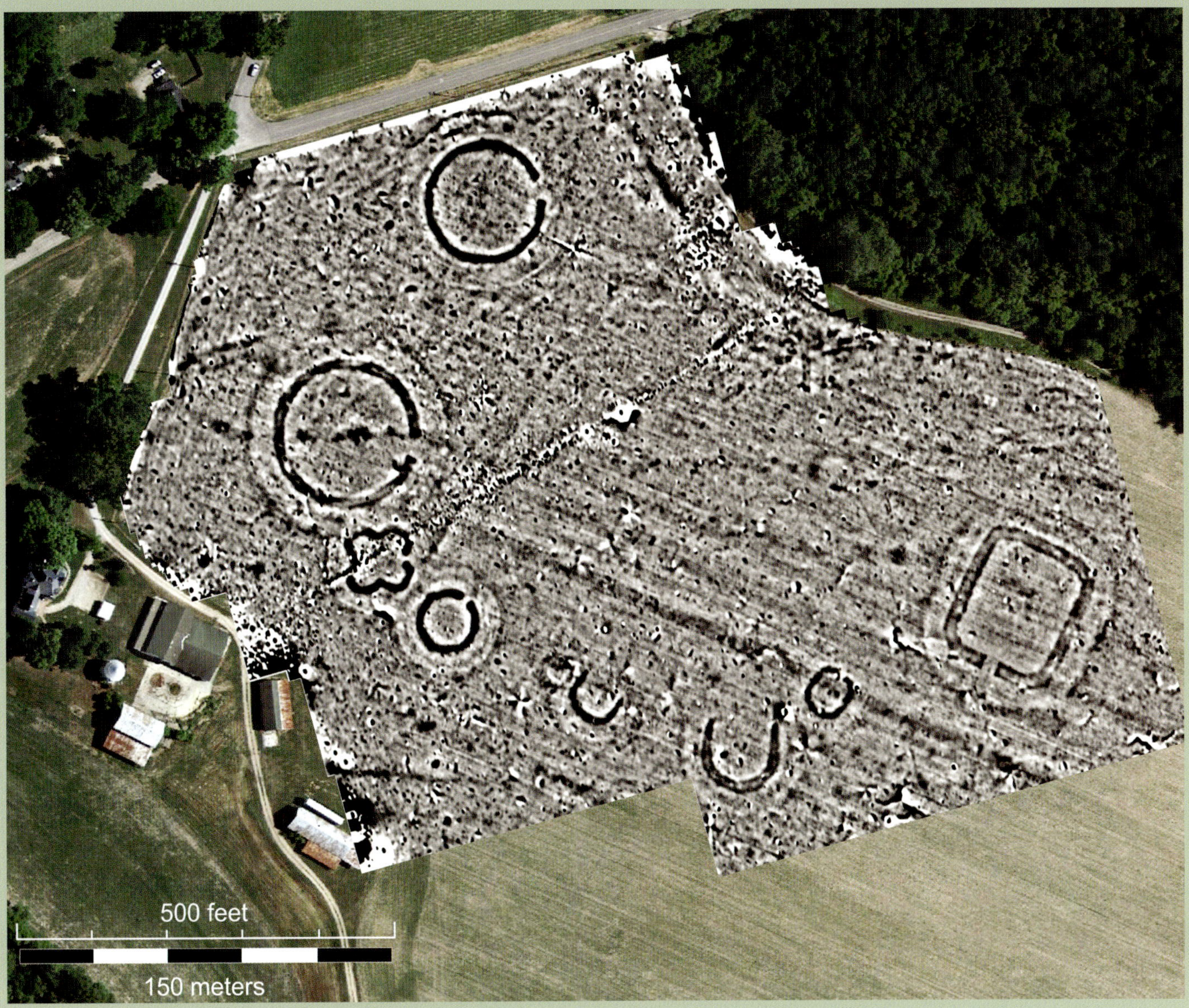

Opposite: In the 1930s, pilot Dache Reeves captured this image of the Junction Group earthworks in a farm field near Chillicothe. Above: Although leveled today, the figures reappeared, along with several more, in the site's magnetic survey data. The stunning new image also helped inspire community fundraising to preserve the site.

pinpointing hearths, cooking pits, or deposits of burned soil. Advances in sensor technology and transport have enabled the creation of magnetometry maps of ever-larger areas and the discovery of many previously unsuspected earthworks.

These tools have changed our understanding of the scope of the ancestors' earthwork building efforts across the region. In Squier and Davis's day, when walking sites with visible earthworks was the only way they could be recorded, many remained unknown—obscured in the forest, damaged during the intervening centuries, or too subtle in relief to begin with. Many sites that were known to early antiquarians and archaeologists but are now obscured or degraded are reappearing with these new tools—along with many more.

When large-scale magnetometry began at Hopewell Culture National Historical Park in 2001, a previously unknown small circle appeared in the middle of the Hopewell Mound Group. The park's landscape-scale magnetic surveys of 2015 to 2017 revealed many previously unsuspected features, such as Hopeton's woodhenge, and a whole array of intriguing features inside the Seip Earthworks—all told, enough to guide new lines of investigation for a least a generation.

Mound City may be at its most beautiful on a frosty early spring morning, as the rising sun tinges the forms with gold.

8.
MOUND CITY

"What power resides in earthen mounds?
Ancestors, wisdom of clan relatives,
astrological continuities, portal to spiritual realities.
The hungry rise of earth imbued with sacred life,
monument, transcendent force
Name this site—holy.
Become in this sanctuary
rich in memory,
humble before mystery."

—KIMBERLY BLAESER (White Earth Nation)

Mound City lies on the high terrace directly across the Scioto River from the Hopeton Earthworks. While Hopeton is far from the river, separated from it by a broad meander and floodplain, Mound City overlooks the river directly. The steep, wooded riverbank beautifully evokes the ancient celebrants' experience of arriving by water in their canoes and climbing directly to the monument. The Scioto Valley at this location has an especially vivid character; its wide Ice Age terraces are overlooked by the distinctive Logan Range to the east.

Arriving at Mound City today from the modern highway also feels authentic. The driveway to the park's visitor center enters deep woods, quickly erasing the memory of the adjacent land uses. The sacred precinct then appears on the right—a well-framed forest clearing filled with serene mounds and rimmed by a low earthen wall. A prominent opening in the wall invites entry. The surrounding forest filters out the modern world and evokes the Woodland context of the builders' culture.

MOUNDS AND BUILDINGS

The monument's two dozen mounds of varying sizes stand within a low, earthen enclosure wall in the shape of a slightly irregular 850-foot square with rounded corners and very gently flaring sides. The wall's uniform cross section measures four feet high and fifteen feet wide at its base. Gateways open in the centers of its eastern and western sides; their positions suggest an axis across the center of the enclosure, parallel to the other two sides and oriented to seventy-eight

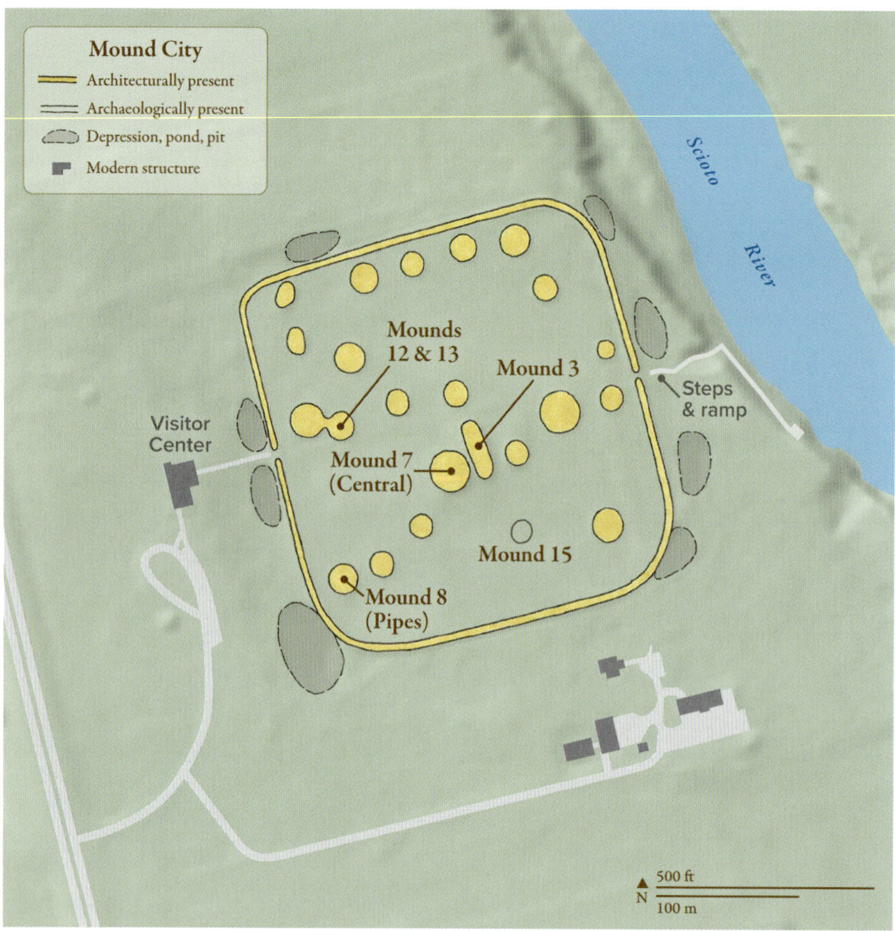

degrees east of north. The enclosure's eastern wall runs near the top edge of the densely wooded embankment, which falls steeply to the Scioto River. Just outside the four sides of the enclosing earthwork wall are eight constructed pits of varying sizes and depths.

People began building the mounds, pits, and enclosure at Mound City in about the year 1 CE. Detailed studies by Squier and Davis in the 1840s, by William Mills and Henry Shetrone in the 1920s, and by James Brown and others in the 1960s and '70s have revealed much about the creation and use of the earthworks. They have also informed the present restorations of all the mounds and walls visible today. One of the mounds (Mound 15) remains unrestored, with short posts set in the ground to mark the floor plan of the building that preceded it.

The circular mounds within the enclosure include both spherical and conical forms, varying from three to eighteen feet in height and from twenty-five to one hundred feet in diameter. Mounds 12 and 13 form a conjoined pair covering the remains of a connected double structure. In the approximate center of the enclosure stands the largest, Mound 7 (the Central Mound), with a precise conical profile and a rounded top. Just to its east is Mound 3 (or the Elliptical Mound), a loaf shape measuring 140 feet long by nearly fifty feet wide. Its long ridge rises to ten feet in a triangular profile with a rounded top.

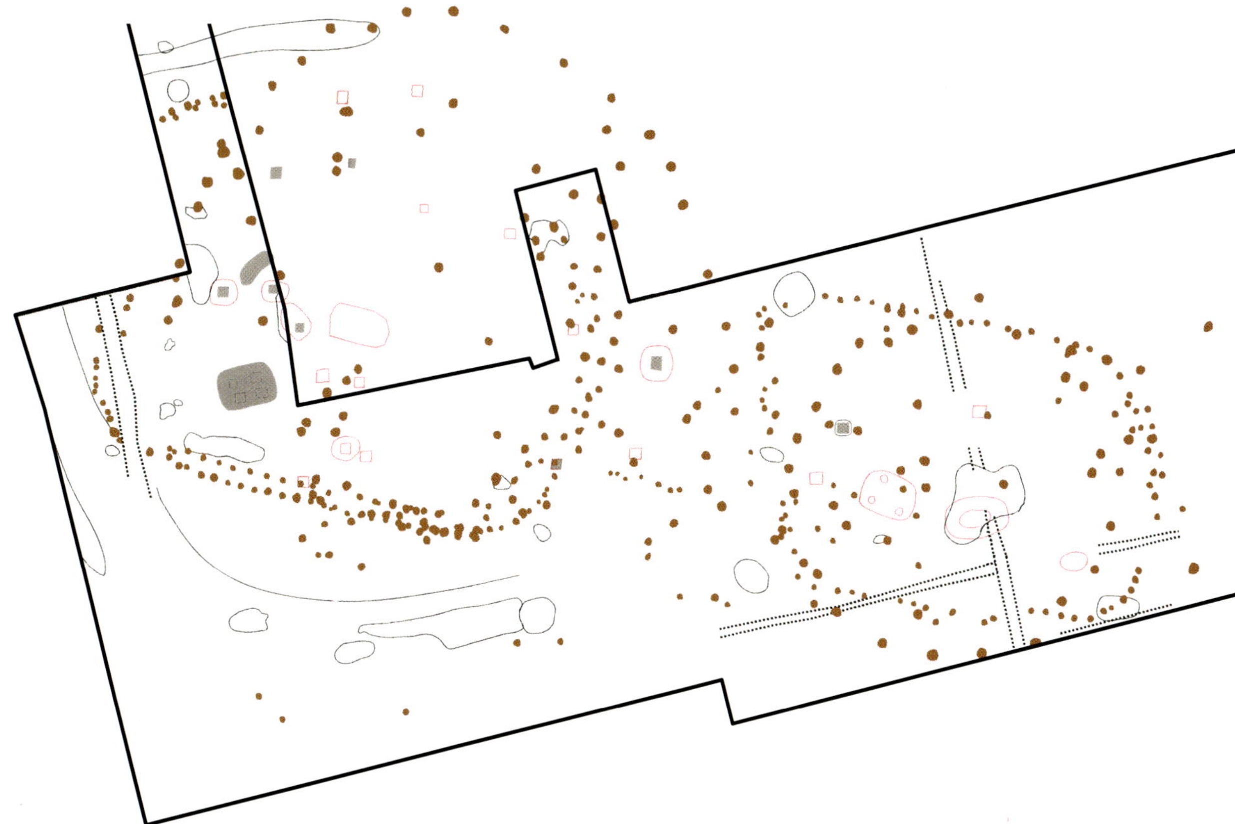

Beneath Mounds 12 and 13 at Mound City, archaeologists found the posthole pattern of a large double building with many interior features.

Each mound covers the remains of a wood-framed ceremonial building. Varying in design, these buildings were nearly all rectangular with rounded corners, with sizes ranging from just under 500 to about 2,500 square feet. The long sides of many of these structures had a double row of posts, with larger interior support posts near the corners and center to support the roof. The doorways were placed in the center of the shorter end walls, sometimes with an exterior extension or portico.

The builders of these structures most likely set opposing rows of heavy posts into the ground, then lashed a lighter bent-pole structure to the uprights, bending them toward each other and lashing them together under tension. They then covered this vault-shaped framework with sheets of bark, or possibly skins or thatch. The floors were carefully made by layering wet clay slurry with fine sand and compacting it through repeated trampling, creating a durable, cementlike surface. When archaeologist William Mills uncovered one of these floors during excavations in 1920, he said it resembled slabs of sandstone. This material, often called "Hopewell concrete," has been found at other sites in the region. In three cases (Mounds 7, 8, and 13), two successive structures were built at the same location; after the first was dismantled, a new floor was created and a second structure built on top.

While Mound City was in use, people would have seen a combination of functioning buildings—with their associated funerals, festivals, and feasts—and others under construction, along with mounds already covering the remains of still others. After the largest, centrally located Mound 7 was completed, it must have had very special significance because the doorways of all the later buildings were oriented toward this new focal point.

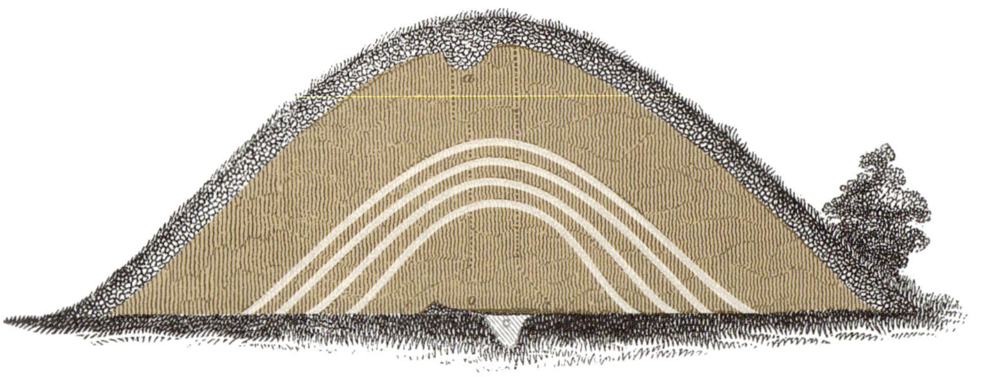

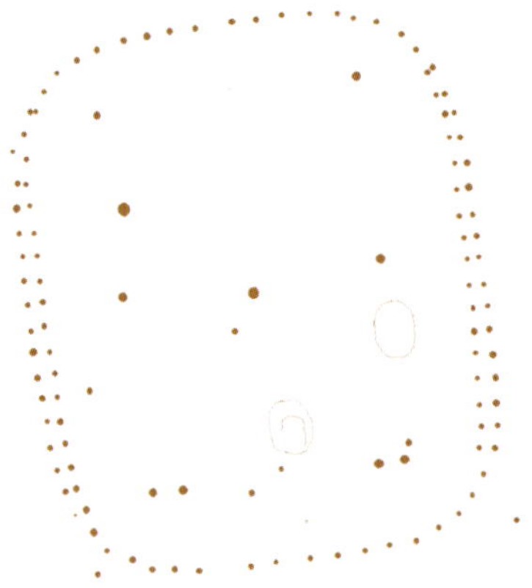

LEFT: Squier and Davis's cross section of Mound 7, the Central Mound, shows thin layers of sand alternating with thick layers of soil (coloration added).

ABOVE: The building floor plan beneath Mound 10 was typical of the others, their shapes all echoing that of the enclosure itself.

CEREMONIES AND TOMBS

Inside these well-framed timber buildings, the ceremonies focused around clay-lined ritual basins. Measuring around four by six feet and slightly recessed into the floor, they held intense fires, which added their heat and scents to the sounds of incantations, rattles, drums, and songs. Probably in the presence of the gathered family or community, ritual practitioners presided over the cremation and disposition of the dead and the breaking and burning of important objects meant to accompany them on their journey. Afterward, the ash and other remains of these ritual fires might be swept up and placed carefully on certain areas of the building floor or on low earthen platforms.

The remains of the deceased were often placed on bark, netting, or animal skins on the floor, along with ornaments and implements perhaps indicating their role in life. They were surrounded by logs or stones, then covered with bark or poles, followed by a small mound. While some individuals were placed alone, others lay in small groups. In a final ceremony, celebrants dismantled or burned the building and built a larger mound over its remains and contents. These final mounds were sometimes constructed in stages, with layers of loamy soil carefully separated by thin membranes of fine sand.

The creation of the Central Mound was an especially elaborate process. The builders began by digging out an elliptical subterranean room five and a half feet deep, thirty feet wide, and forty feet long. A gently sloping ramp led down into this space, which was centered on a crematory basin. At some later point, they filled the sunken room with soil, prepared a new floor over it, and positioned a new basin exactly above the lower one. Across the rest of the area later covered by the mound, they erected an array of low covered tombs, timber-framed shelters, and a partial perimeter fence.

Nine of the larger mounds received mantles of coarse gravel or river cobbles—an effective defense against erosion—usually to a thickness of about one foot, but nearly twice that in the case of Mound 7. River cobbles may have also symbolized water, so central to Indigenous cosmologies and creation stories. Each of these large mounds was at least five feet tall and more than fifty-five feet in diameter.

A large bag buried beneath Mound 8 contained 200 smoking pipes, all purposely burned and broken. Their bowls portrayed a variety of Eastern Woodland creatures (and a few humans), carved from local pipestone with accuracy and great artistry. The creatures sit atop their gently curving, tapered platforms, drilled to convey the smoke; their finely detailed faces look directly at the smoker at close range. Effigy platform pipes were a Hopewell innovation, signaling new beliefs about the relationships between humans and other-than-human beings, which were probably seen as beings themselves, with names, histories, and the power to change the course of human lives. The eye-to-eye intimacy between creature and smoker intensified the tobacco's power to induce spiritual, otherworldly experiences. The communal, sacrificial breaking and incineration of these esteemed beings suggest they needed to be "killed" before being buried.

ENCLOSING WALL AND PITS

The Mound City enclosure forms a flare-sided square with rounded corners, a shape mathematicians call a superellipse. It may seem to be a poorly executed square, but the predominance of this shape across the Hopewell world—most often executed with great elegance—suggests otherwise. It reproduces in monumental form the shape of the wooden structures that preceded the individual mounds. Those wood-framed structures in turn reflect the shapes of the clay crematory basins on their floors. This mirroring, or nesting, of a favored shape was clearly intentional. The frequent use of superelliptical forms across the Hopewell world helps define the transition from Adena buildings and earthworks, which were almost universally circular.

Some evidence at Mound City suggests that the enclosure wall was built after many of the mounds were in place. If so, the superellipse would have been

ANCESTRAL REMAINS AND WORLD RENEWAL

Scholars believe that long-deceased ancestors often bore witness to or participated in living rituals through the presence of their mortal remains. Their bones rested on low clay platforms or in log-lined tombs inside the ceremonial buildings. These sacred relics, much like those of Christian saints, forged eternal bonds between the worlds of the living and the dead. With the ancestors present, the ceremonies ensured the renewal of the world—the continual resurrection of the cosmos, also symbolized in the monumental order and scope of the earthworks.

The cyclical continuity between life and death is dramatized every winter when life seems to die, or hides in the Earth like buried seeds, and then reawakens every spring. Many American Indian groups still place this world renewal at the center of their ceremonial life. Human beings have a responsibility in this renewal: without their ceremonies, the world might die. Sacred fires are extinguished each year and rekindled. Sometimes ancestral spirits are reincarnated in the person of adoptees who recycle the names, roles, and responsibilities of the deceased. The Earth Diver creation story, known across North America, is related: an animal dives to the bottom of the primordial sea to retrieve mud or sand that then grows to create all the Earth. Accordingly, mound and earthwork construction can also be seen as world renewal—a ritual reenactment of the creation of the Earth.

TOBACCO AND RITUAL

Squier and Davis's volume included many beautiful lithographs of the Mound City pipes. They noted that the finely detailed specimen identified as Fig. 173 resembled "the tufted cherry bird."

"Across American Indian cultures, tobacco was cultivated and smoked as a sacrament. Though all plants—like animals—are considered sacred for their power to grow, feed, heal, or even harm us, tobacco is the most potent of all. It is highly prized and given as a gift. Its central role in ceremony is shown by the effigy pipes, where creatures of the Above or Beneath Worlds face the smoker; their spirits, and the smoke, carry prayers and songs up to the Milky Way, the ancestors, the Above World."

—JOE STAHLMAN
(Tuscarora/Pennsylvania Dutch)

Smoking tobacco in the distinctive Hopewell pipes likely played a role in shamanic transformation and communication with other-than-human beings and powers. The native tobacco (most likely *Nicotiana rustica*) contains much more nicotine that the *N. tabacum* used in today's cigarettes, making it highly addictive and capable of producing hallucinatory experiences. The pipes' ceremonial use and sacred status derived from the strong tobacco's power to intensify and alter perceptions, while sending a smoke column skyward.

The pipes share similarities with the *calumet*—a ceremonial tobacco pipe associated with ritual practices among many tribes in the postcontact period. Its stone-carved bowl was attached to a long, wooden stem decorated with the heads and feathers of various birds. The calumet ceremony involved singing, dancing, and drumming, as well as smoking the pipe, most often to solemnize decisions, make peace, cement friendships, or establish alliances.

an established tradition by then for wood-framed structures both domestic and ceremonial. Such monumentalizing adaptations have occurred in many ancient cultures, where the "house" form becomes the "temple"—transformed into the communal, ceremonial prototype. The resemblance of the Mound City enclosure to the irregular square at nearby Hopeton suggests similar thinking about how to shape ceremonial space.

Builders began constructing the wall by removing the topsoil layer, as elsewhere in the Scioto and Paint valley earthworks, and leveling the site. The base layers of the wall contained midden (waste, refuse) including charcoal, broken pottery, and animal bone. Such signs of feasting may suggest that preparing and building the earthwork was a community activity, initiated by shared ceremonies. Where the walls adjoin the adjacent constructed pits, the builders took special care to line the continuous surface with soil types that would resist erosion.

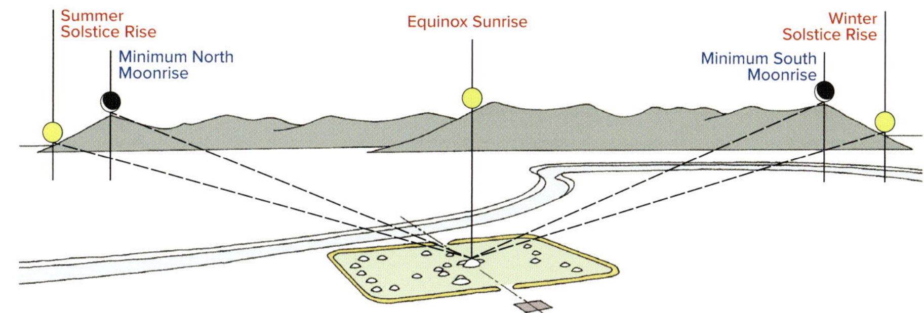

ABOVE, RIGHT: An artist's photomontage of one of the western pits at Mound City shows how it would have appeared in wet seasons with its clay lining intact.

RIGHT: From the center of Mound City, the annual extremes of sunrise positions and the minimum swing of monthly lunar rises align over the defining features of the Mount Logan Range.

The eight large pits positioned outside the wall, even after centuries of erosion, were still quite deep in the mid-1800s. Squier and Davis recorded the depth of the largest one, next to the southwestern corner, as eighteen feet. The most thoroughly researched pit, outside the southeastern corner, is fifty by eighty feet wide and six feet deep. The placement of the pits around the enclosure wall resembles the positioning of eight large marine shells found surrounding one of the human burials beneath the Central Mound. Once again, a repeated pattern at a different scale suggests an important, meaningful relationship.

These were once assumed to be borrow pits—sources of soil to build the mounds—but their depth and their clay linings show that the builders meant them to hold water. They excavated deep into the glacial sand and gravel beneath, then imported clay to create more impervious linings. Because the topsoil is very shallow on these glacial terraces, they would not have been digging very deeply to get material for mound building. Instead, they were creating intentionally designed vessels—windows into the watery Beneath World, or sources of fresh water for the gatherings, or vernal pools to draw animal, bird, and insect life, filling the Sky and Earth with sound and color. Or all these things at once.

A uniform, forested perimeter helps to create Mound City's mood of serenity.

GEOMETRY AND ASTRONOMY

What looks like a somewhat irregular outline still reveals some of the Hopewell architects' penchant for geometric order, shared dimensions, landscape positioning, and cosmic alignments. Each diagonal of Mound City's enclosure wall approximates one OCD. Its orientation angle and central axis are the same as those of the similarly sized square at the Hopewell Mound Group five miles to the west-southwest. The enclosure's southeast to northwest diagonal aligns to the summer solstice sunset.

The forested hillsides defining the Scioto River valley at this location have a particularly vivid profile. Mound City's eastern horizon is dominated by the distinctive Logan Range, the westernmost mountainlike formation of the rugged Appalachian Plateau. As seen from Mound City, its symmetrical features calibrate both the annual solar and the generational lunar cycles. From the center of the site, observers could watch the moonrise position moving back and forth each month. Every 18.6 years, the end peaks of this symmetrical mountain profile pinpoint the Moon's minimum arc before it expands outward again toward its maximum. And every year, the sunrise moves between its summer and winter solstice positions aligned over the outer base points of that same mountain profile.

MODERN HISTORY

The site had long been reclaimed by forests by the time the first Euro-American settlers arrived at the end of the 1700s. The nearby town of Chillicothe began to develop as a major center, and in 1803 it became the first capital of the state. As early as 1798, a 1,300-acre land parcel containing Mound City was surveyed as a land grant for William Davies, in consideration of his service as a colonel

During Mound City's use as part of Camp Sherman in the late 1910s, the Central Mound was the only feature preserved in its complete form.

in the American Revolutionary War. Mound City was first described in 1808, in *Richardson's Chillicothe Fredonian*, as an "ancient fortification" surrounding "twelve or fifteen mounds, supposed to have been the repositories of the dead."

In the early 1830s, the Ohio–Erie Canal route connecting Lake Erie to the Ohio River passed just west of Mound City. The completed canal encouraged rapid settlement of the area and accelerated the clearing of farms, yet Mound City remained forested for at least another twenty-five years. In 1832 (concurrent with Indian Removal), George Shriver purchased the land, and the Shriver family held title to it until 1920.

Squier and Davis, who were from nearby Chillicothe, mapped and partially excavated the still-pristine, forest-covered site between 1845 and 1847. Their findings formed the basis for much of their *Ancient Monuments of the Mississippi Valley*, where they described cremated burials, the smoking pipes, and many other beautiful, exotic objects. This established Mound City as the defining exemplar of what was called "Moundbuilder" culture—the place where the sacred, ceremonial purpose of the earthworks was first understood. The site's preeminence stood for more than fifty years, until the appearance of the even more spectacular finds from the Hopewell Mound Group in the 1890s. Soon after their investigations, the Shrivers finished clearing the trees and the land came under the plow.

During the American Civil War, from 1861 to 1865, the land at Mound City became "Camp Logan" for the training of Union soldiers. After the war, it reverted to use as Shriver's farm until 1917, when the US War Department took control of about 2,000 acres north of Chillicothe. The nation's entry into World War I again required the construction of a training site, to be called Camp Sherman. A small city unto itself, its nearly 2,000 buildings accommodated 40,000 men—with barracks, a hospital, a railroad, its own prison, and sanitary and farming facilities.

Roads and two-story wooden buildings were built across the site, but Henry Shetrone, William Mills, and Albert Spetnagel of the OSAHS met with army officials to determine an approach that would minimize disturbance of the mounds. The construction and three-year occupation of Camp Sherman damaged many above-grade features, but much remained intact. The Central Mound was left untouched. Mound City remained under federal ownership after the war, and local and state preservationists mounted efforts to set it aside as a national monument.

RESTORATION AND RESEARCH

Working around the Camp Sherman buildings, the OSAHS undertook excavations at the site in 1920 and 1921. By this time, the scientific community understood that American Indian ancestors had built the region's earthworks. William Mills directed the work, assisted by Henry Shetrone. Their results demonstrated that despite damage to most of the mounds, the archaeological record had survived Camp Sherman in surprisingly good condition. They reaffirmed Mound City's importance, bringing to light new evidence of the timber-framed buildings beneath the mounds, their clay cremation basins, and their tableaus of finely crafted artistry.

Important artifacts from Mound City now included many pieces made from exotic raw materials—outsized obsidian blades, mica mirrors, and copper sheets hammered into relief effigies of falcons, ramshorns, deer antlers, turtles, and animal claws. All these animals, so finely wrought, suggest a powerful, reverent connection between humans and other-than-human beings—animal spirits associated with various aspects of life, knowledge, and ceremony.

Mills and Shetrone's work at Mound City reignited public interest in Hopewell studies and launched a drive to preserve the mounds and earthworks here and elsewhere. These efforts succeeded in 1923, when the Mound City Group National Monument was created. With this designation, the land remained federally owned, but the War Department licensed the OSAHS to "care for, preserve, protect, and maintain" the site. The restoration of the mounds began in 1925, immediately following the removal of the Camp Sherman buildings. Workers carefully plowed the site to find traces of the nearly leveled mounds and the enclosure wall. They located twenty-three of the mounds mapped by Squier and Davis, restored eleven of them to their 1840s dimensions, and identified remnants of the stone caps over Mounds 3 and 7. Restorations continued over the next two years, using the best available evidence from Mills and Shetrone as well as Squier and Davis.

Mound City State Park opened to visitors in 1929, with picnic areas, shade trees, and open lawn on the mounds. The federal government transferred the administration of national monuments from the War Department to the National Park Service in 1933, though OSAHS management continued until 1946. That year, the Park Service began a long-term program to enhance the visitor experience at the site—planting the surrounding forest, adding more land parcels, and building a new museum and visitor center in 1960.

In 1963, the Park Service initiated a research program intended to discover any still-intact archaeological resources and correct known inaccuracies in the 1920s restorations. The locations of the enclosure wall and gateways were

OPPOSITE: With Camp Sherman gone and the mounds newly restored, the 1920s view of Mound City and the Logan Range made their resemblance to each other especially obvious.

RIGHT: A steep, wooded embankment, now fitted with paved walks, connects Mound City's high terrace to the swiftly flowing Scioto River, evoking the Ancients' experience of arriving by water.

reconfirmed and corrected. The large southeastern pit was reconstructed. The exact locations of all twenty-three mounds that had been shown on the Squier and Davis map were verified, including several smaller ones that had disappeared during the decades of cultivation and Camp Sherman. Each mound excavation also revealed the intact posthole pattern of its corresponding building plan, along with substantial new evidence of its associated ritual and mortuary activities. Two more mounds appeared that had been missing from the 1848 map, bringing the total number of mounds within the enclosing wall to twenty-five.

AUTHENTICITY AND EXPERIENCE

With its relatively small size, restored mounds, enclosing wall, and wooded perimeter, Mound City presents to modern visitors the most iconic architectural image in the series. The gathering of mounds within this enclosure echoes the gatherings of the builders and celebrants, and of the generations of ancestors whose remains were interred here. The setting creates a bounded enclave, filled with a quiet sense of reverential antiquity. The earthen forms offer an eternal image of communal identity and peaceful rest—the sacred atmosphere of a clustered Hopewell necropolis, of which this is the only surviving example.

In winter, the Logan Range appears through bare trees; besides its resemblance to the mounds themselves, it forms the only astronomical alignments in this series clearly calibrated to a distant horizon. The forested riverbank—rushing water, tangled trees, and inclines—prompts reflection on the ancestors' waterborne arrivals.

More than 150 years of archaeological knowledge have informed Mound City's meticulous restorations. Now also joined by modern Indigenous perspectives, that knowledge illuminates the meanings of this sacred place—its ceremonial uses and the contexts of many of the finest expressions of Hopewell artistry.

LIFE, DEATH, CEREMONY

"Much Indian knowledge involved the technique of reproducing the cosmos in miniature and invoking spiritual change, which would be followed by physical change. . . . Wherever possible the larger cosmos was represented and reproduced to provide a context in which ceremonies could occur. Thus, people did not feel alone; they participated in cosmic rhythms."

—VINE DELORIA JR. (Standing Rock Sioux, 1933–2005)

People came to Mound City to participate in ceremonies of loving remembrance for their deceased kin, whose remains were prepared through the skills of spiritual leaders for the journey to the world beyond. For the gathered community, the elaborate rituals of mourning and celebration strengthened their own bonds and their understandings of life and death. Ritual and ceremony have an underlying universal role across cultures: the elaboration, size, ornament, and detail draw the community's attention to the sacred dimensions of the actions, message, and beliefs. Preparations of the dead—their bodies for burial and spirits for the journey—call for solemn rituals steeped in the community's sacred traditions, and in expressions of love and shared belief.

We cannot know with certainty the details of their ceremonies, or what Mound City's creators and visitors believed about the journey from life to death, but ongoing American Indian traditions can suggest what preparations of the body may have been required and where the deceased spirits were going. For many contemporary tribal nations, the view of death, of moving from this world to the next, is not something to be mourned but rather something to be celebrated and undertaken in a good way; steps taken for the body's preparation and inhumation facilitate the journey.

The body, or its ritually prepared remains, must return to Mother Earth. If at any time the decaying remains are disturbed, moved, altered, or unnaturally destroyed, the soul of the person can be lost on its journey. This enduring tradition explains why the tribal nations have objected to the excavation or destruction of their ancestors' graves and have been adamant that their views must be taken seriously.

In some Native beliefs, a person has more than one soul: a "free soul" that leaves the body at the time of death and takes the afterlife journey, and one or more "body souls" that inhere in the bones and remain after death. This is why the continued presence of human remains in museum collections is such a problem: they are not the inanimate bones of science, but instead contain the body souls of the deceased and must be treated with respect and reburied. Reincarnation, another widespread belief, meant that mourning was closely tied to ritual adoption. Requickening ceremonies were common, in which captives or others were adopted to replace dead kin, taking on their names and social responsibilities and so reconstituting the community.

Although the interment customs of today's tribes vary greatly, one common thread of contemporary Indigenous life is that customs for the dead in the community prepare the person's spirit for a journey to the afterlife. Often spoken of as "walking on," "passing over," or "sending them home," the purpose of the rituals is to help the spirit have a successful journey—and not linger among the living or look back. A hole might be put in the casket so the spirit can escape; some favored clothing, possessions, or signs of a person's trade might be put in with them, or boots or moccasins for the spirit's walk-on.

After a prescribed period of mourning, the deceased's personal belongings might also be given away, broken, or burned; the breakage of personal belongings is also symbolic of sending people on—severing an attachment to this plane, discouraging any who might not want to take their walk-on.

Like the broken objects, destruction of the body can also aid the journey to the afterlife. Through cremation, the rising smoke transforms the body into spirit and sends it skyward. What remains, being of the Earth, returns to the natural world. At the Hopewell sites, evidence of fire and destruction—of the body and of objects—shows that their rituals likely had a similar purpose: a transformation to help facilitate the sending on from this earthly realm to another mythic place or time.

Not all ceremonial life at the earthworks was about death, although creating a set of combined burials, or reburials, of their deceased relatives was a way for otherwise dispersed communities to signify alliances. The shared interment of ancestral remains symbolized group unity, reinforced by the enclosure's spatial order and its marking of cosmic rhythms. The gatherings also served other functions, bringing communities together

Left: In this image by Talon Silverhorn (Eastern Shawnee), ceremonial leaders wear distinctive regalia reflecting their individual roles in a ritual story re-enactment—based on both Hopewell evidence and continuing Shawnee traditions. Right: A man is enjoying his pipe in this digital portrait, wearing bear fur and a copper gorget. His facial tattoos are based on a human effigy pipe from Mound City.

for social networking, forming and sustaining alliances including marriages, and allowing wise elders to settle disputes. Like today's tribal powwows, they were probably scenes of general reunion, with storytelling, passing on knowledge, infant naming and youth coming-of-age ceremonies, weddings, commerce and trade, and perhaps even sports like lacrosse or stickball.

The celebrants gathered at the earthworks from many places, often from far across the Hopewell world, speaking many languages and having otherwise many different customs. For those far away to know when to leave home, and for the hosts to know when to have the grounds and food ready, skywatchers would mark the seasonal Sun cycle or the appearance of certain stars. Weeks in advance, caretakers prepared the site by burning off the prairie grasses that had grown up since the last gathering. Others harvested crops and wild plant foods, captured fish with weirs and nets, and hunted white-tailed deer and other game to feed the many participants who would come.

"At the core of American Indian cultural values is the understanding that all things—humans, animals, plants, rocks, water, air—are living, are connected, and deserve respect. So everyday tasks, as well as special occasions, are marked by honor and reflected in ceremonies. The legacy of the Hopewell tradition shows the importance of ceremonial life in all things—extravagance in material artistry, precision in earthwork design, and elaboration in the rituals of death and burial.

Marking the paths of the Sun and Moon, the earthworks determined the times for ceremonies, when (as still today in Native communities) large gatherings included feasting, gift-giving, dancing, and ceremonial games. Ceremonies convey traditions, knowledge, and philosophy; they emphasize the sacred, and the connectedness of people with their beliefs, families, ancestors, and communities—and with the natural world."

—MARTI CHAATSMITH (Comanche/Choctaw)

Subtle remains of High Bank Works' large circle lie in this open field. The neck connecting the two figures appears as a small hump in the farm road; the slight rise beneath the tall tree (right of center) marks the apex of the earthwork's main axis.

9.

HIGH BANK WORKS

"There's such a complexity, and it gives me great pride to know that. Too many times the word that I read in Ohio history, and on signs in Ohio, on statues, on monuments, my people are often referred to as 'savages.' [But] there had to be such intellectual capacity here . . . there had to be so much knowledge of so many different subjects. And so there's an intellectual, there's an emotional, there is a spiritual... [achievement here] and it gives me immense pride."

—CHIEF GLENNA J. WALLACE (Eastern Shawnee Tribe of Oklahoma)

A few miles south of Chillicothe, the High Bank Works occupy a high, level terrace some thirty feet above the Scioto River floodplain, directly opposite the Paint Creek confluence. The "high bank" after which the site is named shows evidence of huge meander loops where the Scioto has carved the western edge of the terrace into steep, arcing embankments. On this wide terrace, the Ancients planned and constructed a geometrical and astronomical masterpiece equivalent to Newark's Octagon, which it closely resembles in both form and function.

High Bank is maintained as a research preserve, and public access is limited. Its isolated, rural site is an open former agricultural field, ringed on all sides by trees. Just beyond the eastern edge of the earthwork, a sixteen-foot-high railroad embankment separates the site from a modern highway and the low hills beyond. Distant horizons open to the north and south. Nearly two centuries of cultivation have spread the soil of the walls out into wide, gentle rises clearly detectable in LiDAR data but visible today only with considerable effort or expert guidance. Yet high-resolution magnetometry data gathered since the turn of the twenty-first century reveal the extent, precision, and underground integrity of High Bank's circle, octagon, and other features.

SITE FEATURES

The High Bank Works were obviously designed and built in a way related to Newark's Octagon Earthworks. As with all the geometric enclosures, they lie atop the deep, well-drained, gravelly subsoils typical of these glacial terraces. The circle is identical in size to that at Newark and is linked by a short, narrow

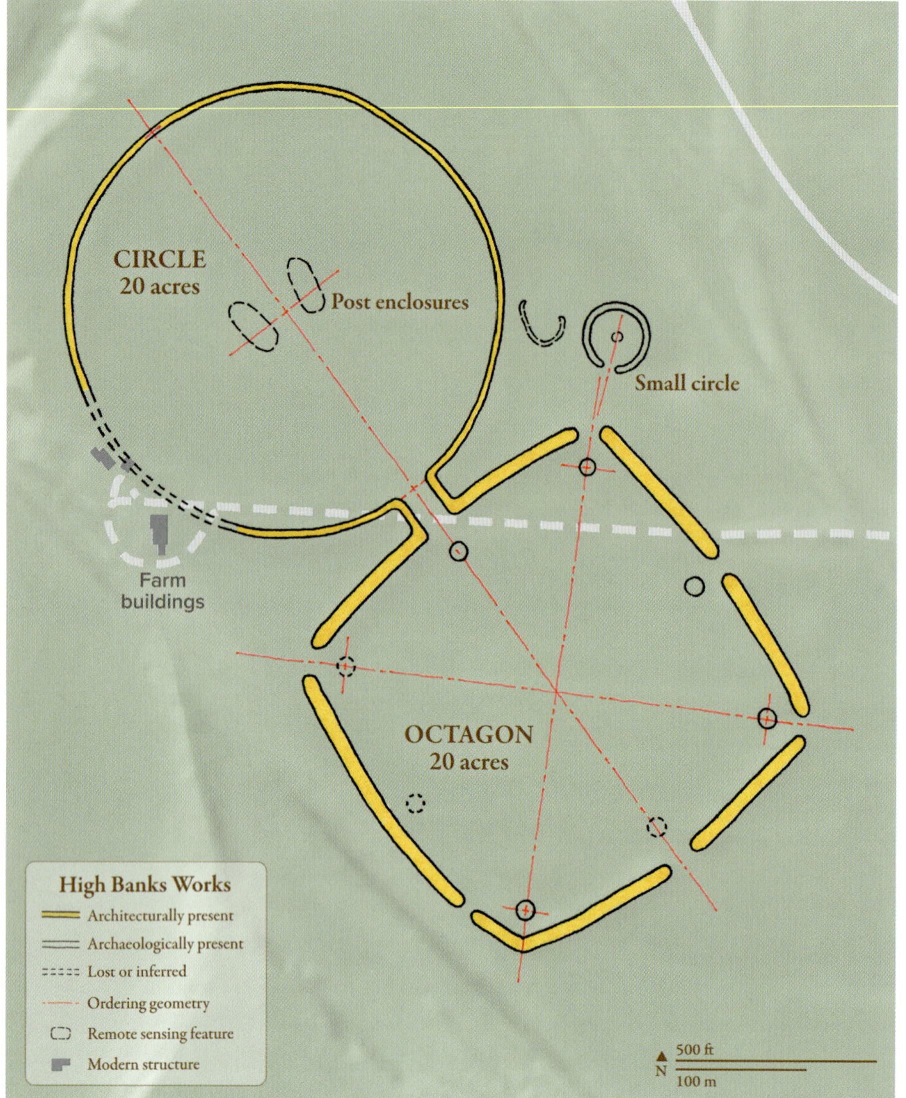

OPPOSITE, LEFT: A 2008 LiDAR image of the High Bank Works shows that despite appearing obscure on the ground, the ruins of the earthen walls are still present.

OPPOSITE, RIGHT: Magnetometry data from High Bank reveal the precise widths of the walls' foundations, plus other subsurface features yet to be investigated.

neck to a slightly irregular, open-cornered octagon. The circle and octagon have nearly equal areas and total just over forty acres.

Just outside the northern corner of High Bank's octagon are the subsurface remains of a small circle, 148 feet in diameter, with an interior ditch and a gateway aligned toward the octagon's open corner. The partial underground remains of a rounded-corner rectangular feature lie nearby. The outlines of two large post enclosures straddle the center of the large circle. Squier and Davis noted the small circle, but these other features have only recently appeared in the remote sensing data and have not yet been investigated.

A complex set of roughly parallel walls, circles, and geometric fragments extended far to the southwest from the octagon, roughly parallel with the terrace edge; their partial circles suggest they may have been truncated by erosion at some point. Described by Squxier and Davis as "reduced but traceable" in their day, these features have long since disappeared on the surface, although some of their outlines appear in LiDAR images and magnetic data.

CIRCLE AND OCTAGON

In the mid-nineteenth century, the wall of High Bank's nearly perfect twenty-acre circle stood about five feet high, similar to Hopeton's. At its apex, corresponding to where an equivalent of Newark's Observatory Mound would be, the ground swells slightly, suggesting that the design included a similar feature to mark the head of the monument's major axis. Traces of two huge (60 by 130 feet) oval post-enclosures lie in the ground on either side of the large circle's center point. A very short neck, just 100 by 100 feet, connects the circle to the octagon.

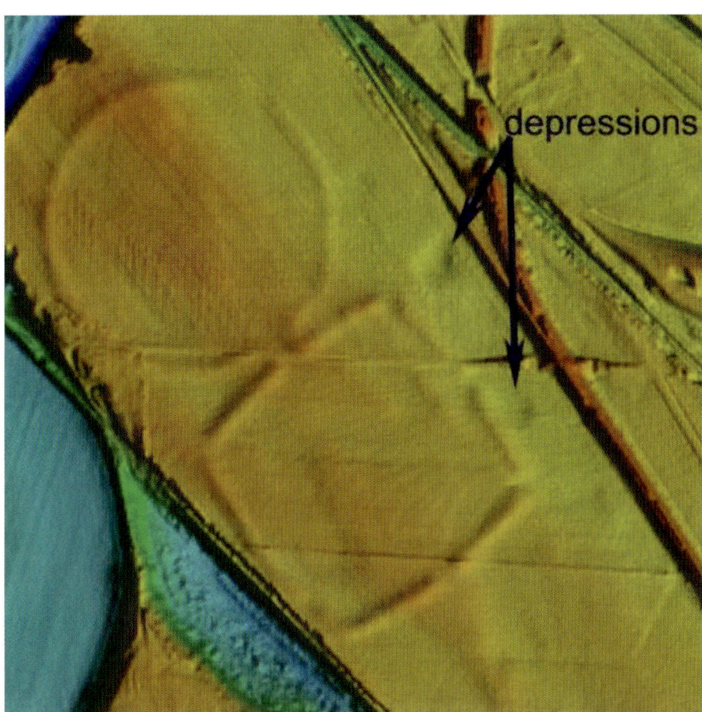

Squier and Davis recorded the walls of the octagon as twelve feet high, similar to those of Hopeton's square. Today, they average less than five feet and are difficult to discern. Eight mounds stood just inside the octagon's corners, six of them aligned in the typical manner with the wall's open gateways. Instead of a gateway at the southernmost apex, one wall extends at an angle to form an offset gateway on the southwestern side. The adjacent, southwestern apex (actually a subtle arc) has no gateway opening, but its mound lies on the octagon's cross axis. The interior mounds are not visible today.

GEOMETRY AND CONSTRUCTION

The large circle at High Bank has the same diameter as Newark's Observatory Circle (1,054 feet—the OCD) and, though somewhat less precise, it still varies less than six feet from the shape of a perfect circle. The corner mounds inside High Bank's octagon form a square with a diagonal of one OCD. High Bank's primary central axis, though not aligned to any astronomical event,

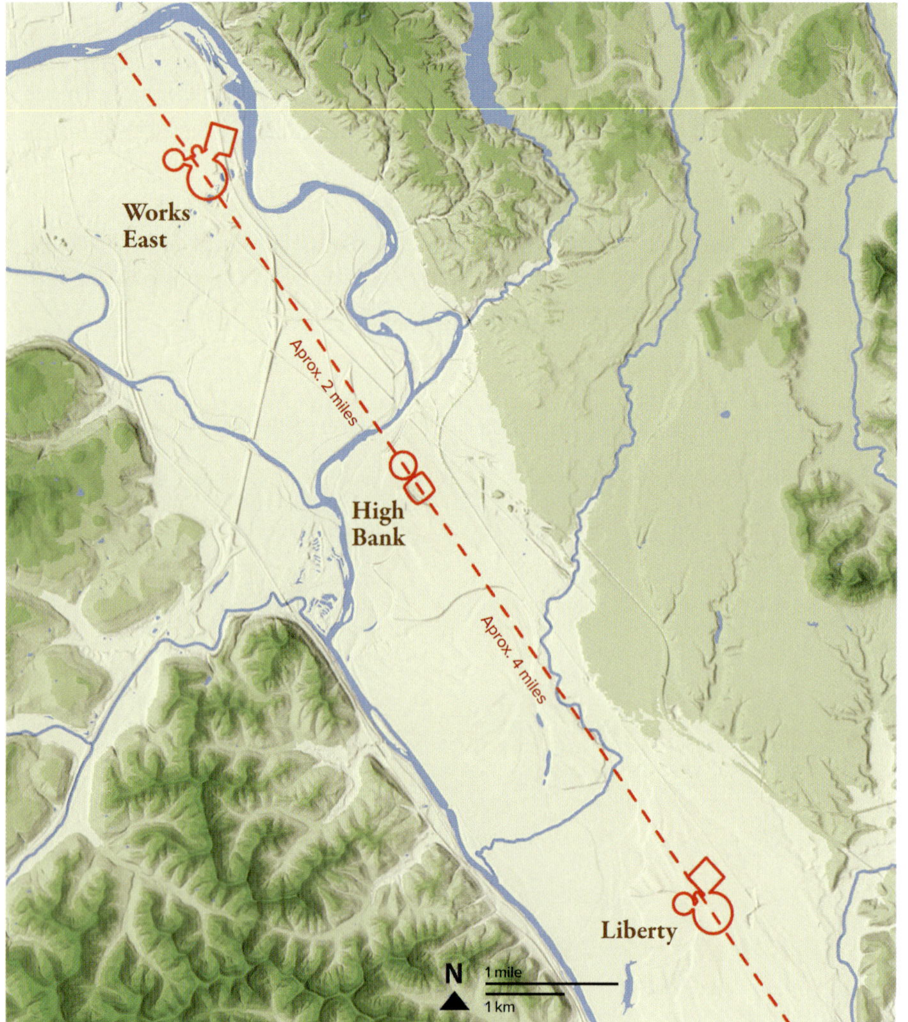

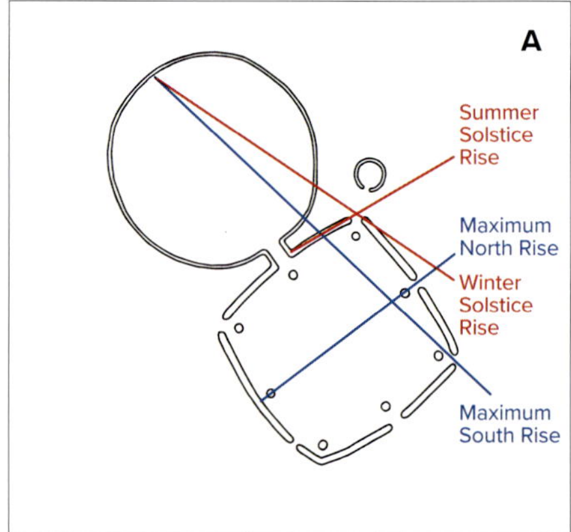

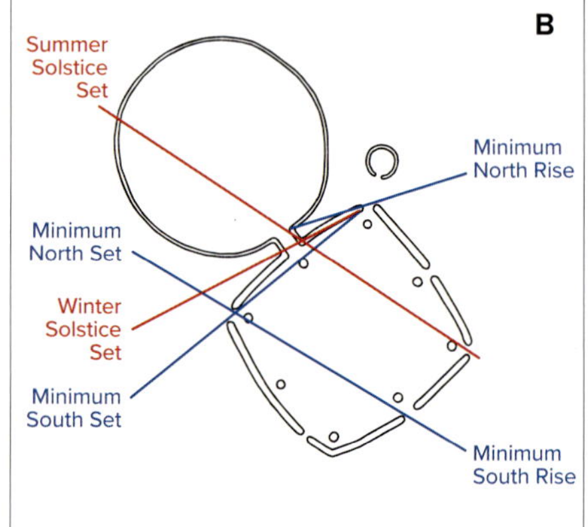

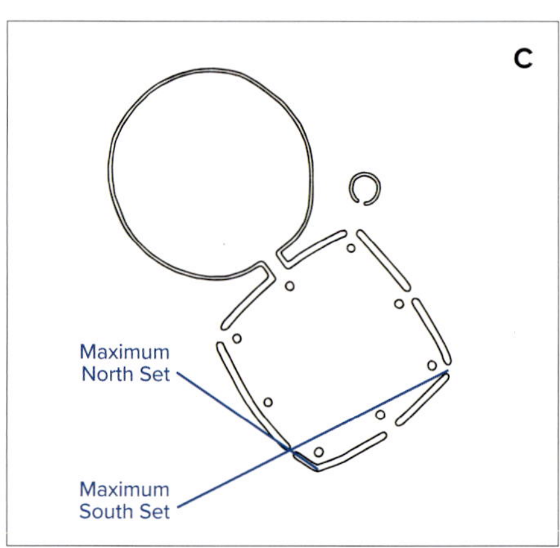

points precisely toward the locations of two other now-destroyed geometric earthworks in its immediate vicinity—Works East, which stood just over two miles to the north, and the Liberty-Harness Earthworks, whose scant remains lie four miles to the south. This axis also corresponds to the southeasterly bearing of the dramatically wide and unusually straight Scioto (Teays) Valley itself. It is also exactly perpendicular to the main lunar axis of Newark's Octagon Earthworks, fifty-eight miles away.

Limited excavations are beginning to shed light on High Bank's construction process. As at Hopeton and the other Paint and Scioto Valley earthworks, the builders began by clearing away the surface topsoil. In this case, they brought in various sandy clays and loams to create the wall, with mixes of sand and gravel, some of which came from the features west of the octagon labeled by Squier and Davis as "dug holes." Excavations at the large circle's apex showed that wooden posts were erected and then removed before the earthen wall was built. Similarly, excavations of the large circle's southern arc, just west of its connection with the octagon, indicated a fence of closely set oak posts that were also dismantled prior to wall construction.

ABOVE, LEFT: Three earthworks south of Chillicothe were lined up along a seven-mile axis, also matching the long straight section of the ancient Teays Valley in which they lie.

The builders capped all the walls with a silty clay loam, over underlying construction that otherwise varied. For the octagon, they used a mixture of red and yellowish soils, but for the large circle they placed the red soil beneath, with a layer of yellow silty clay loess over it. The area of the wooden fence had also been overlaid with thin layers of gravel in alternating colors. These complex variations show that High Bank's architects intentionally selected, combined, and placed specific materials for practical or symbolic purposes.

LUNAR AND SOLAR ALIGNMENTS

Like Newark's Octagon Earthworks, High Bank encodes the extreme rise and set points of the Moon at its latitude. But High Bank also captures all four of the solstice sunrises and sunsets. The cross axis of its octagon, perpendicular to the site's principal axis, marks the Moon's northernmost rise, while one of the octagon's north walls aligns to the summer solstice sunrise. From the point on the large circle at the top of the site's main axis, the position corresponding to Newark's Observatory Mound, alignments to the far left and near left corners of the octagon mark the maximum southern lunar rise and the winter solstice rise, respectively. By setting up these four eastern-horizon alignments (diagram A), the site's architects were able to derive the overall shape and orientation of the earthwork.

ARCHAEOASTRONOMY AND ITS CRITERIA

The Hopewell-era Moon watchers' mastery of the complete long lunar cycle appears to be unparalleled in human history, judging from two reports (in 2010 and 2017) by the International Council on Monuments and Sites (ICOMOS), the body that advises the UNESCO World Heritage Committee on criteria standards. Entitled *Heritage Sites of Astronomy and Archaeoastronomy in the Context of World Heritage (thematic studies 1 and 2)*, they summarize knowledge about the world's ancient, astronomically aligned monuments, which are overwhelmingly solar. The few conjectures about Moon alignments are related mainly to seasonal rise and set positions, and most are acknowledged to be imprecise. They mention the long lunar cycle mainly to suggest that its complexity is likely the reason for its absence from all cited examples.

Lead author Clive Ruggles, in the 2010 report, also specifies standards for judging the intentionality and precision of any alignment claims, cautioning against gratuitous or random "astronomical alignment hunting." First, there should be "geographically and chronologically well-defined clusters of architecturally similar constructions where systematic analyses can be, and have been, undertaken." Second, only "a clearly identifiable principal axis or other major structural orientation" should be taken as deliberate rather than incidental. The alignments at the Hopewell Ceremonial Earthworks meet both standards and within a 1.5-degree angle of precision. Both solar and lunar alignments are marked comprehensively (at the Octagon Earthworks and High Bank Works), and at multiple sites (also at Mound City and Fort Ancient).

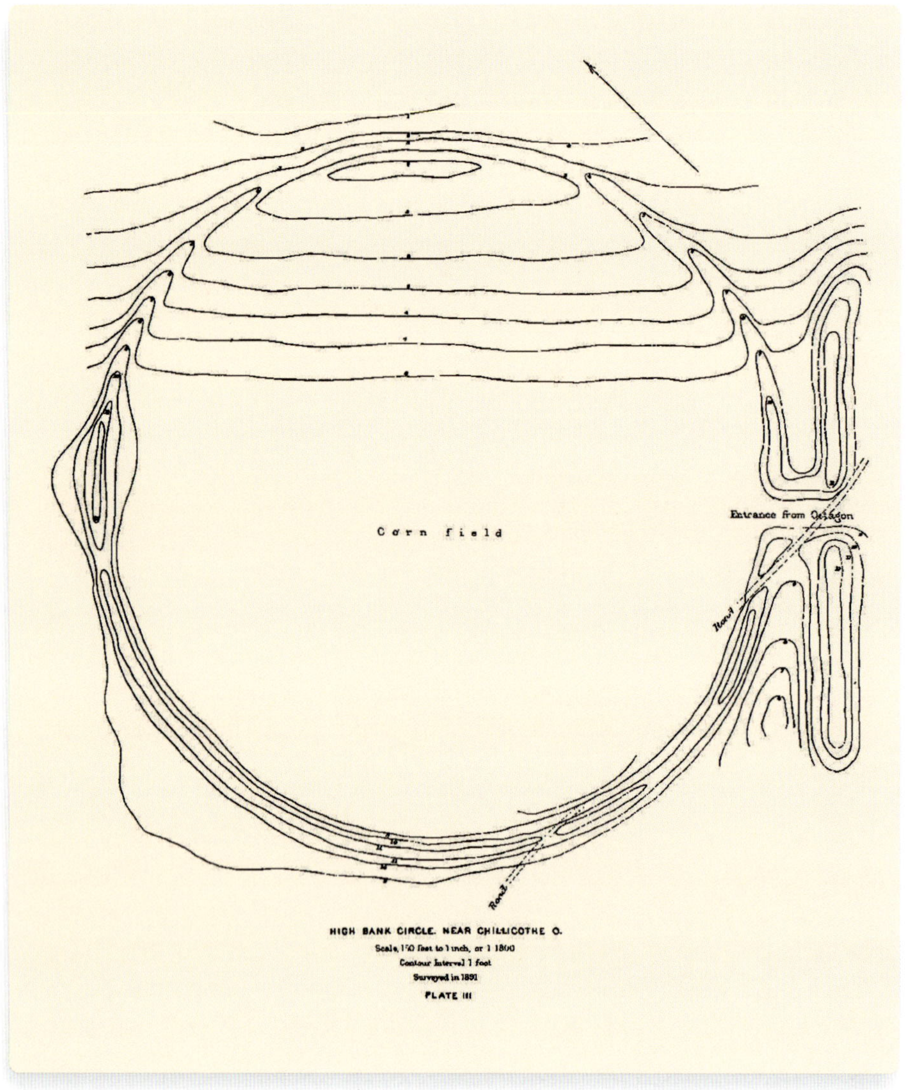

An 1891 contour map of the High Bank circle shows what may have been an Observatory Mound comparable to Newark's at the apex of the site's main axis (left).

With the Sun's four and the Moon's eight, there are twelve standstill positions in total. Of the eight remaining, three occur between corners of the octagon: north to west captures the maximum south moonset; west to southeast the minimum south moonrise; and the reverse (southeast to west) the minimum north moonset. Three more involve the defining points of the connecting avenue: the octagon's north apex marks the minimum northern moonrise when viewed from the avenue's northern corner. The avenue's eastern corner aligns to the winter solstice sunset when viewed from the octagon's northern apex. This same eastern corner marks the summer solstice set when viewed from the octagon's eastern apex (diagram B).

Finally, the two remaining alignments are captured by what otherwise looks like a design flaw. The minimum southern moonset, viewed from the eastern octagon apex, occurs through the oddly displaced gateway at the southern corner, and the seemingly distorted angle of the short adjacent corner wall places it into alignment with the maximum northern moonset (diagram C).

MODERN HISTORY

High Bank, like the other great Hopewell centers, was gradually covered by the forest following the end of Hopewell ceremonial practices. There is no evidence of later use or occupation by other Indigenous groups. Over the centuries, the shifting course of the Scioto River apparently eroded the subsidiary features extending southwest of the octagon.

The site was part of a large tract deeded to the frontier surveyor Nathaniel Massie in 1796, which then changed hands and was subdivided during the first half of the nineteenth century. By the late 1840s, Squier and Davis's map showed the site cleared of trees, with a farm building west of the earthworks near the terrace edge, and what were then recent property boundaries. They reported that the walls of High Bank's octagon that had "been least subjected to cultivation . . . (were) between eleven and twelve feet in height, by about fifty feet base." This would make them comparable to the walls of the square at nearby Hopeton.

Forty years later, Cyrus Thomas noted that the site had "been cultivated almost annually since 1845. The walls of the circle and octagon are still quite prominent, and are respectively two and five feet high." A contour survey of the large circle around 1890 detected the slightly wider and taller profile at the circle's axial apex (the "observatory mound" position), although no other records had yet noted this feature.

MORE THAN OBSERVATORIES

Our modern idea of an observatory—a facility for observing astronomical phenomena—does not fully capture what these earthworks were. Instead, they were more like cathedrals or mosques—sacred places with meanings related to their alignments (to the east, or to Mecca). The cosmic connection helps to sanctify these places even when it is not being directly observed. Yet at the earthworks, observances of the Sun's and Moon's turning points would also have mattered: they were the key realignments of powerful spiritual beings whose comings and goings were filled with special meaning. Many people probably came, not just to observe but to assist by presenting ritual offerings, helping to ensure that those realignments occurred successfully.

The earthworks were arenas for interactive performances. What could be more dramatic than standing with a crowd, in the dark, while the Moon or the Sun slowly appears, exactly where the architecture—already inspiring in itself—says it will, and understanding that appearance as an affirmation and renewal of the cosmos? Obsidian bearers from Wyoming, for example, could plan their months-long trip to Ohio with knowledge of the Moon's long cycle, and of its seasonal presentation: the dramatic northernmost risings of the near-full Moon occur in the fall and winter, and the southernmost ones in the spring and summer. A Moon-watching culture also knew they had at least three consecutive days each month when the moonrise would repeat within one or two degrees of its extreme position.

PRESERVATION AND RESEARCH

Through most of the twentieth century, High Bank's walls, like Hopeton's, were subjected to more significant degradation by ever-more-powerful agricultural machinery until the site's preservation in the 1980s. On the National Register of Historic Places since 1973, it was one of three earthworks to join Mound City in the establishment of Hopewell Culture National Historical Park in 1992, finally taking it out of cultivation. LiDAR topographic data and aerial photography show the walls' remains, although the soils composing their original profiles have been spread far out across the ground. Magnetometry surveys since 2012 clearly delineate the inner and outer margins of the earthworks, indicating that the original base layers of the walls remain intact.

LEFT: A digital rendering restores the features of the High Bank Works.

RIGHT: The High Bank octagon's walls and gateways surrounded most of this large meadow, seen here from the top of the adjacent railroad embankment.

Little archaeological research has been done at High Bank. From the mid-1990s to 2010, N'omi Greber of the Cleveland Museum of Natural History led the most extensive investigations, revealing that, like its sister site in Newark, High Bank has a pronounced lack of artifacts. Yet of the major Hopewell earthworks, High Bank has one of the greatest potentials for yielding new knowledge. Its chronology remains unproven, and many features now revealed by remote sensing—structure walls, floors, post enclosures, and cooking pits—need to be field verified. These and other questions are particularly important given the earthwork's size, elaborate geometry, astronomical alignments, and probable connections with the Newark Octagon.

AUTHENTICITY AND EXPERIENCE

Even without readily visible earthworks, High Bank's wide, tree-rimmed terrace site conveys, like Hopeton's, the vast spatiality of the Hopewell cultural landscape—expansive vistas across level terraces, along the river's huge valley and riparian corridors, and out to the distant hills beyond. These are the wide horizons toward which the ancient builders calibrated alignments not only to the Sun and Moon, but in this case also to the dramatic valley landforms in which they lie. Despite nearly two centuries of cultivation, the High Bank Works retain some topographic relief, evident in LiDAR data and aerial photography, and detectable on the ground in optimal conditions.

Like its sister site, the Newark Octagon, High Bank is extraordinarily complex. Its astronomical alignments are at least as astonishing, capturing not only all eight lunar rise and set alignments, but also the four key solar ones. The site's substantial archaeological integrity is revealed by geophysics and ensures that future research will yield important results.

ANCIENT SKY KNOWLEDGE

Hopewell astronomical genius is embodied most convincingly in the similarities between High Bank Works and Newark's Octagon Earthworks. Both calibrate the long lunar cycle with similar shapes and comparable precision, and both mark certain key alignments with otherwise inexplicable formal anomalies. Neither could have been conceived without generations of continuous, motivated intellect and persistent, careful recordkeeping. What were they doing, and why?

In today's world of enclosed spaces and technological comforts, we seldom notice the Sun's movements, even though its relatively simple daily and annual patterns control day, night, and the seasons. The Moon's changes are more elusive; when we notice it at all we are usually surprised by its shifting position, phase, or brightness. For ancient people, these celestial cycles were immediate and directly experienced—there in the Sky, not objects in an astronomer's diagram or in today's mental models of the solar system. In most ancient societies, the Sky's observed patterns were both timekeepers for life activities and messengers of a spiritual domain.

The Sun's annual cycle of rising positions and day lengths is easily observed. It creates the seasons in our northern hemisphere's midlatitudes. In the summer, it rises in the northeast, crosses the Sky in a high arc, through a long day, and sets in the northwest. In the winter it rises in the southeast, follows a low arc during short days, and sets in the southwest. At the two equinoxes, the Sun crosses from due east to due west with equal day and night. Marking sunrise or sunset positions through this straightforward annual cycle allowed ancient people to predict the seasons, telling them when to plant and harvest, when the rains would come or the animals would migrate, and when to plan their greatest festivals.

Lunar cycles are harder to decipher and predict, and thus less practical for timing seasonal activities like planting. The Moon's phases could be readily observed—its cycle of growth and disappearance (waxing and waning) marked out a clear, regular interval still important for Indigenous timekeeping today. But the Moon's rising positions move through a complex pattern lasting 18.6 years, swinging from northeast to southeast and back again every month, through an angle that expands slowly for 9.3 years, and then contracts again at the same rate. Modern astronomers will explain that the Moon's phases result from its position in its orbit relative to the direction of the Sun's light, and that the generation-long pattern of rising positions is caused by a five-degree tilt between the plane of the Moon's orbit and the plane of the Earth's movement around the Sun.

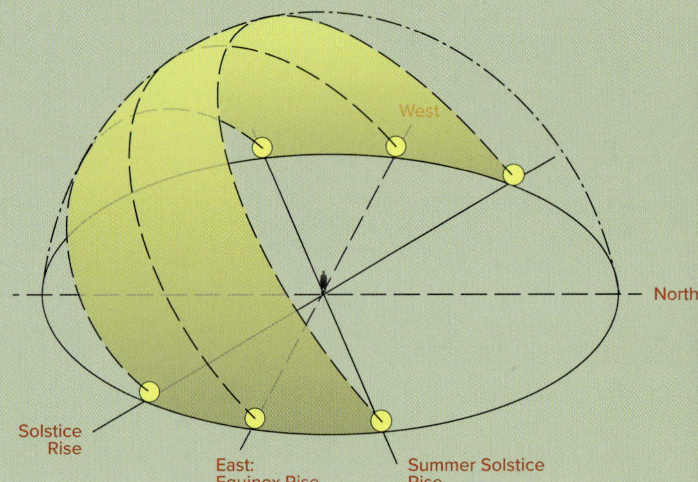

The Sun's seasonal rising positions move between the northeast and the southeast, with corresponding changes in the height of its path across the sky.

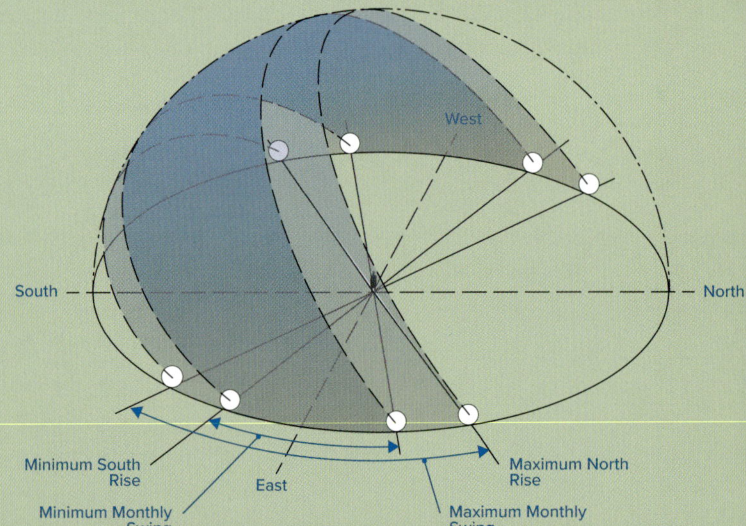

The Moon's rising positions move through a similar horizon angle—but monthly—also with corresponding altitudes of its overhead arc. But the angle between its monthly extremes expands and contracts slowly over 18.6 years.

Stonehenge remains the most famous ancient astronomy site in the world, although its encoded knowledge of the long lunar cycle is far from complete.

But ancient observers did not envision tilted planes. They saw, instead, the shining Moon growing and diminishing every twenty-eight days, while its path across the Sky changed rapidly from low in the south to practically overhead and back again during the same period. They would have seen the difference in arc positions first—it is quite pronounced—and probably turned to the observation and marking of the corresponding rise and set positions as a method for recording their extremes.

Just as the Sun's observable rising position at each solstice (standstill) lasts about six days, so the Moon's observable monthly maximum and minimum positions remain within a tiny, one-degree range throughout a "season" of around thirty months (and for two or three days each month). Those positions vary by tiny amounts, in irregular patterns, approaching an outer limit (the "scientific" maxima) which, for either them or us, is of practically no observational consequence.

The singular achievement of the Hopewell-era skywatchers was figuring out how these Moon positions (arc altitudes and rise points) change over their long, 18.6-year cycle. It would have required decades of recorded observations. Only after several repetitions of the cycle—with phases, time of day, and cloud cover affecting its visibility—could the northernmost rising of the Moon be confidently marked. That means several generations recording observations even after the value of doing so had been established in the first place. Complex recording systems would have been needed, most likely poles erected as foresights and backsights (with vistas cleared to the horizon) and then adjusted over time. Once the key alignment points were determined, and verified probably by at least one more cycle, soil was brought in for the final monument.

A digital restoration of the Hopewell Mound Group shows its large forest clearing, with the North Fork of Paint Creek (far left) and the water-filled ponds along the northern walls (right).

10. HOPEWELL MOUND GROUP

"The vast majority of Indian tribal religions . . . have a sacred center at a particular place, be it a river, a mountain, a plateau, valley, or other natural feature. This center enables the people to look out along the four dimensions and locate their lands, to relate all historical events within the confines of this particular land, and to accept responsibility for it."

—VINE DELORIA JR. (Standing Rock Sioux, 1933–2005)

In a rural setting five miles west of downtown Chillicothe, a narrow country road crosses a small tributary of Paint Creek's North Fork before rising to a broad level terrace. Gentle wooded hills surround this quiet valley, and in a huge clearing above the creek's floodplain lie the remains of the Hopewell Mound Group, the place that gave this brilliant ancient civilization its modern name. This seemingly remote and peaceful valley was the preeminent sacred pilgrimage and ritual center of the entire Hopewell world. Of all their earthwork complexes, this one contains the most mounds, the largest mound, one of the largest enclosed areas, and the greatest variety of earthen architecture. Two and a half miles of earth and stone embankments enclose 137 acres, combining hilltop, geometric, and irregular forms.

The site overlooks the active floodplain of the small stream to the south, where the elevation drops steeply just beyond the scant remains of the earthwork's southern wall. The scope of the enclosure is well defined by the surrounding tree lines on the south, west, and east. To the north, the best-preserved walls climb into the forest and along the top of the hill—an ancient glacial moraine. Unique among the sites in this series, the earthwork perimeter here engages both the wooded hillsides and the steep terrace edges so authentically associated with Hopewell spatiality. Beginning in the mid-100s CE and over at least two centuries, the Ancients embellished this high terrace with a succession of increasingly elaborate ceremonial activities, tombs, buildings, artistry deposits, walls, and mounds. Their commitment to this sacred site continued until around 400 CE, the end of the Hopewell era.

Today, tree lines define the vast space of the Hopewell Mound Group, focused on the distant, subtle profile of the unrestored Mound 25 (center). Preserved walls climb along the wooded hillside (right).

THE GREAT ENCLOSURE

The large, roughly rectangular space called the Great Enclosure averages 1,900 by 2,900 feet, encompassing within its 119 acres all of the site's major ritual remains. These include three smaller enclosures—a D-shape and two rings—and more than twenty mounds. At least half of its western wall survives, though less than two feet high, running adjacent to an intermittent waterway connecting the hillside with the terrace edge to the south. The condition of the southern wall is not well known; it is difficult to access because it follows the edge of a steep scarp, which drops to the floodplain and has been vulnerable to erosion and possible impacts from the construction of an 1870s rail line below.

The eastern wall and ditch of the Great Enclosure form the western side of an adjacent square; the wall's height, now reduced by decades of plowing to just over two feet, was recorded in the mid-nineteenth century at about five feet. Though farming and erosion have leveled out their profiles, the original base layers of the wall and ditch are well preserved. Their exact widths and positions have been revealed by geophysical data, and excavations have uncovered the materials and techniques of their construction.

For the wall, the builders chose distinct soils and used them in at least two major construction episodes. They first stripped away the upper layer of topsoil

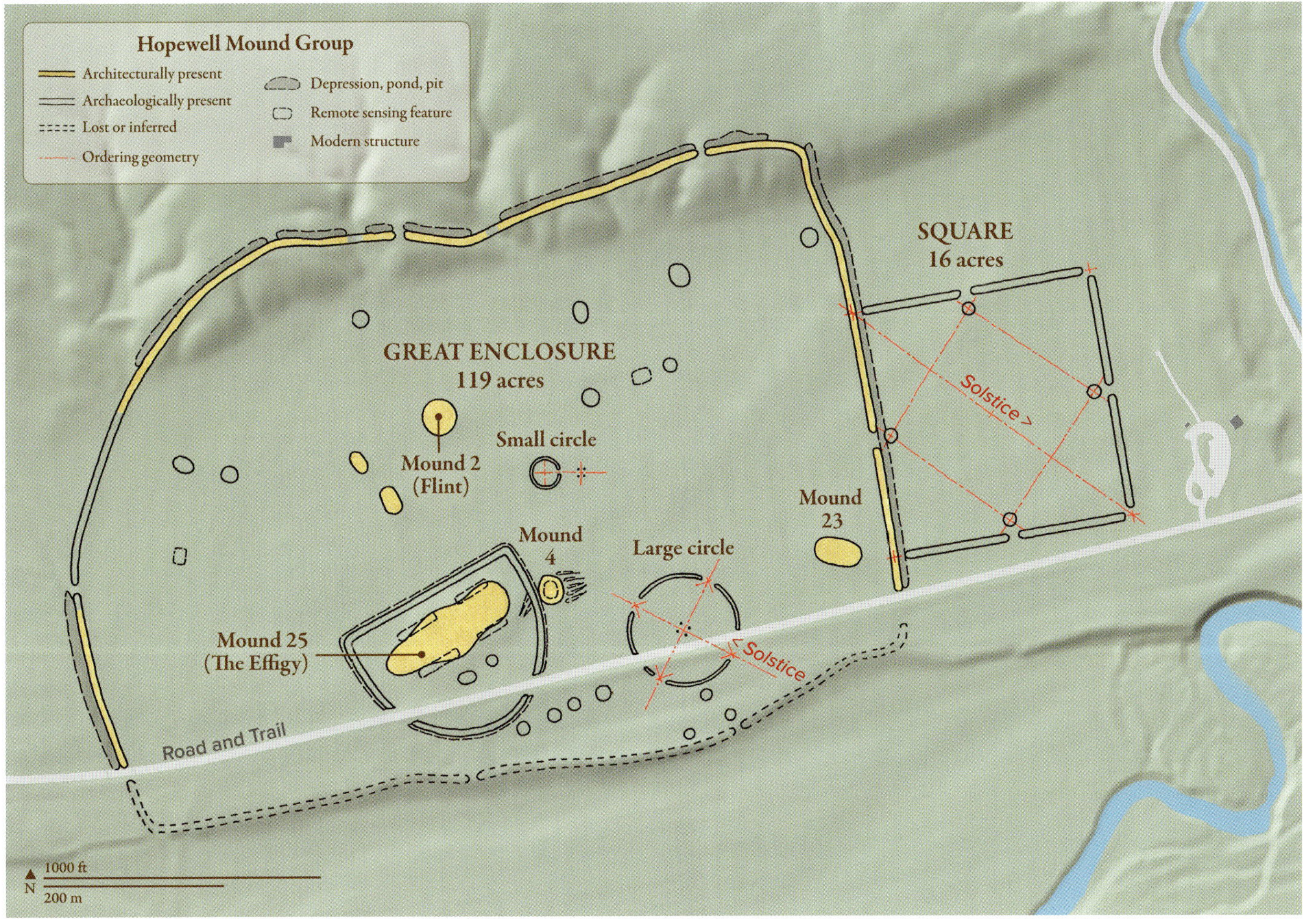

before depositing their carefully selected materials—first yellow-brown and then reddish-brown soils—creating distinct strata and taking care to keep the colors from mixing. The soils were not quarried from the adjacent ditch (which would have been the loose and unconsolidated sand and gravel typical of these glacial terraces) but were brought instead from other locations in the vicinity. The builders dug into the gravelly subsoil, then lined the ditch with a clay loam, also brought in from elsewhere, stabilizing the sloping surface so it would hold water.

The northern wall of the Great Enclosure ascends some thirty-three feet to the crest of the moraine, where, along with an exterior ditch, it crosses the hilltop and undulates in and out of small ravines. This northern section is well preserved, having been subjected to little if any plowing. The largest portions are about thirty feet wide and stand about five feet above the surrounding level. The adjacent ditch still reaches a depth of nearly three feet, creating a total relief from bank to ditch of about eight feet today, equivalent to when it was first recorded in the mid-nineteenth century.

The ditch's water-retaining linings remain undisturbed and effective in wet seasons. Near the northwestern corner of the Great Enclosure, the builders had also redirected a nearby spring to increase the flow of water in the channel outside the western wall. This apparent desire to complete a water boundary is consistent with design intentions at Newark's Great Circle and at Fort Ancient.

GEOMETRIC ENCLOSURES

A sixteen-acre square adjoins the eastern wall of the Great Enclosure, incorporating its straight section as one of its sides. Its walls measured six feet high in the mid-nineteenth century but are reduced to near invisibility today. Their subsurface traces appear in geophysical images, and the National Park Service presents them to visitors through differential mowing. The similarly reduced remains of small mounds stand inside the square's midpoint gateways, though not in its corners. The soil of the square's walls is noticeably red, possibly from burning, similar to that of other squares at the region's geometric earthworks. The subsurface remains of a cluster of borrow pits lie next to the square's central, north-facing gateway, each around twenty feet in diameter.

Although the Great Enclosure and its mound placements appear irregular, the square and other features reveal the usual Hopewell precision. The four faces of the perfect 850-foot square are each bisected by a gateway, whose corresponding mounds define a square of one-half an OCD on a side. (If there were mounds at the corners, they would be diagonally one OCD apart, as is the case with those in the octagon at High Bank.) The square's east-northeasterly axis aligns, through a very evident gap in the surrounding hills, in the precise direction of Mound City, which shares the same orientation angle. A diagonal line connecting the northwest and southeast corners of the square aligns with the winter solstice sunrise, a phenomenon shared with the squares at Hopeton, Mound City, and the Seip Earthworks.

The largest feature inside the Great Enclosure is a D-shaped figure measuring 690 feet across, with its straight side facing to the north-northwest. This figure appears in geophysical imagery as the footprint of a sixteen-foot-wide earthwork with a narrow exterior trench. A few small mounds stood inside its southern arc, but the enclosure's geometric clarity and spatial framing primarily serve to enhance the honorific status and monumental presence of the large mound at its center—Mound 25.

MOUND 25, "THE EFFIGY"

OPPOSITE: From above the north wall and its accompanying ditch, views through the forest open to the huge expanse of the Great Enclosure below and the wide valley beyond.

RIGHT: Four previously unknown features give Mound 25's earlier name (the Effigy) new credibility: Magnetic anomalies suggest the stylized paws of a huge, crouching animal.

In antiquity, the huge, triple-lobed mass of the largest mound ever built by the Hopewell culture dominated the wide-open space of the Great Enclosure. Called the Effigy by early archaeologists (and Mound 25 today), it rose to a maximum height of thirty feet above a base of 180 by 500 feet. Excavations of this mound in the 1890s yielded the spectacular artifacts displayed at the 1893 World's Columbian Exposition in Chicago. The soil from those excavations was replaced, although not as a restoration of the mound's original shape but instead as a large pile only about ten feet tall and spread across a wider area. Magnetometry data show a symmetrical set of rectangular features along its original outline, which have not yet been investigated.

This giant mound was the culmination of a long process—the growth, use, decommissioning, and covering of the site's primary ceremonial spaces. It reflects the most elaborate planning and development process of any Hopewell project, all sanctified and embellished with the greatest care and artistry. In the open, level center of the site, the builders removed the topsoil to reach a clay layer, then mixed clay and water to create a hard floor surface (Hopewell

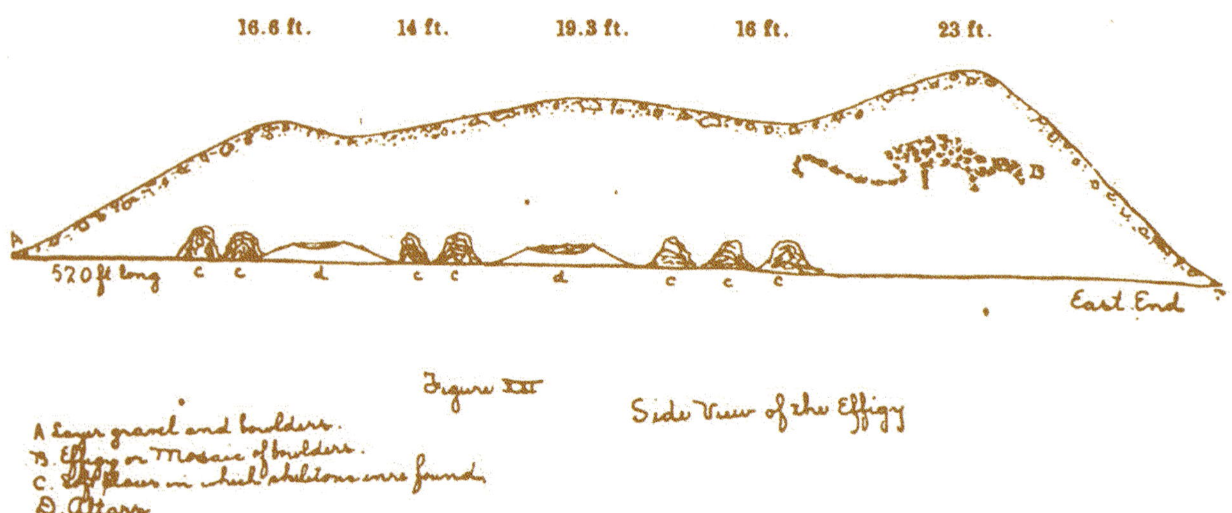

LEFT: This artist's collage envisions the variety of abstract, geometric, and figurative shapes crafted from Lake Superior copper and buried together in a ceremonial deposit beneath Mound 25.

BELOW: Warren King Moorehead's 1892 field sketch of Mound 25 depicts a large rock mosaic of a panther.

concrete again) across the area of the future mound. They decorated it with colored and fire-altered sediments. Over several generations, people performed ceremonial rituals here that involved digging pits, building fires, and covering certain areas with stones or multicolored clay.

They erected buildings of various sizes across this prepared floor to shelter or enclose their ceremonies, leaving open plazas between them where other performances took place. As at Mound City, many of their ritual activities focused around prepared clay basins. They placed human burials on and under the floors of several wood-framed buildings, possibly interconnected yet sometimes individually decommissioned and mounded. Each of these great timber halls was eventually dismantled, and its floors, basins, and tombs covered by a larger mound. Eventually they piled up the final, gigantic, three-lobed form,

A digital reconstruction shows the flint discs stacked neatly in the center of the flint cache building that preceded the construction of Mound 2.

and decorated its southern face with an unusual boulder mosaic depicting a long-tailed panther.

The graves in Mound 25 contained the remains of at least 102 people. The celebrants arrayed them with a prodigious variety of copper, obsidian, mica, and other exotic materials, fashioned into beautiful abstract and figurative shapes. Also on the floor of Mound 25, they laid down two elaborate sets of objects (called the Great Deposits), many ritually broken and burned. The pieces were arrayed in a set of dualistic contrasts: all the black obsidian, for example, was placed in the eastern deposit, and all the white pearls in the western one. A massive collection of copper artifacts found beneath Mound 25 included what the archaeologist Moorehead called "the largest worked copper object made by prehistoric man in the world"—a twenty-two-inch ceremonial axe weighing thirty-eight pounds.

OTHER MOUNDS AND DEPOSITS

Near the southeastern corner of the Great Enclosure, the oblong form of Mound 23 is the second largest of the group, originally more than 150 feet long and

17 feet tall. Today, its height is reduced to only three feet, but geophysics and soil coring have shown that much of its floor and cobble stone mantle remain beneath the surface. All the mounds at Hopewell Mound Group that were originally over six feet tall retain the remnants of a mantle—a rim or covering of stream cobbles and gravel—similar to that on Mound 7 at Mound City.

The slightly visible form of Mound 4 stands immediately next to the eastern edge of the D shape. Magnetic data show a pattern of several unusual lines extending from it to the east and west, looking rather like the bear-paw motifs known from Hopewell artistry. North of the D shape, three mounds, including the relatively large Mound 2, also remain visible, with subtle profiles approaching three feet.

Beneath Mound 2, also called the Flint Mound, the people assembled more than 8,000 nearly identical flint discs, arranging them in little bundles—each about as much as one person could carry—and laying them down carefully on the floor over a bed of fine gravel. This whole assemblage covered the central floor area of a timber building, which was later dismantled while leaving the flints to be buried. This massive collection was assembled here from several different flint sources in Tennessee, Illinois, and Indiana—some as many as 400 miles away.

A small mound near the northern edge of the Great Enclosure covered two other raw material deposits. Like the Great Deposits, they were deliberately arranged in a contrasting duality—all the silvery mica lay on a square stone tablet, and all the shiny copper on a round stone disc. At least twenty other mounds stood inside the Great Enclosure, with an astonishing variety of dedicated functions and lavish deposits—including more mica—and a huge cache of obsidian pieces from the Yellowstone Valley. The spectacular quantity, material variety, and impressive artistry of the ceremonial deposits placed at this site have no equal at any other location in the Hopewell world.

LARGE AND SMALL CIRCLES

Within the Great Enclosure lie the hidden remains of two earthen circles. The larger one, about 390 feet in diameter, has an interior ditch and, inside that, the posthole traces of a closely spaced ring of large-diameter timber poles—a woodhenge. Though its form is not visible on the surface, investigations in 2017 revealed three gateway openings toward the northeast, northwest, and southwest, with a fourth to the southeast obscured but likely. They pass like causeways across the interior ditch. At the center of this circle, magnetic traces of four gigantic earth ovens form a square pattern aligned with the ninety-degree cross axes defined by the gateways. Each subterranean oven was nine feet in diameter and six feet deep—large enough to cook huge feasts for the gathered community.

This circle reveals the characteristic Hopewell precision. Its diameter is half the dimension of the nearby square, and an inscribed square connecting its gateways is one-quarter OCD on a side. The large circle's northwestern gateway frames the summer solstice sunset when viewed from

BELOW, TOP: Magnetometry data of the large circle show its ditch (black ring), three of its four gateways, its four central ovens, and the regularly spaced postholes of its woodhenge (along the right edge).

BELOW, BOTTOM: This 2012 geophysical image shows the small circle's gateway pointing toward a square cluster of features, probably ovens like those at the center of the large circle.

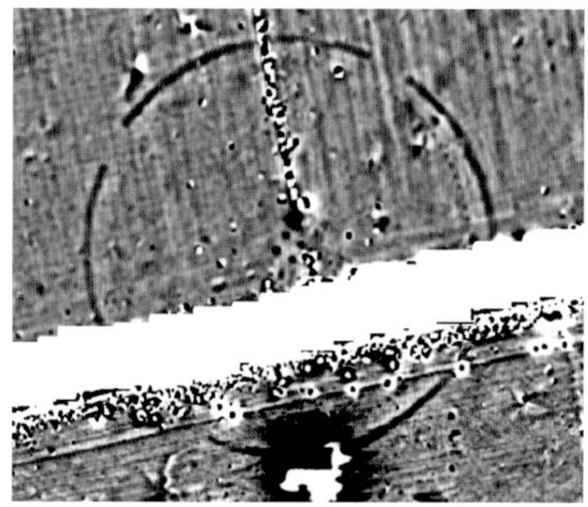

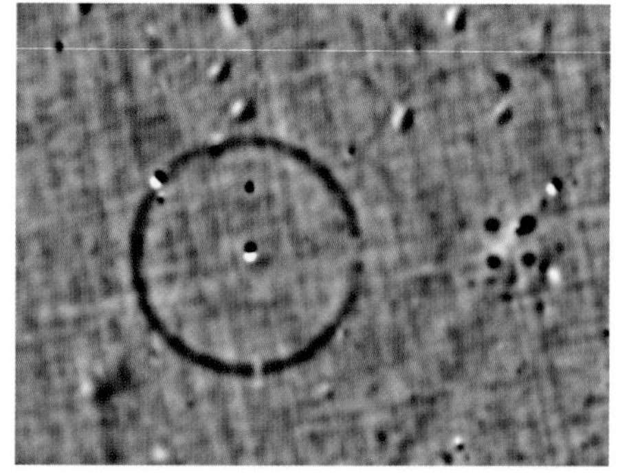

WORLD CENTER SHRINES

The Hopewell Mound Group's large circle, with its cross-axial gateways, reflects the symbolic associations of "world center shrines" or "earth navels"—ceremonial centers that served as portals to the Above or Beneath World, places where one might communicate with the powers of nature or ancestral spirits. Many examples exist across Indigenous North America, including some in active use today: Sun Dance grounds, the boulder outline on New Mexico's Chicoma Mountain, and Great Plains medicine wheels (stone circles with spokes) including the well-known Big Horn example. Also called "six directions altars," these shrines are typically circular and divided through a center point into four quadrants (normally north, south, west, and east). They often have a central post or pit—an axis mundi—to connect the Above and Beneath Worlds.

"The concept of the world center shrine offers a powerful metaphor for understanding the form and purpose of the Hopewell Mound Group's large circle as a colossal cosmogram; a place for prayer where the powers or blessings of the setting solstice Sun might be accessed, captured or channeled; or a sacred center where one might communicate with the Sun, the Moon, or the powers of the four quarters, or of the Above World and the Beneath World."

—BRET RUBY

or across the circle's center, suggesting that the feasting crowds were there for longest-day celebrations.

A smaller, 100-foot-diameter circle lies about 500 feet northwest of the larger one, also invisible on the ground but with an intact underground signature. It remained unnoticed, even by Squier and Davis in the mid-1800s, until a remote-sensing survey brought it to light in 2001. Sixty feet away and directly in line with this circle's east-facing gateway, a square group of underground features looks identical to the feasting ovens at the center of the large circle.

MODERN HISTORY

When the first Euro-Americans began to arrive in the area, forests had been reclaiming the Hopewell Mound Group site for nearly 1,500 years. In 1796, it stood on Virginia Military District lands given to Nathaniel Massie (the founder of nearby Chillicothe) and was then subdivided and sold several times throughout the 1800s. The earliest well-known map and description of the earthworks were made by Caleb Atwater for his 1820 American Antiquarian Society report. Since then, archaeological investigations at this site have been among the most important not only for understanding the builders' culture, but also for developing the theory and methods of American scientific archaeology.

Squier and Davis's 1848 depiction was more detailed than Atwater's, and shows the land almost entirely cleared of forest by that time, with two farmsteads on the property. All the lands on the level terrace were cleared and divided into agricultural fields, while the portions of the Great Enclosure on the northern slopes remained forested. A road linking the nearby towns of Chillicothe and Frankfort crossed the southern portion of the Great Enclosure and is still in use today. Squier and Davis also conducted the first excavations at the site. They opened at least four mounds and identified several characteristics that shaped their conception of the builders' culture—the prepared clay altars apparently devoted to sacrificial rites, and the highly refined sculptures and ornaments in materials from distant parts of North America.

Farming continued throughout the 1800s, and more infrastructure arrived, including two rail lines. In 1851, a route from Marietta to Cincinnati was laid across the site adjacent to the road; it has since become a recreational trail. About three decades later, another line crossed the floodplain immediately beneath the Great Enclosure's southern wall; its construction may have undermined the steep bank and that portion of the enclosure.

In the early 1890s, the young Warren King Moorehead came to this mound-covered terrace (just recently purchased by Mordecai Cloud Hopewell) to find specimens and art objects for the Chicago World's Columbian Exposition. Guided by Squier and Davis's work of a half century earlier, and given its objective, Moorehead's excavations yielded spectacular results. Over several months, his teams took down at least seventeen of the mounds, including about a quarter of the large mass of Mound 25, enabling him to establish the defining characteristics of the culture: in particular the bewildering variety of symbolic objects skillfully crafted from exotic materials. Visitors to the Chicago exposition were enthralled by the abundance and exquisite craftsmanship of the artifacts from Mr. Hopewell's farm, and the concept of the Hopewell culture was born. After the exposition, many of the objects from the site were stored or displayed in Chicago's newly created Field Museum of Natural History.

OPPOSITE, TOP: Squier and Davis's map shows the 1840s condition of the "North Fork Works," later to be named the Hopewell Mound Group and, in turn, to give its name to the entire culture.

OPPOSITE, BOTTOM: The three-lobed form of "the Effigy" had been under cultivation for decades before this photo was taken in 1891, just before Moorehead's excavations.

NAMING INDIGENOUS PLACES

There is a clear dissonance between this ancient, sacred, American Indian place and its modern name derived from a nineteenth-century landowner.

"We can't know what the earthwork builders who labored here, who crafted beautiful objects to leave with their beloved kin, who sculpted the earth into enduring monuments, called themselves, or what they called this place—but we know it wasn't 'Hopewell.' The fact that it now carries the name of a Chillicothe merchant is, on some level, objectionable.

Names define the things in our world. Names have power. Many tribes have names in their Indigenous languages that mean 'The People.' The names of clans or specialists are often related to a particular trait or skill in extended family groups. When a person receives a name, it often occurs in a ceremony with relatives in attendance. We don't know the language of the earthwork builders, but we can be sure that this significance of naming would apply to places, especially sacred places."

—MARTI CHAATSMITH (Comanche/Choctaw)

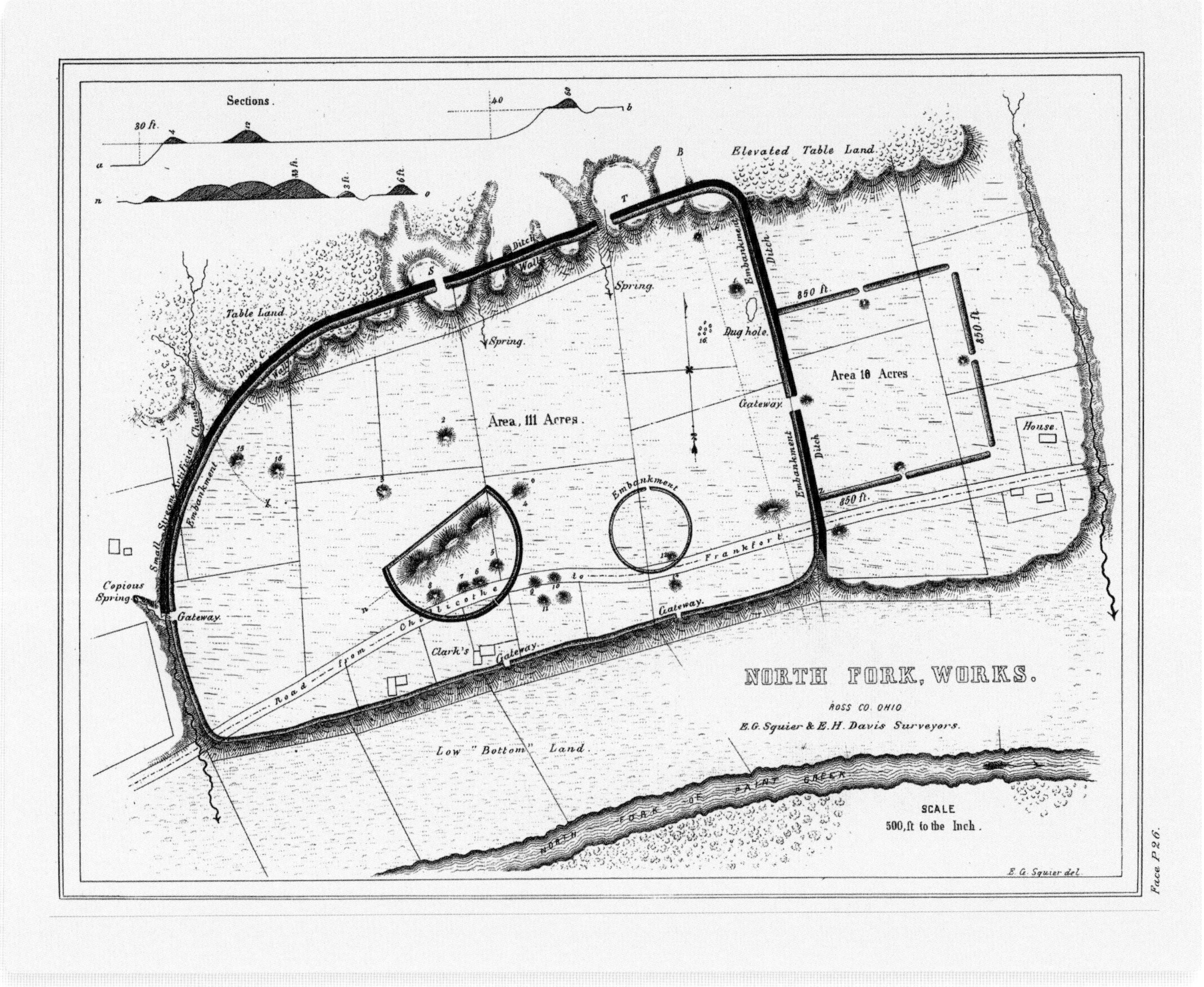

NORTH FORK, WORKS.

ROSS CO. OHIO

E. G. Squier & E. H. Davis Surveyors.

SCALE
500, ft to the Inch.

E. G. Squier del.

Face P. 26.

Sections.

Elevated Table Land.

Table Land

Area, 111 Acres.

Area 16 Acres

Low "Bottom" Land.

North Fork of Paint Creek

Road from Chillicothe to Frankfort

Copious Spring

Spring.

Dug hole.

House.

Clark's

Gateway.

Embankment

Ditch

Wall

850 ft.

Small Stream Artificial Channel

PRESERVATION AND RESEARCH

From 1922 to 1925, the Ohio State Archaeological and Historical Society conducted work at the site under the leadership of Henry Shetrone. He more systematically excavated all the extant mounds and re-excavated those incompletely explored by Moorehead. Shetrone's improved field methods and record-keeping helped him to locate the mounds and earthworks more accurately, and to create more detailed floor plans of several submound structures. His work remained the authority on the Hopewell Mound Group until the advent of new remote sensing surveys after the turn of the twenty-first century.

The Hopewell Mound Group remained in private hands, and mostly under cultivation, until 1980, when The Archaeological Conservancy purchased 160 acres, including most of the mounds and earthworks. No professional archaeology had been conducted at the site since Shetrone's. Through these decades, the northern wall was the least affected part of the earthworks, lying mainly in forest and pastures. In 1974, the site joined the National Register of Historic Places, and in the 1990s and early 2000s the National Park Service acquired essentially all of it. Within ten years of the site's acquisition by the Park Service, magnetometry and resistivity surveys sampled wide areas across the enclosure. They showed no evidence of long-term settlement inside the walls but did reveal features suggesting specialized ceremonial activities—including the small circle, which had not been recorded on any previous surveys.

Larger, higher resolution magnetometry surveys followed from 2012 to 2015. The last of these (in partnership with the *Deutsches Archäologisches Institut*, Bournemouth University, SENSYS GmbH, and Ohio Valley Archaeology, Inc.) was at the time the largest archaeological magnetic data set ever compiled in North America, covering the entire area of the Great Enclosure and the square. It showed the previously mapped features in richer detail and revealed many previously unknown subsurface features. These magnetic surveys demonstrate substantial archaeological integrity, even though much of the earthen architecture has been removed by excavations and degraded by decades under the plow.

BELOW: A 1930s aerial photograph by Dache Reeves shows the Hopewell Mound Group's northern walls and ditches (right) and portions of the Great Enclosure and the square in use as a hay field.

OPPOSITE: The beautiful northern walls and their often-waterlogged ditches crown the Hopewell Mound Group's forested hillside, today a highlight of the two-mile hiking trail.

AUTHENTICITY AND EXPERIENCE

The extravagant embellishment, monumental power, and compelling importance of the Hopewell Mound Group can seem rather elusive today. Out in the open meadow, the sheer volume of built-up earth is now evident only in the subtle, unrestored bulk of the largest mounds. The space of the Great Enclosure is so large that even if its low perimeter walls were still intact, their distant forms would not be perceptible from much of the interior. But the procession of the trail up and across the wooded hillside reveals more: The expansive overviews grant a fuller comprehension of the immense scale, as defined by the distant tree lines, and of the enclosure's overall setting in the terraced valley. Impressive sections of the northern walls and ditches run parallel to the pathway across undulating terrain.

Descending again to the open terrace, we can reflect on the sheer volume of soil moved and the depth of care expended to commemorate important events and individuals. A sacred destination for much of North America, this was the repository of the largest quantity of exotic materials and the most exquisitely crafted ceremonial artistry ever assembled by Indigenous peoples on this continent—evidence of their makers' superlative aesthetic and technical genius, the richness of their ceremonial traditions, and the continent-wide reach of their influence.

SOCIETY AND LEADERSHIP

"In our communities, Chiefs, Sachems, clan matrons, medicine people, bone setters, dreamers, and others, attain their roles only through efforts of persuasive speech—attracting followers, and then through the counsel of other community members taking on their roles as 'leaders.'"

—JOE STAHLMAN (Tuscarora/Pennsylvania Dutch)

The archaeological records from the Great Mound at Hopewell have been decisive for understanding Hopewell social organization. The distribution and treatment of the deceased and the sensational arrays of honorific artistry—apparently gifts or regalia, or both—suggest much about the communities that gathered here, their activities, and their leaders. Treatments of the deceased varied widely. Some of the remains were first burned in another location, then the remaining ash and bone swept together and redeposited here. But most were buried unburned, stretched out in log tombs. About eighty of the graves under Mound 25 were placed in three clusters, each thought to represent members drawn from one of three communities who chose to cement and symbolize a tripartite alliance by burying their dead together.

The objects found with each of these groups were distributed widely, and in highly variable quantities. Many people had honorific burials, but the symbols of those honors varied greatly, suggesting an egalitarian social structure and a wide range of leadership roles. Leaders earned their positions of authority, which were tied to specific roles and domains of action, mostly sacred rather than secular. Certain individuals acquired and exercised leadership through spiritual knowledge, which may have been obtained in a variety of ways, including long journeys to special places where they also obtained valuable materials.

The power, knowledge, and prestige of these various roles were displayed through symbolic objects and ritual regalia. The quantity and quality of such goods increased enormously at the beginning of the Hopewell era compared with those at earlier Adena sites. During ritual performances in the timber-framed buildings, and around the carefully prepared clay basins, spiritual leaders called on the powers of nature and their relationships with other-than-human beings to serve the community's needs—animal spirits, for example, who could help foster the people's health and nutrition. The exquisitely crafted objects and exotic raw materials helped to establish ties of obligation and reciprocity; by symbolizing acquired status and expertise they helped to secure commitments to cooperative projects such as mound and earthwork building.

With much feasting, drinking, and smoking, the events and performances at the Hopewell Ceremonial Earthworks brought together groups from hundreds of miles away as well as nearby. The elaborate rituals created an aura of spiritual power, knowledge, and prestige, amplified by the eternal spatial and temporal orders embodied in the earthworks. This convergence of place and ceremony helped maintain social relationships among groups of people who gathered only periodically, coming from distant places and speaking different languages. The large offerings and material deposits (the huge piles of copper and flint, for example) were community gifts, symbolizing connections of belief and purpose; they were not any individual's wealth.

Squier and Davis illustrated this exquisitely sculpted effigy pipe from Mound City. It may portray an important leader who, like the animals on other pipes, comes face-to-face with the smoker.

In this digital portrait by Talon Silverhorn (Eastern Shawnee), a man wears a copper headplate, earspools, hair knots, and facial tattoos based on a human effigy pipe from the Tremper Mound.

All this evidence indicates a broadly egalitarian social structure, despite distinctions between individuals who were accorded burial inside an earthwork versus those who were not, or among burial facilities or accompaniments in different mounds. There were leaders, but no class stratification, coercion, or royal families; without more burials of honored children, it seems clear that leadership roles were not inherited.

Moreover, studies of skeletal markers of physiological or dietary stress, disease, or trauma show that everyone, even people buried with much honorific regalia, ate the same foods and worked just as hard as everyone else. Although more men than women were buried in the mounds, the ancestor accompanied by the second largest quantity of associated regalia was a woman. Finally, there were no large, complex settlements to manage. Hopewell communities numbered only in the several dozens and had no large dwelling houses or "palaces" befitting a king—or even a mayor. These features contrast sharply with the powerful hereditary chiefs who, 700 years later, controlled Cahokia and other Mississippian towns and cities.

The very large mound at the center of the Seip Earthworks echoes the forms of the surrounding hills.

11.
SEIP EARTHWORKS

"Indigenous mapping practices . . . (unlike Western cartography) are 'process-oriented,' 'dispersed,' and 'embodied' so that visitors—either in the ancient past or in the future—are themselves 'mapmakers' who may contribute to a continually regenerative mapping process that was begun by earlier generations."

—MARGARET WICKENS PEARCE (Citizen Potawatomi Nation)

A few miles west of Chillicothe, Paint Creek meanders through an especially beautiful, rural landscape—an enclosed valley formed by wide, generally level glacial terraces, ringed by a complete circuit of forested hillsides, and dotted with farms and small villages. In antiquity, several geometric figures lined this idyllic setting, overlooked from the east by the low stone walls of Spruce Hill, the largest Hopewell hilltop enclosure ever built. The layered terrace settings here resemble those at Hopeton and High Bank, although the Paint Valley is more intimately defined. At the valley's western end, near the nineteenth-century village of Bainbridge, stands one of the largest earthen burial mounds in North America. Now called the Seip-Pricer Mound, it was restored following excavations in the 1920s.

From the roadside parking area, a peaceful grove of trees frames an inviting approach into the site. The large mound dominates the scene, echoing the rounded shapes of the surrounding hills. In antiquity, it anchored the three connected geometric shapes that constitute the Seip Earthworks (pronounced "SIPE"), spreading out across the wide and faintly undulating terrace toward the riverbank. Today, long lines of unmowed grasses and wildflowers outline those huge enclosing forms. The wooded riverbanks frame the open space, approximating the extent of the earthworks on the west and south. High hills stand close to the south while the prominent, vertically striated, mineral-rich cliffs of Copperas Mountain rise a mile to the southeast.

SITE FEATURES

Seip's geometric figures and their connecting spaces total 100 acres. A large, partial circle is 1,621 feet in diameter and connects to a smaller and very precise square, 1,079 feet on each side, and a smaller, 948-foot-diameter circle. An irregular section of the wall completes the enclosure, connecting the square

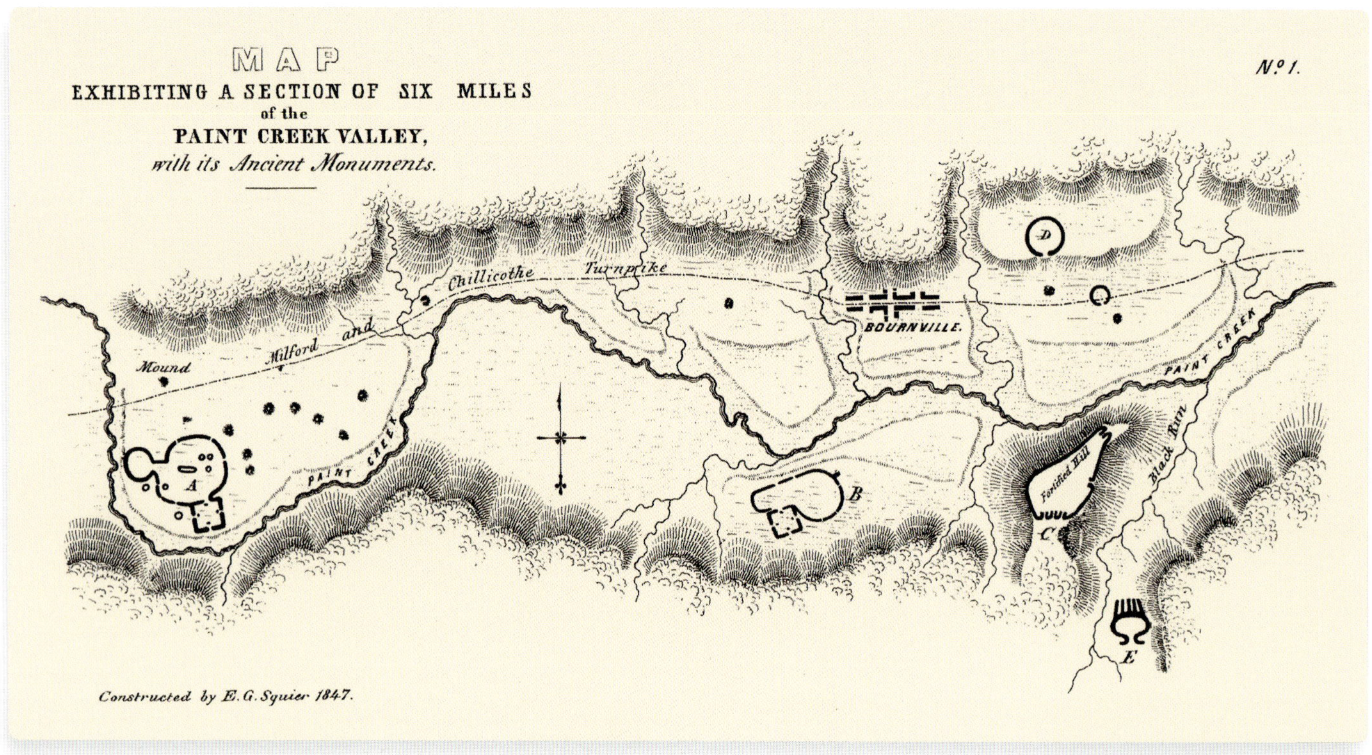

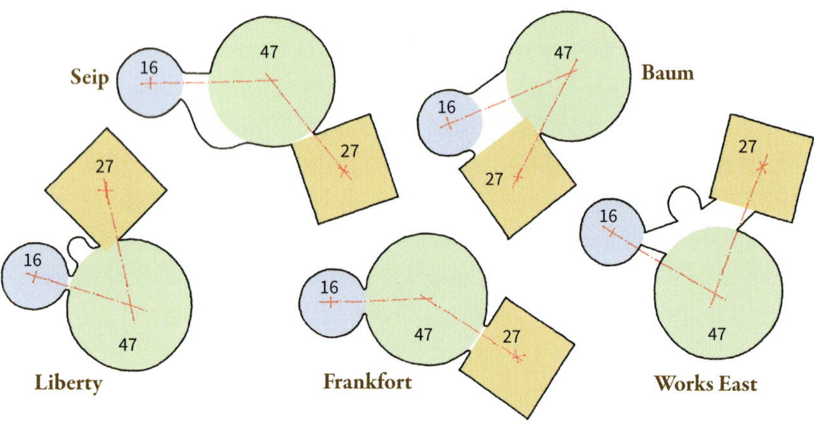

ABOVE: Squier and Davis's 1847 map of the Paint Creek Valley shows the similar earthworks of Seip (far left, at A) and Baum (center bottom, at B); prominent among several other works is Spruce Hill (lower right, at C).

LEFT: Five tripartite earthworks built in the immediate Scioto and Paint Valley region were composed of equivalent shapes with nearly identical areas, noted here in acres.

with the smaller circle. Though now degraded, much of the northern and northeastern sections remain visible, and their locations, profiles, and soil compositions have been confirmed by archaeological investigations. Magnetic data reveal the clear outline of a tapered, reentrant gateway toward the northeast. Four borrow pits lie outside the western walls of the large circle; many more were recorded along the circle's perimeter in the mid-1800s. The remains of many other features lie inside the combined enclosure, some recorded while they were still visible and others appearing only in recent geophysical data.

GEOMETRY AND CONSTRUCTION

Like the Hopewell Mound Group, this complex was built over many years, serving the civic and ceremonial life of an extended community over several

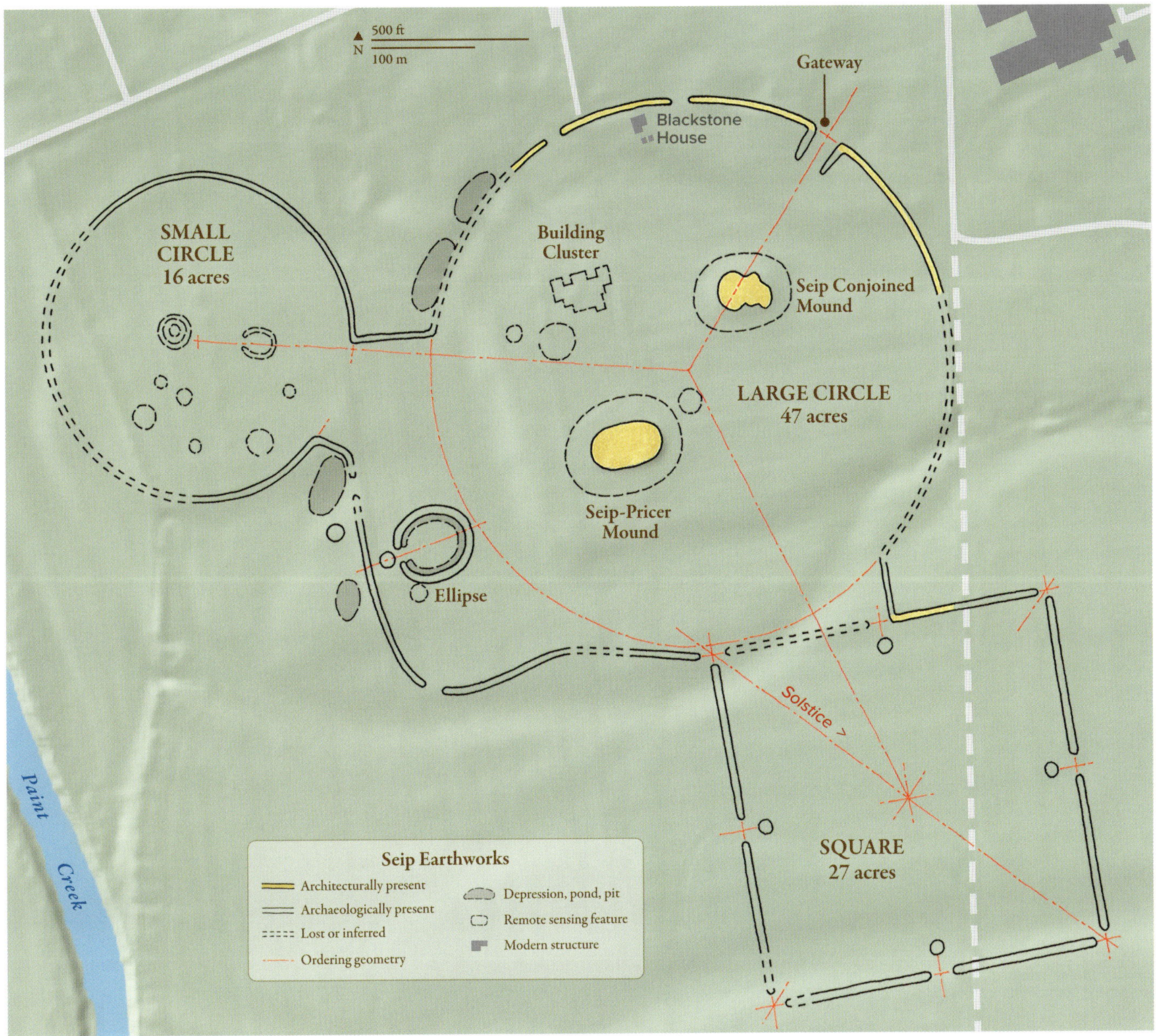

generations. As the architecture accumulated here, the builders used shapes and dimensions shared by four other, similar earthwork sites clustered in a twenty-mile area of today's Ross County. All five of these "tripartite" earthworks (as they are called) were composed of a twenty-seven-acre square about one OCD on each side, a forty-seven-acre large circle about 1.5 OCDs in diameter, and a sixteen-acre smaller circle. They must have been designed and directed by the same team of architects, who had attained an advanced knowledge of geometry and precise methods of execution.

The arrangement of the three figures varies among the five tripartites. At Seip, lines connecting the center points of the three shapes are of nearly equal length and form an angle exactly bisected by the axis of the large circle's northeastern gateway. Of the five, Works East and Frankfort are entirely obliterated today, while Liberty and Baum have scant remains. As a set, these five earthworks help to reveal the ancient architects at their most advanced, with refined techniques, reliable tools, and clear intentions.

The walls of the square were interrupted by eight gateways at their corners and midpoints, with small mounds (now lost) standing inside their midpoint openings. The winter solstice sun rises in alignment with its northwest to southeast diagonal, as it also does at Mound City, Hopeton, and Hopewell Mound Group. This apparent attention to the diagonals may be linked to their importance in the process of constructing perfect squares.

Though degraded today, the enclosing walls of Seip's three figures have shown evidence of the construction process used nearly universally for the Scioto and Paint Creek Valley earthworks. Preliminary investigations document a process in which the builders first stripped off the topsoil to create a cleared, level surface, then carefully arranged at least two contrasting soil colors to form the wall. In at least one location, they removed a fifty-foot-wide strip of subsoil along the path of the wall, then laid down a low, wide layer of yellowish soil. The wall's profile was then formed by building up a narrow ridge of darker, reddish-brown soil over it. Both soil types were sourced from a series of borrow pits outside the large circular enclosure.

The floor plan of the ceremonial building at the Liberty Earthworks—another of the tripartites—had a symmetrical, three-chambered, gridded structure similar to the one found at Seip.

SEIP-PRICER MOUND

Near the center of the larger circle stands the Seip-Pricer Mound, named after two landowners whose shared boundary line once bisected it. Crews restored it to its recorded nineteenth-century dimensions following thorough excavations in the 1920s. It is the second largest Hopewell mound in the Ohio heartland, its loaf shape measuring 246 by 148 feet at the base, and 32 feet tall. Beneath the mound are the remains of the builders' prepared floor surface and the posthole pattern of an elaborate, precisely gridded, three-chambered, timber-framed building.

Like most Hopewell-era burial mounds, this one covered the dismantled remains of a ceremonial building—in this case, at 72 by 155 feet, a very large one. The floor plan was almost identical to another discovered at the nearby Liberty Earthworks south of Chillicothe: three symmetrical chambers organized along a central axis. By stripping away six to twelve inches of topsoil, the builders exposed a coarse clay and gravel surface in the shape of the final

ANCIENT DRUM STONES

"In 2014, while consulting with several tribes at a meeting in Oklahoma, I began a conversation with Chief Ben Barnes of the Shawnee Tribe, about the Shawnee drum, which is used in all their most important ceremonies. As a drum maker, he explained how they attach the leather drumhead to the shell by wrapping its edges around a series of round, black pebbles, which they then tie off and attach one to another with cordage wrapped under and around the shell. This reminded me of the similar round, black soapstone spheres that Henry Shetrone excavated from Seip Mound in the 1920s; he supposed that they were marbles—though without evidence that precontact American Indians ever played that game.

Five round, incised stones found beneath the Seip-Pricer Mound, and first thought to be marbles, could well have been part of the fastening system for an ancient drum skin. The versions rendered here were created by artist Talon Silverhorn (Eastern Shawnee).

After months of research, Ben and I agreed that they were probably part of a Hopewell drum, constructed in much the same way as the modern Shawnee ceremonial drums. If we're right, it's the oldest evidence of a drum in eastern North America, and a path-breaking example of how Indigenous knowledge can help us interpret these ancient places and the people who built and used them.

It should come as no surprise that the Hopewell culture used drums in their ceremonies, but since drums are made mostly from perishable materials, such as wood and leather, they leave little for archaeologists to find after centuries in the soil. The five stone spheres from Seip Mound, nearly identical in size and color to Shawnee drum-stones, may be all that remains of a Hopewell drum."

—BRAD LEPPER

mound, then laid down layers of dark clay and sand. Then they erected the building's gridded timber framework, lashed it together, and covered it with skins, mats, or sheets of bark.

Laid down inside this impressive timber temple were many log tombs, at least 125 cremation and inhumation burials, prepared clay basins, and elaborate ceremonial deposits. They constitute one of the most spectacular collections of Hopewell material remains ever encountered, nearly comparable to those from Hopewell Mound Group and Mound City. Among them are copper breast plates; objects of silver, galena, and meteoric iron; flint and obsidian blades; and organic remains including alligator and shark teeth, tortoise-shell artifacts, shell and pearl beads, and intact samples of Hopewell cloth woven of milkweed fibers.

BURIED CEREMONIES

The development and uses of this impressive shrine building, and the processes of its eventual burial, were complex. Most of the burials on its floor had been cremated first. Among the few to be laid out unburned were four adults—two males, two females, and two infants—that were placed together within a log burial chamber at the building's western end. Thousands of freshwater pearl beads surrounded the adults, and the whole burial chamber was then covered with a fabric canopy pinned in place by more than 100 sharpened bone stakes.

Next to these burials, a massive deposit of ceremonial regalia was laid down in a large basin and burned. It included more than 5,000 objects, including thousands of shell beads, copper breastplates, canine teeth of bears and mountain lions, alligator and shark teeth, flint points, ceramic sherds, a considerable quantity of charred fabric, fragments of leather, and several animal bones—especially from deer. But conspicuously absent were any bones from Indigenous ancestors. It may be that these objects were regalia used in the rites associated with the special burial of the six people: At the conclusion of the ceremonies, the celebrants placed their regalia in the shallow basin, set it on fire, and then buried it all beneath the floor.

Ultimately, they dismantled the building and buried it beneath three feet of earth. At some point, the burial chamber collapsed under the weight of the mound, leaving a depression on top. Ceremonial leaders then filled the depression and placed, directly over the collapsed chamber, five large pipes carved into the shapes of two dogs, two birds, and a bear. The style and material of the pipes indicate they came from the Tennessee River Valley, nearly 300 miles to the south; their presence here, along with examples of complicated stamped pottery, suggests that the people at Seip had distant cultural connections. The community then built up the final form of the mound with a thick mantle of soil that more than doubled its height, encircling it with a twelve-foot-thick stone slab retaining wall, and capping it all with a mantle of small stones up to two feet thick.

PRESERVED TEXTILES

Most of the copper plaques excavated at Seip had been carefully wrapped in fabric and fur before being buried. Contact with the corroding metal preserved substantial fragments of these perishable materials. Research by Katherine Jakes and her colleagues at Ohio State University has identified rabbit hair, twined fabric of milkweed and other fibers, and evidence of fringes and leather. To study remnants of the large fabric canopy that was placed over one of the main burials, they use forensic photographic techniques to scan for colors and patterns now faded to the point of being invisible to the eye.

The textile fragments are so fragile that they can fall apart when touched, so techniques borrowed from crime labs allow Jakes and her team to reconstruct the vibrant colors and patterned designs—some with precise, circular-patterned geometries reminiscent of the earthworks.

Clothing and accessories worn by modern American Indians are often colorful; this work on ancient textiles suggests that their Hopewell-era ancestors also mastered vivid hues. They adorned their clothing, regalia, and other ceremonial fabrics with colors, using applied pigments and chemical dyes made from plant, animal, and mineral sources.

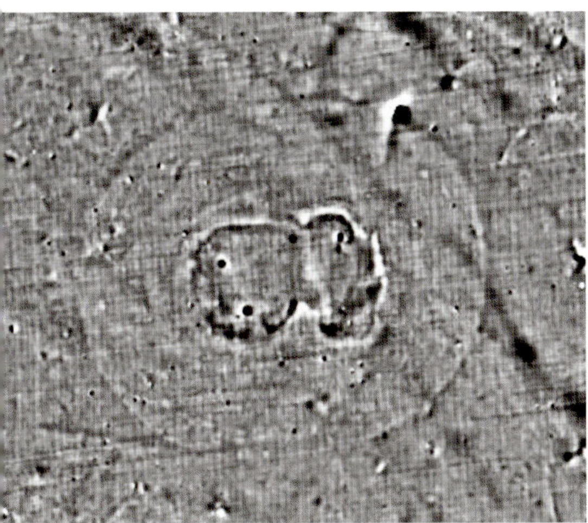

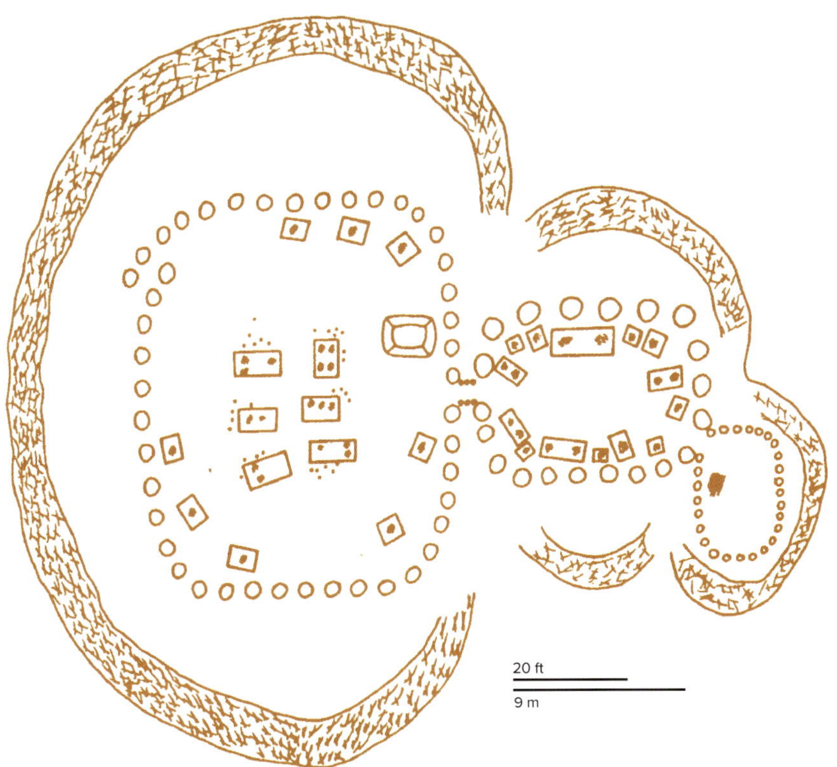

ABOVE, LEFT: Magnetometry of the Seip Conjoined Mound shows its overall shape plus the subsurface remains of a surrounding oval embankment.

ABOVE, RIGHT: An archaeologist's plan of the three connected buildings beneath the Seip Conjoined Mound also shows the enclosing gravel band defining the mound's perimeter.

SEIP CONJOINED MOUND

About 500 feet northeast of the Seip-Pricer Mound, still within the large circle, stands the Seip Conjoined Mound (Seip Mound 2). Its three lobes covered the remains of three superelliptical ceremonial buildings and measured thirty-two, twelve, and six feet high in the nineteenth century. Today the unrestored mound crests at about six feet. Magnetometry reveals the underground remains of a narrow embankment wall and accompanying trench forming an oval surrounding the mound at a distance of about sixty-five feet.

The three connected buildings had timber frames erected above a prepared floor. They contained several log tombs, forty-three cremated burials, and artifacts including copper breast plates, earspools, and axes; cut and drilled bear canines; ornaments and implements of shell, bone, and freshwater pearls; marine shell and decorated pottery vessels; and chipped flint implements, mica cutouts, and still-intact pieces of cloth. After burning the buildings, the people built up the three lobes of the mound with loamy soil and outlined the combined perimeter with a band of gravel. They capped the tallest section with limestone slabs interspersed with gravel and built a stone staircase to the summit along its northern slope.

ELLIPSE AND BUILDING CLUSTER

On the opposite side of the large enclosure, near the irregular connecting wall, are the subsurface remains of an elliptical enclosure measuring 210 by 246 feet. It had an interior ditch, a ring of posts, and a small mound standing just outside its west-facing gateway. Magnetometry data gathered between 2015 and 2017

Before excavations began in 1906, the Seip Conjoined Mound stood thirty feet tall in an open agricultural field.

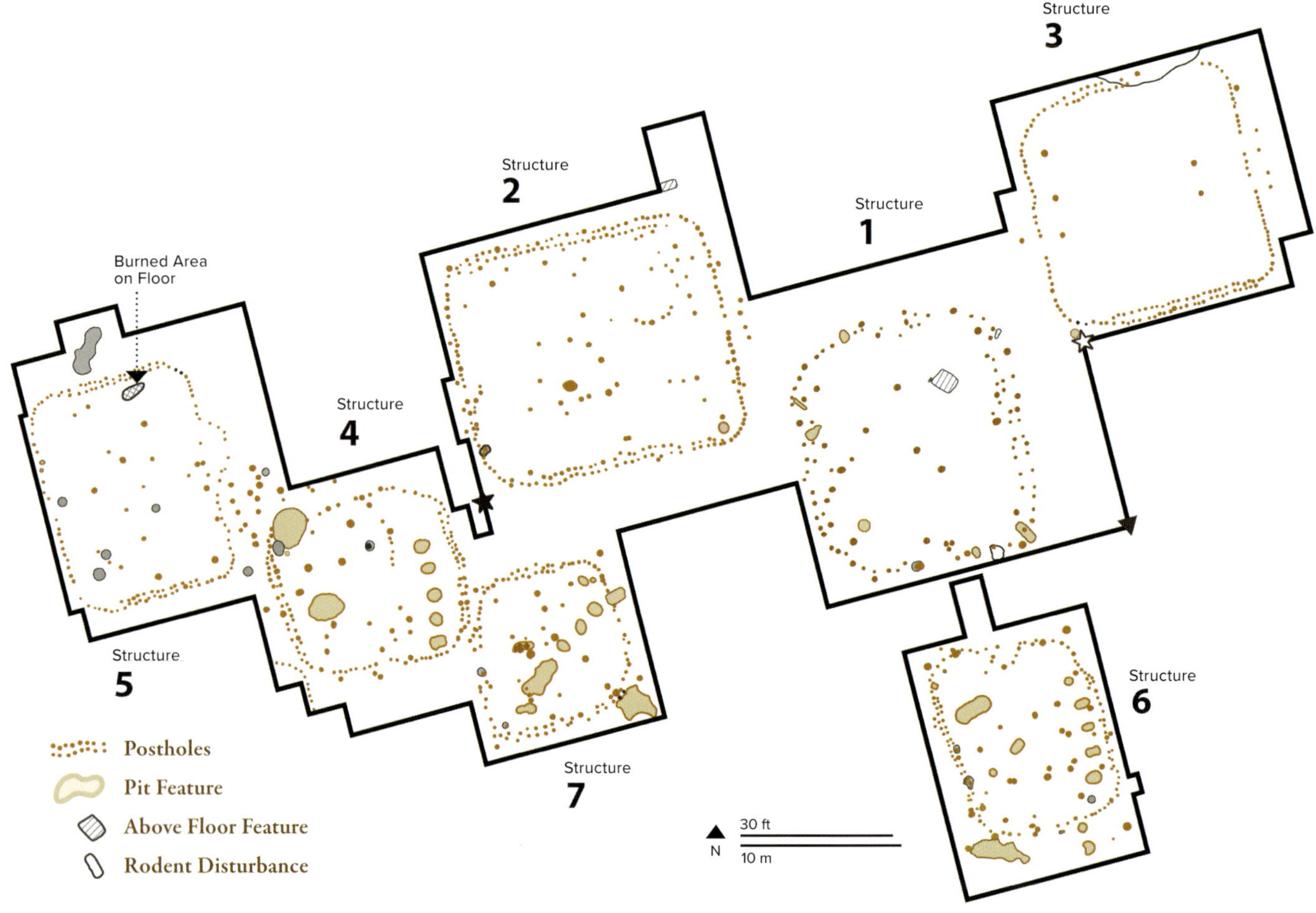

revealed more characteristically Hopewell features, including another mound near this ellipse, and several post circles and ditched enclosures concentrated in the southern two-thirds of the smaller circle and the western portion of the large circle.

North of the Seip-Pricer Mound and halfway to the enclosure wall, an intensive activity area included several large buildings, ranging from 590 to more than 1,400 square feet. The builders left few clues to indicate what they did in these structures, although eventually they dismantled them and carefully covered each one with a low mantle of soil and gravel. Later, between about 200 and 500 CE, several large timber post circles were also built and dismantled here, and the empty post pits were carefully filled with cobbles. The subsurface remains here suggest one of the most intensively used areas yet known at any Ohio Hopewell site.

ABOVE: Evidence from a cluster of buildings in the northern area of Seip's large circle may suggest that they were craft-working facilities.

OPPOSITE: Squier and Davis's map of the Seip Earthworks shows how the earthwork drops onto slightly lower terrace levels—unusual for a geometric earthwork—probably carved by rare, catastrophic floods over millennia.

MODERN HISTORY

Like most sites in this series, the Seip Earthworks were reforested after 400 CE and remained so until after 1800, when they stood within a 1,000-acre Virginia Military District tract given to one Simon Morgan. Caleb Atwater's 1820 map and description noted the exact geometric equivalencies between the squares

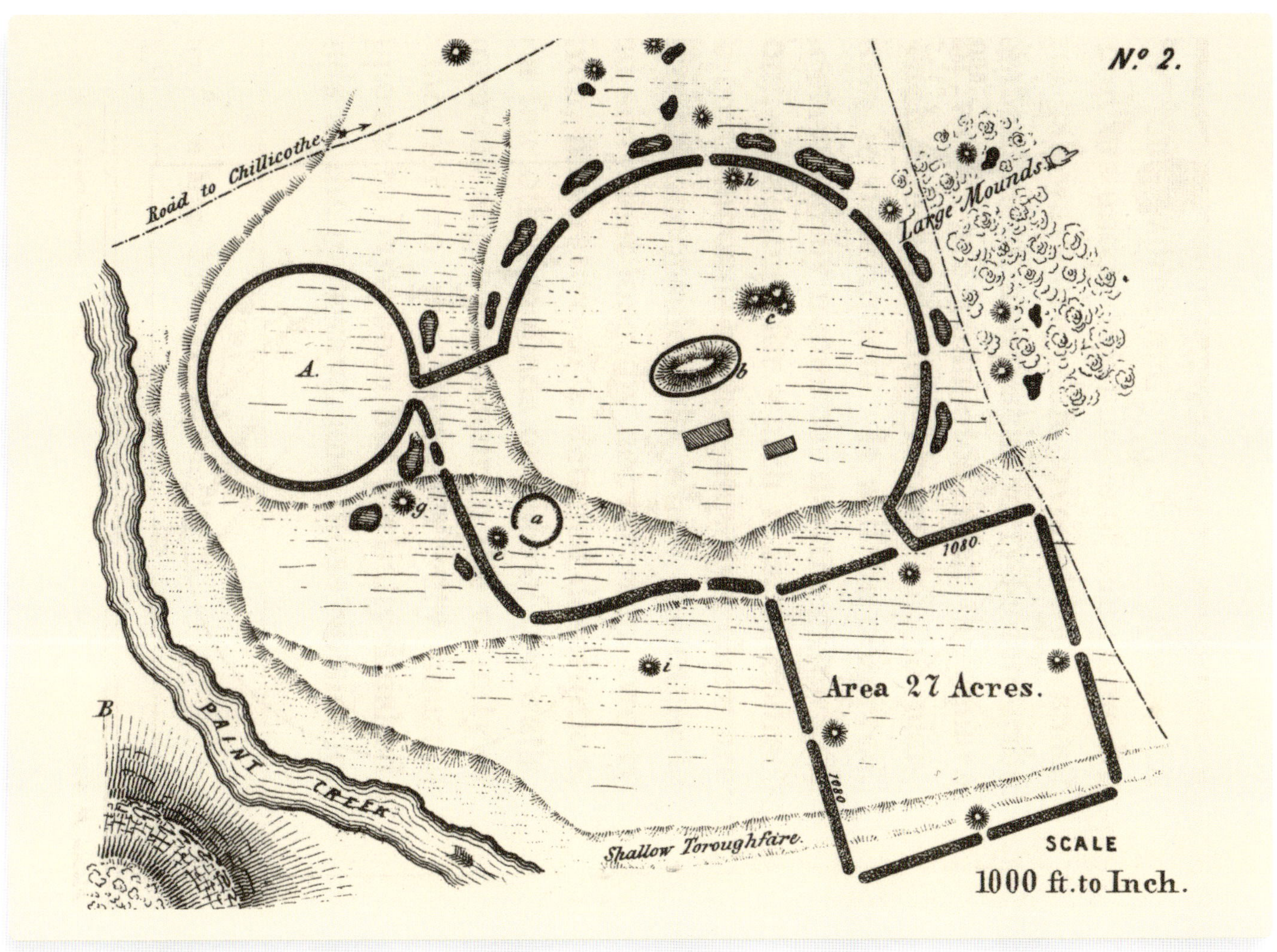

at Seip and at nearby Baum, and that the Seip-Pricer Mound appeared to be "composed mostly of stones." He described another mound nearby as "composed entirely of a red ocher, which answers very well as a paint. An abundance of this ocher is found on a hill not a great distance from this place; and from this circumstance, the name of the fine stream in the vicinity, in all probability, is derived. It is called 'Paint Creek.'"

In the 1840s, Squier and Davis recorded the "Road to Chillicothe" passing by to the north (now US Highway 50), and two now-vanished structures standing south of the large mound. They found some earthwork features difficult to trace because of agricultural plowing. The square, they reasoned, being situated on a slightly lower level than the circles, had apparently been "invaded by the water" during the centuries since its construction—likely the result of rare but extreme flooding caused by slippage on the steep cliffs across Paint Creek from the site.

Thomas and Hannah Blackstone purchased a narrow parcel in 1852, stretching from what is now Highway 50 south to Paint Creek and between a line cutting through the Seip-Pricer Mound to what is now a small road. Within five years, their small brick house stood, as it does today, with its front directly atop the north wall of the large circle. Farming operations continued among

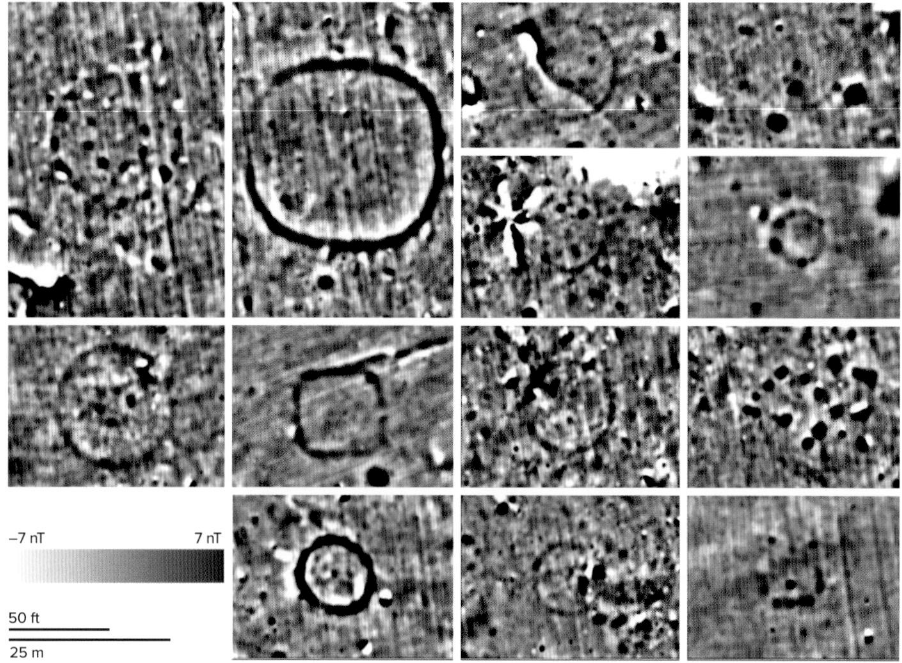

Thirteen magnetometry details from Seip show an unusual quantity and variety of characteristically Hopewell circular and superelliptical rings, ditches, and post patterns.

what an 1871 county history called "the ancient works." In 1883, the Seip family bought the Blackstone property and held it until 1990. The Pricer family owned the neighboring parcel to the west, resulting in the mound's hyphenated name.

PRESERVATION AND RESEARCH

From 1906 to 1908, William Mills of the OSAHS excavated the Seip Conjoined Mound, revealing the ancient, charred remains of its large, three-roomed structure and its many tombs and artifacts. Today, the excavated soil has been redistributed, though not as a restoration of the mound's original form. In the late 1920s, Henry Shetrone and Emerson Greenman, also on behalf of the OSAHS, excavated the Seip-Pricer Mound, revealing the posthole patterns, fire pits, and burials across the full layout of the large submound building. They also found Seip's most iconic artifacts, including the copper pieces with their preserved fabric wrappings. The Seip-Pricer Mound was reconstructed in 1927 to the dimensions measured by Squier and Davis in the 1840s.

Shetrone and Greenman's excavations highlighted the importance of the Seip Earthworks and led to their preservation as a public park. Seip Mound State Memorial was established in 1927 with the acquisition of a ten-acre parcel stretching from the highway to the Seip-Pricer Mound, plus an additional small parcel donated by the Seip family. A small roadside rest area and parking lot were added in the 1930s, of which only a rustic picnic shelter remains today. Archaeological work resumed in the 1960s and 1970s, when one of the first nonmound investigations at any Hopewell earthwork revealed the building cluster north of the Seip-Pricer Mound.

The site expanded significantly in 1990, when the last Seip family heir bequeathed a large tract to the Ohio History Connection. Two years later it became part of the newly established Hopewell Culture National Historical

LEFT: In this view of the Blackstone House, from the west, the subtle trace of the large circle wall is detectable crossing from the center right of the image and up to the front wall of the house.

RIGHT: A differential planting and mowing plan initiated in 2016 at the Seip Earthworks helps visitors to visualize the enclosure wall locations.

Park, with land now totaling more than 360 acres. Since 2016, the park has maintained an interpretive mowing and landscape plan, helping visitors to envision Seip's spectacular scope and geometric complexity.

Pioneering remote-sensing work was first done at Seip in 1979, followed by a comprehensive LiDAR survey in 2012 and the huge magnetometry surveys completed in 2017 in collaboration with the *Deutsches Archäologisches Institut*. These have confirmed the precision of the geometric layout and dimensions and revealed the startling array of still-unexplored subsurface features within the enclosure.

AUTHENTICITY AND EXPERIENCE

The large, restored mound dominates the Seip Earthworks today, approached through a restored gateway of the circle. The iconic vista evokes a dramatic ceremonial approach and, with the rounded hills beyond, suggests clearly the mounds-to-mountains analogy. Beyond the mound, the earthwork geometry extends far, far into the distance, taking the spatial scale to an almost astonishing level. The long enclosure walls, marked by plantings, seem to reach for the horizon; the spaces they enclose seem nearly incomprehensible. Unlike Hopeton, they cannot all be seen at once, and unlike Hopewell they cannot be sensed from the surrounding tree line. Only extensive walking among the walls and gateways (if somehow staying oriented) brings the site's vast conception into focus.

The Seip Earthworks are a geometrical masterwork. As the best surviving example of the five similar tripartite enclosures, Seip demonstrates the Hopewell architects' most consistent and sophisticated techniques of earthwork design and execution—an advanced genius approaching that evident at ancient Newark. Here also is the memory of elaborate ceremonial facilities and offerings, and the quiet setting in one of Ohio's most beautiful valleys.

GEOMETRIC CONSTRUCTION

"Clearly, the Hopewell had a great interest in exploring the geometric and spatial relationships between circles and squares, and they were fairly sophisticated in their understanding of those relationships. In fact, interconnected relationships between circles and squares may have been at the very heart of . . . [their] belief system and worldview."

—WILLIAM ROMAIN

Geometric order was presented directly to all ancient societies in the structure of their experience—living on the Earth and watching the Sky. The horizon is a circle; the perceiving human is its center. The movements of Sun, Moon, and stars, of day and night, present other circles overhead, ordered by symmetry axes—north, south, east, and west, the cardinal points. Cosmic shapes and symmetries become the archetypal patterns for making sacred space: circles, squares, and axes both horizonal (movement, orientation) and vertical (the axis mundi). Given already by creation or by the gods, these perfect orders naturally inspire the design of sacred monuments. Among the hills and valleys of southern Ohio, the Hopewell Ceremonial Earthworks captured this cosmic perfection on a vast scale.

The Seip Earthworks and the original Newark complex are brilliant works of interconnected geometry. As with all ancient architecture, the simple answer to the question "How did they do it?" is: "With sticks and strings" (or at full scale with poles and cords). Even the Greek Parthenon, with its famously sophisticated and harmonious proportions, is based on an easily derived ratio of 4:9 (a double square's short side to its diagonal)—drawn on parchment or animal skin with a short string and a piece of charcoal, or laid out on the ground with a long cord and some poles. To lay out a huge design like the Seip Earthworks, the "strings" had to be very long indeed.

The forest provided plenty of "sticks": wooden posts probably would have defined the shapes first, with their placements adjusted over time to calibrate the alignments. Only after much observation had finally confirmed their correct positions would any earth be piled up. Woodhenges like those at Hopewell Mound Group and Hopeton suggest a calendrical cycle, with observations from their centers aligning across marked locations on the perimeter. The prevalence of the OCD, and its halves and quarters, suggests that Hopewell architects traveled the region with calibrated cords—braided plant fibers or deer hide, strong and nonelastic, marked off with knots or dyes into some common interval. The smallest increments probably related to an average or ideal human body—a height, a foot, or a pace.

From earlier Adena architecture, with its rings and circular mounds, the simple method for making circles would have been well known: Fold a cord of the desired diameter around a central post, hold its two ends, and walk around in a circle to mark the perimeter. Squares are only slightly more complicated. Carpenters construct perfect right angles by making a triangle with sides of 3:4:5 (the 3:4 corner is ninety degrees)—easily done with a cord marked into twelve equal units.

But even that method is not necessary: the simpler principle, also known to all modern carpenters, is that a square's two diagonals are equal. Square builders, with any cord marked into four equal lengths (that is, folded twice), could walk those points out and adjust the corner positions until the diagonals were equal. That set of interrelated cords (side/perimeter and diagonal) contains the key proportion for squares (known as the square root of two), and any perfect square could be constructed with such a set, whether the intent was a certain side length, a certain perimeter, or a certain diagonal.

James Marshall, an engineer who analyzed the geometries of scores of Hopewell earthworks in a 1987 essay titled "An Atlas of American Indian Geometry," posited two persistent lengths that were widely used: 187 feet and the diagonal of a 187-foot square, which is 264 feet (and one-quarter of the OCD). We could call them the A-unit (side) and the B-unit (diagonal). Either would have been easily derived from the other, creating a set of earthwork layout tools. Diagonals were apparently important, intentional features of Hopewell squares: the several cases where they mark a solstice alignment suggest that laying down the B-cord was the first step in positioning a square rather than setting up the sides, perimeter, or mid-point axes, and that construction teams walked out their four-part A-cord afterward with the B-cord's ends as fixed points.

Hopewell design shows a mastery of the relationships between squares and circles and an ability to manipulate these shapes with precision. Ray Hively and Robert Horn, in their 2019 essay "Hopewell Topography, Geometry, and Astronomy in the Hopewell Core," show how the Newark Earthworks' principal figures are circles inscribed in squares and vice versa. The set of layout cords described here produces these relationships easily: a square's diagonal cord is the diameter of its circumscribing circle, and its side cord is the diameter of its inscribed circle.

Analyses of the Newark complex have also revealed matched perimeters among its square and circular figures. This can be done with mathematics' irrational number, pi, but also in the field with poles and cords. Wrap a circle (perhaps marked by posts at regular

Matching the areas of squares and circles, an ancient mathematical conundrum called squaring the circle, is more complex. Newark's square and Observatory Circle shared the same area, and the Great Circle's area matches that of a square with a side of 1,054 feet—the OCD. In his essay, "The Geometry of the Newark Earthworks," John J. Volker explores how this could have been achieved. Citing Marshall's dual-unit system of relating sides and diagonals, he points out a surprising relationship: a square with a diagonal of five B-units has the same area as a circle with a diameter of four B-units (264 feet each). So, using four-fifths of the Newark square's diagonal cord as the diameter of the Observatory Circle (or the reverse) produces their equal areas.

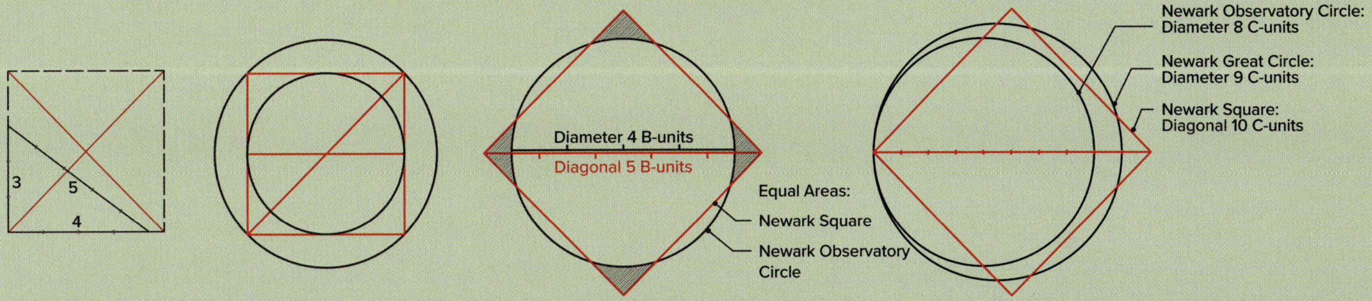

Left to right: 1. A triangle with sides of three, four, and five units will provide a perfect right angle; a square will be perfect when its two diagonals are equal. 2. Matching a circle's diameter with a square's side or its diagonal easily creates the relationships among nested circles and squares, as for example those of the Newark Earthworks. 3. A square and a circle have essentially equal areas if the circle's diameter is four-fifths of the square's diagonal. 4. A simple dimensional relation unifies the main elements of the Newark Earthworks. If the square's diagonal is ten units, the diameters of the Great Circle and the Observatory Circle are nine and eight units, respectively.

intervals) using its diameter cord; it will need to be placed end-to-end three times with a remainder of one-seventh. The circumference cord, then, is three-and-one-seventh diameters—essentially pi. (Perhaps coincidently, the diameter of the small circle at Newark is one-seventh of the OCD.)

To lay out a square with the same perimeter as a given circle—such as Newark's square, assuming the Great Circle already existed—fold the circle's circumference cord (three and one-seventh diameters) in half twice, mark those quarter points, and then walk them out taut and confirm the diagonals. (Such procedures could also be done at a smaller scale and then multiplied out to the final size.)

The diameter of the Great Circle is also neatly calibrated in this system, at four-and-one-half B-units. Volker suggests splitting Marshall's units so that the ratio of the OCD to the Great Circle's diameter to the square's diagonal is a simpler relation—8:9:10—where each unit is now 132 feet, or one-eighth of the OCD. It is the B-unit cord folded in half, or call it the C-unit cord. Dividing by halves has a certain logic resulting from the obvious field technique of simply folding the cords. This method ensures that all elements are harmonized using simple whole-number units on the same cord. The C-cord hypothesis would also suggest that this unit (or further divisions created by more folding) might have been used to measure features at other Hopewell sites.

STOP

12.
FORT ANCIENT

"Walking inside the Fort Ancient and Newark earthworks . . . one is confounded by a multiplicity of sensations: that here are the greatest works of art on the American continent . . .; that here in the seductive Ohio Valley are perhaps the greatest art monuments in the world."

—BARNETT NEWMAN

Fort Ancient is the only earthwork in this series located in the Miami Valley region of southwest Ohio, where another significant concentration of Hopewell earthwork building took place. Several geometric enclosures, including the Turner Earthworks, once lined the Little Miami Valley but have been destroyed beneath the eastern suburbs of Cincinnati. Yet twenty miles farther upstream, the immediate visual surroundings of Fort Ancient are well preserved—steep hillsides, entirely and densely forested. A road crosses the northern portion of the site, from the west climbing up out of the river valley, and on the east entering from a level plateau. From either direction, it passes through large earthen gateways giving access to the site entrance, parking, and a museum.

Southwest Ohio's topography resembles that along the border of the Appalachian escarpment, but here the relief is formed by subtraction: a generally level surface has been carved, sometimes dramatically, by rivers. During the last Ice Age, glaciers dammed up the older rivers of the Teays system, causing them to find or create new channels. One of the steepest and narrowest of these gorges now carries the Little Miami, where it is overlooked by the walls and gateways of Fort Ancient.

Ringing two adjacent plateaus high above the river, this is the finest surviving example of a Hopewell hilltop enclosure. Fort Ancient's elaborate stone and earthen forms, and their accompanying ponds, meander through the forest in an intricate choreography with the steep slopes dropping off in nearly all directions. To the west and south, the land falls away into the Little Miami's gorge nearly 300 feet below, and to the north and east into the deeply cut, densely wooded ravines of two intermittent tributary streams, Cowan and Randall Runs. Only to the northeast, outside the enclosure's largest walls, lies level land—where a few widely spaced, semirural residences are set among open lawns and fields.

A reflecting pool near Fort Ancient's Great Gateway hints at the site's extraordinarily complex variety of walls, gates, and water features.

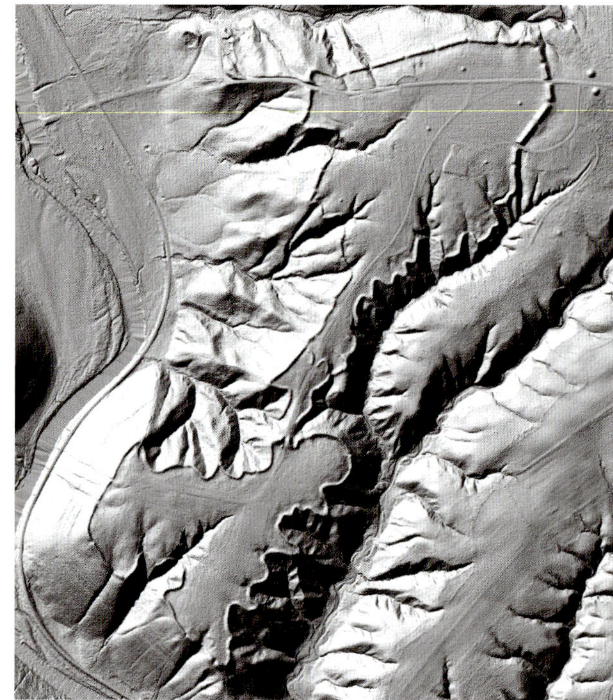

ABOVE, LEFT: A digital restoration of Fort Ancient shows the continuous string of ponds accompanying the walls, from a vantage point above the South Gate (lower right).

ABOVE, RIGHT: By seeing through the forest cover, this LiDAR relief image of Fort Ancient shows its complete perimeter of intact walls and interior ditches and its rugged adjacent topography.

SITE FEATURES

Hopewell hilltop enclosures were designed in response to the forms of their elevated sites, following the natural topography and adapting to its unique features. The walls of Fort Ancient have a total length of three and one half miles and are divided by gateways into eighty-four segments. They enclose a total area of more than 100 acres, in three distinct zones named the South, Middle, and North Forts, in the order of their construction. Three monumental twin-mounded gateways articulate these spaces.

The walls range in height from five to twenty-three feet and, except for the tallest walls facing the northeastern plateau, they undulate along the irregular crests of the hillsides, sometimes dipping slightly below the rim. Some segments follow the crest of the bluff, built mainly with soil scraped from the surface of the plateau and with ditches dug along their interiors. Others were placed partway down the hillside so that a similar ditch would be formed as a natural result of this placement. Limestone slabs, brought up from the riverbank far below, cover the outer faces of many of the walls.

Stone-reinforced openings separate the wall segments, some creating monumental gateways to the enclosure while others connect to precarious spurs or overlook steep ravines. Most gateways form elevated crossovers in the gaps between the walls, reached by ramps crossing between the interior ditches. Only where the five largest walls separate the North Fort from the level terrain to the northeast do the accompanying ditches shift to the exterior. All the ditches were lined with clay and stone to create a continuous necklace of water-filled reservoirs and reflecting pools.

The early settlers named these hilltop structures "forts" in the early 1800s. But with so many openings, and with their "moat" on the interior, these walls would

Randall
Run
Twin Mounds
House
Foursquare
Moorehead Circle
Museum
NORTH FORT
55 acres
MIDDLE FORT
7 acres
North Overlook
Great Gateway
Picnic area
Village site
SOUTH FORT
38 acres
Little
Miami
River
Run
Cowan
South Gate
Fort Ancient
Architecturally present
Ordering geometry
Depression, pond, pit
Remote sensing feature
Modern structure
1000 ft
N
200 m

ABOVE, LEFT: A pair of very large mounds forms the South Gate and frames its elevated passage—the site's original ceremonial entrance—here viewed from the interior.

ABOVE, RIGHT: Along the exterior faces of Fort Ancient's walls, here near the South Gate, large limestone slabs can be seen among the leaf litter.

have offered little protection from invaders. Fort Ancient was never used for defense; it was created as a ceremonial enclosure, just like the valley-terrace geometric sites, and some of its elaborate ritual facilities have only recently come to light.

CONSTRUCTION

Fort Ancient's design involved a variety of techniques and materials, apparently carried out in at least three phases. The southern plateau was ringed first, making the South Fort the oldest part of the enclosure; the North Fort and the connecting passage or Middle Fort were added later. The construction spanned the entire duration of the Hopewell era, evident from radiocarbon dates as far back as 100 BCE. Pollen analysis from that early date suggests extensive cultivation of edible plants near the interior ponds, and a surrounding landscape already cleared of forests and covered with Big Blue Stem prairie grass.

The construction of the walls required more than 700,000 cubic yards of soil, with an estimated equal amount also moved for other design purposes like leveling hilltops or filling the ravines beneath the Middle Fort. The whole northern plateau was stripped down to the clay subsoil to make it flatter and to provide material for the walls. The natural gullies cutting into the plateau were also blocked by continuing the walls down through them, creating more ponds.

Many of the walls were built in stages, identifiable in the archaeological record by the presence of an interim layer of vegetative soil. At least one wall of the North Fort was built on a cleared and prepared clay floor, first with three low earthen parallels followed by alternating layers of orange and dark gray soil,

ABOVE, LEFT: The two mounds of the Great Gateway, seen here from inside the South Fort with an adjacent small mound, have framed a modern road since the early 1900s.

ABOVE, RIGHT: In the center of the Middle Fort—here looking south—two crescents frame the passage in the middle distance; beyond, the modern road rises to pass through the Great Gateway.

and a final layer of brown-gray silt on top. Excavations have been limited, but in one location, postholes were found beneath the wall suggesting that a timber palisade preceded the construction of the earthwork; in another, the wall's gray clay had been derived from maintaining the nearby ponds.

Fort Ancient also contains a lot of stone. Flat slabs of limestone were stacked along the exterior perimeter and then extended farther up the wall surface. Archaeologist Warren King Moorehead referred to a stone "backbone" around the entire enclosure of the South Fort. Flat, stacked limestone slabs also reinforced the slopes on both sides of some of the gateway passages and were used to construct or cover interior mounds, circles, paths, and other features.

The building of Fort Ancient spread over many generations and required up to six million hours of human labor. From the complexity and duration of the construction and the extensive evidence of human activity both inside and outside the walls, the enclosure apparently served as a place of ceremony and assembly throughout the entire Hopewell era.

SOUTH AND MIDDLE FORTS

The walls of the roughly triangular, thirty-eight-acre South Fort closely follow the edges of the hilltop, negotiating the many small gullies, as well as one very large ravine in the middle of its southern flank. The South Fort had two principal gateways, both formed by the swelling of two adjacent wall segments into large, matching spherical mounds framing an elevated passage. The largest is the South Gate, where the mounded walls rise to a height of nineteen feet above the adjacent interior, framing a monumental passage at a height of thirteen feet. From the crest of this dramatic elevated gate, the remains of a limestone-paved path extend down toward the riverbank nearly 300 feet below. Visitors today view the South Gate from the interior, from within a beautiful grove of trees, but in antiquity its impressive, symmetrical form was approached from the exterior, the culmination of a long, steep climb from the river below.

A similar but smaller gateway frames the entry to the South Fort from the narrow isthmus at its northern end. Although somewhat less grand than the South Gate, it is traditionally called the Great Gateway. Here, the pair of mounds added on top of the walls rise to sixteen feet above the adjacent South Fort interior. A road has crossed this passage since the early 1900s, with the resulting cuts into its paired mounds reinforced with short, stone retaining walls. Moorehead found many burials directly beneath what would have been the interior ramp, meaning that celebrants passing in and out of this gateway would literally have been walking (to borrow John Low's words on this book's frontispiece) "on the bones of their ancestors."

The Middle Fort frames a narrow isthmus, 1,400 feet long and varying in width from about 100 to 330 feet. It connects the South Fort, via the Great Gateway, to the larger plateau to the north. Its narrowest portion was constructed by adding fill to the adjacent ravines, requiring (as estimated by archaeologist Robert Connolly) an amount of soil equal to that in all the rest of Fort Ancient. The earthen walls lining the Middle Fort's irregular edges are generally lower than those elsewhere in the North or South Forts, though their sinuous beauty is more easily appreciated. Near the center of this isthmus stand two low, crescent-shaped earthworks, their curvatures opening southward toward the Great Gateway. They seem to channel the movement of visitors in that direction. Within the curve of the eastern crescent is a small mound covered in stone slabs. A cluster of stone-paved circles and rings lies nearby.

SACRED INDIGENOUS PLACES

"The structure of [American Indian] religious traditions is taken directly from the world around them, from their relationships with other forms of life. Context is therefore all-important for both practice and the understanding of reality. The places where revelations were experienced were remembered and set aside as locations where, through rituals and ceremonials, the people could once again communicate with the spirits. Thousands of years of occupancy on their lands taught tribal peoples the sacred landscapes for which they were responsible and gradually the structure of ceremonial reality became clear.... Regardless of what subsequently happens to the people, the sacred lands remain as permanent fixtures in their cultural or religious understanding. Thus, many tribes now living in Oklahoma, but formerly from the eastern United States, still hold in their hearts the sacred locations of their history."

—VINE DELORIA JR.
(Standing Rock Sioux, 1933–2005)

The large open space inside the North Fort is enclosed on its eastern side by the site's tallest walls; they face the level exterior on the other side.

NORTH FORT

The largest of Fort Ancient's three zones, and the last to be built, is the fifty-five-acre North Fort. Its northeastern walls, facing the level plateau, are the site's largest at twenty-three feet high and seventy feet wide at their bases. State Route 350, the early nineteenth-century coach route from Lebanon to Chillicothe, crosses the North Fort, passing through gateways on each side. Highway upgrades over the years have cut into the walls (and afforded brief archaeological investigations). The northern walls run just below the top edge of the large ravine of Randall Run, and at the northwestern corner they rise and turn to form the site's most intact water retention pond. Where the road penetrates nearby, the adjacent walls rise to a height of nearly twenty feet. A steep wooded ravine bisects the western flank of the North Fort, with the earthwork walls passing nearly to the bottom.

Inside the North Fort are more earthworks and other features. A small crescent lies next to the paved highway in the northern section; from its focal point the equinox sunrise aligns through the large eastern gateway and the Twin Mounds beyond. Several small, circular stone features, similar to those in the Middle Fort, lie near the North Fort's southeastern walls, behind the museum. Prior to the museum's construction, excavations revealed at least seven apparently domestic, superelliptical structures; they likely predate the construction of the North Fort's enclosing walls.

FOURSQUARE AND MOOREHEAD CIRCLE

Four stone-covered mounds form a nearly perfect square in the open, level, eastern section of the North Fort. In a site otherwise determined by its topography, this decisively geometric Foursquare stands out, its 520-foot sides approximating one-half of the OCD. The four identical mounds were covered with limestone slabs on which huge fires had burned. Now restored and resurfaced, two of them serve as backsights for lunar and solar alignments. The southwestern mound aligns through three adjacent northeastern gateways—framing, from left to right, the northern maximum moonrise, the summer solstice sunrise, and the northern minimum moonrise. (The site's staff maintain a view shaft through the forest outside the solstice gateway so the sunrise can be seen; celebrations occur every June 21.) From the square's northwestern mound, the winter solstice sunrise appears through another gateway of the North Fort.

In an open meadow southwest of the Foursquare, a 2005 remote sensing survey revealed the remains of a 197-foot-diameter woodhenge and its associated ritual facilities. Over the following decade, archaeologist Robert Riordan led teams from Wright State University in an investigation of the site. He named it the Moorehead Circle after Fort Ancient's early archaeologist

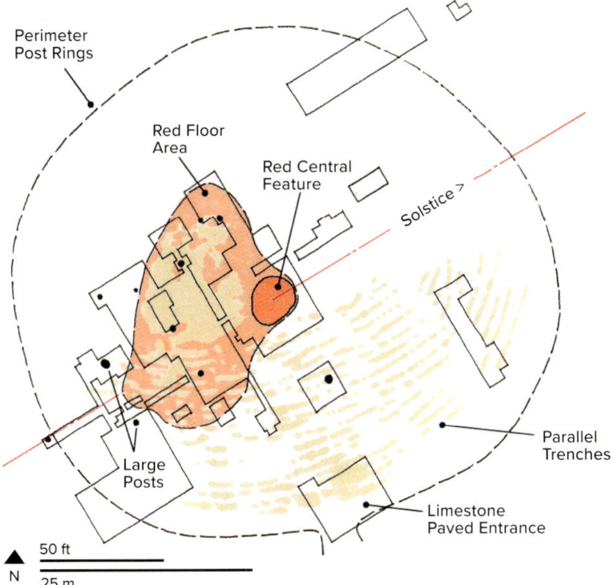

ABOVE, LEFT: A composite excavation plan of the Moorehead Circle shows its post ring, paved entrance, red central feature, and concentric arcs of limestone.

ABOVE, RIGHT: The Moorehead Circle excavations revealed its central deposit of astonishingly bright red-orange soil, transformed by burning.

OPPOSITE: Inside the North Fort, this stone-covered mound and three others like it form a square one-half OCD on each side.

and preservation advocate. Here, next to the North Fort's deepest ravine, the builders created three rings of timber posts (possibly at different times), setting each one more than three feet in the ground and chinking it with limestone slabs. They brought extra soil in to level the northern portion of the circle, toward the ravine; that extra effort, when there was ample level land nearby, suggests that their circle's ceremonial function required that it stand in this exact location.

They paved the post enclosure's main, south-facing entrance with stone. At its center, they dug a shallow, sixteen-foot-wide pit, and then filled it with a large deposit of sterile, burned, astonishingly bright red-orange soil. Around this dramatic central feature, they laid down parallel arcs of limestone slabs, alternating them with gravel bands. The whole arrangement included more timber posts and more reddened soil spread across the central area. After the last ceremony was performed here, they decommissioned the site by removing the wooden posts and burying the entire circle beneath layers of gravel hauled up from the riverbed far below. The decommissioning of this ritual facility did not include the creation of a mound or earthwork to cover its remains; this explains why it remained unknown until its magnetic signature appeared in 2005.

NORTHEASTERN PLATEAU

Outside the large northeastern gateway of the North Fort, facing the plateau, stands the last of Fort Ancient's monumental gateways to be built. Like the South and Great Gateways, a pair of large mounds frame a passage, but this time they were set apart as freestanding forms. These Twin Mounds are 148 feet apart center-to-center, and virtually identical at more than ten feet tall and eighty feet in diameter. They occupy the highest point facing the adjacent plateau and have framed the modern road since it came through in the early 1800s. Small, constructed ditches connected these two large mounds with the adjacent ravines on either side; their intermittent flows to Randall and

Cowan Runs, and on down to the river far below, completed an external water boundary to complement the interior one formed by the string of ponds.

Just beyond the Twin Mounds, according to nineteenth-century maps, a straight, parallel-walled ceremonial avenue extended more than 2,700 feet to the northeast and reportedly terminated in a loop around a small mound. These walls have been subjected to decades of farming and are no longer visible. Their course was centered along the subtle ridge dividing the upland drainages of Randall and Cowan Runs. As recorded, this ceremonial avenue resembles those at other Hopewell earthworks, notably Hopeton and Newark, and would have framed a view to the winter solstice sunset. At least one traveler in the early 1800s recorded hearing from the local farmers that other parallel embankments had been in the vicinity, but no evidence for them has come to light.

MODERN HISTORY

The forest on the plateau had been entirely cleared by the earthwork builders, as required both for digging and placing soil, and for measuring and recording astronomical alignments. But after about 400 CE, trees returned to engulf the walls. Much later, between 1000 and 1450 CE, a group of American Indians built a village in the western arm of the South Fort. Typical of that period, their stockaded settlement had many houses surrounding a central plaza. Some of the residents' burials were also interred within the walls of the adjacent earthwork. It was the discovery of this village that gave this later maize-growing culture its "Fort Ancient" name, when it was wrongly assumed that they had built the earthwork.

Euro-American settlement in the area began immediately after the 1795 Treaty of Greenville ended American Indian claims to this part of Ohio. The nearby towns were established between 1796 and 1803—the year that Warren County was formed from three large parcels of the Virginia Military District. In 1804, a stagecoach route was created to link the new settlements of Lebanon and Chillicothe, traversing the narrow gorge, climbing the steep bluff, and cutting through the earthworks and between the Twin Mounds—later to become Ohio State Route 350.

The monument gained national attention five years later when the Philadelphia *Port Folio* published a map and description, calling it an "Ancient Fortification." Fort Ancient was next featured in 1820, in Atwater's report for the American Antiquarian Society, and within a few years there were calls, including from national figures like Daniel Webster, for its preservation. By the mid-1800s, a small village called Fort Ancient had grown in the valley below, with a bridge, a hotel, and a railroad station.

EARLY ARCHAEOLOGY

Squier and Davis featured Fort Ancient in their *Ancient Monuments of the Mississippi Valley*, incorporating John Locke's "faithful survey" and description originally published in 1843. They continued to interpret the site as a work of defense, noting that "it must have been impregnable." Despite the early calls for its preservation, most of the 1800s saw the earthworks divided among several landowners who cultivated crops and pastured their livestock within the enclosure.

The first "Overlook" structure was positioned to open and frame a long view into the Little Miami River gorge.

Although people had been digging into the mounds for decades, the first recorded archaeological excavations were done by Lewis M. Hosea in 1874. He spent only a few days examining the site, yet made many important discoveries, which he reported in the *Cincinnati Quarterly Journal of Science*. He remarked on the extensive use of stone pavements, suggested there were solar alignments, and rightly surmised that the village remains in the South Fort were newer than the earthwork walls.

Increasingly detailed investigations were undertaken later, especially Moorehead's; his thorough 1890 publication on Fort Ancient remained the definitive account of the site for decades. Besides his archaeological work, Moorehead also advocated successfully for the site's preservation, and in 1890 it was purchased by the state and a year later became Ohio's first state park. By 1908, all land parcels necessary to protect the enclosure had been acquired.

MANAGEMENT AND RESEARCH

As a state park, Fort Ancient came under the management of the Ohio State Archaeological and Historical Society, though it still saw varied uses. In the summer of 1910, the Ohio National Guard held military exercises there; perhaps the only time it resembled a fort was when soldiers practiced "storming the walls" along the steep northern rim of the South Fort. Early site management efforts included brush clearing and plantings to help prevent erosion. Fort Ancient quickly drew both casual explorers and scholars, including, on some occasions, visitors coming to witness special excavations carried out by Moorehead and other archaeologists. In the 1920s and '30s, annual visitation grew to more than 100,000, creating an urgent need for improved infrastructure.

Much of that infrastructure was created by the 1930s Civilian Conservation Corps. They installed concrete drains to allow water—then still

One of Fort Ancient's largest and best-preserved water-holding ponds is in the far northwest corner of the North Fort.

collecting in many of the ponds as the builders had intended—to escape down the hills. They built the picnic shelter and the caretaker's house and restored some of the mounds and earthworks to their recorded mid-nineteenth-century dimensions.

In 1967, soon after Fort Ancient became a National Historic Landmark, its first public museum was built in the North Fort, with exhibits focusing on both the Hopewell and Fort Ancient cultures. The Ohio History Connection renovated and enlarged the building in 1998, with new exhibits on the state's broader Indigenous history. The lobby frames angled views toward two of the Foursquare's stone-covered mounds, and the adjacent garden showcases crops grown in the region one and two millennia ago. Preparations for the museum's expansion uncovered evidence of several houses, one of which is now reconstructed in the garden. The fifteen-by twenty-five-foot structure required seven tons of clay for the wattle-and-daub walls and nearly three acres of prairie grass for the roof.

Archaeological work in and around Fort Ancient has yielded important insights about its construction history, wall composition, domestic areas, water features, landscape modifications, and ritual facilities—all from exploring a relatively small proportion of the site. Much more undoubtedly remains, and since Fort Ancient was subjected to relatively limited, brief, and shallow plowing, any other below-ground features will be well preserved for future research.

AUTHENTICITY AND EXPERIENCE

Surrounded by its steep, densely wooded ravines and enclosed by its elaborate, intact walls and gateways, Fort Ancient retains a primordial timelessness. For many, its magnificent scope, commanding setting, extensive forest cover, and seasonal water features make it an especially compelling sacred place. The steep approach from the Little Miami River and the broad vistas over the valley add drama to the experience of its elevated position. The wall and gateway configurations display a seemingly endless variety and intricacy as they negotiate the plateau's many cuts and ravines. The vernal ponds are beautiful when full, their mirrored reflections offering the best surviving evocations of the interactions among the Beneath, Middle, and Above Worlds of American Indian cosmology. The three monumental gateways—all variations on a shared theme of walls, thresholds, water features, and paired mounds—enhance the ceremonial impact of entering a sacred precinct.

Fort Ancient's excellent state of preservation illustrates the builders' genius with a very different type of ceremonial enclosure. As monumental as the geometric sites, if not more so, its hilltop setting called for very different ideas about form and order. The design drew from a complex repertoire of wall, ditch, pond, ramp, ravine, and hillside elements, while construction entailed various combinations of soil and stone, the careful placement of stone and timber ritual facilities, and massive quantities of landscape modification and earth movement unequalled anywhere else in the Hopewell world.

PRESENTATION AND REPRESENTATION

"For too many North Americans living in the early twenty-first century, Indigenous earthworks are either completely invisible or, if seen, an illegible presence, a ghostly sign or a sign of forgotten ghosts. They appear to bear no inscribed meaning. Sighting thus evokes the great difficulty for most contemporary viewers to perceive earthworks in terms of the complexity of their interrelated structures, the conceptual power of their designs, the beauty of their architecture."

—CHADWICK ALLEN

The earthworks' full conceptual and formal power can be elusive; it does not present itself easily to our modern understandings of space or our implicit expectations of what great cultural monuments are supposed to be and do. Fort Ancient, for example, although very well preserved, appears to us only in fragments—peeking out of the woods, usually just a few seemingly random walls or gateways at a time. Newark's Octagon, though pristine in form, is so complex that our eye-level perceptions alone cannot readily assemble it into a coherent whole. The Great Circle at Newark is spatially simpler, and well preserved, but so large that we barely sense its enclosing form. Only the compact, restored forms at Mound City present us with a coherent, graspable image. (It is no accident that photographs of Mound City are most often chosen to represent this series of earthworks.)

Accordingly, site managers and interpretive planners have two challenges. One involves "presentation"—how to enhance the earthworks' visibility for visitors as much as possible, as by maintenance, restoration, or plantings. The Park Service's mowing program at Seip and Hopeton helps to do this. The other challenge is "representation"—how various visual media can help visitors with these sites' unique challenges of orientation, visualization, and comprehension—how, in other words, to connect *perceptions* (of an earthwork's subtle, fragmentary, or forested features) with a *conception* (of its overall scope, form, precision, and brilliance). Map guides and media visualizations can help with this.

From the Philadelphia *Port Folio* of 1808 to this book, discourse about the sites has relied on various types of representation. Early survey maps like Squier and Davis's emphasized their plan forms; early photographs could show them cleared of trees. The increasingly accurate records of twentieth-century archaeology were of great scientific value but added little to the sites' visuality. Since 2000, geophysical imagery has emerged with a beauty of its own: once-hidden sites leap out from unexpected places or in unexpected detail. Aerial digital reconstructions can show the overall scope and scale of the works in wide landscape contexts and with atmospheric effects, while imaginative paintings can evoke their ceremonial uses.

All these types of representation are used in this volume, in abundance, and for a reason. As World Heritage sites, the Hopewell Ceremonial Earthworks have a new role as global symbols of a distinguished culture. Most of the world's iconic monuments—the Parthenon, the Pyramids, Chartres Cathedral—don't have comparable problems of visibility; they can be seen for miles. And most iconic landscapes—Versailles, the Forbidden City—are huge and horizontal, but also visible, graspable.

Monumentality, by definition, is big and impressive; iconicity, by definition, is vivid and memorable. Helping these earthworks take their place in the public imagination as the iconic monuments of their brilliant makers will require special attention to their visuality—treatments helping them to be seen, felt, understood, and remembered. For a century and a half, Squier and Davis's beautiful lithographs were generally the best available. But the abstraction of a map or plan goes only so far; iconicity depends on evocations of "being there"—identifiable, vivid, and relatable with our lived experience.

The earthworks' elusive spatiality also begs the question: Did the builders and the celebrants possess visualization skills that we don't have? Gathering within enclosures whose scope and complexity barely "enclose" at all suggests they had spatial conceptions almost unknown among other cultures, including our own. More questions arise about how these vast, subtle shapes were "presented" for the ceremonies: Were they maintained in low-growing ground covers and "weeded" constantly, or were they burned off periodically—perhaps timed so that new green growth would appear for the scheduled event? Or were their interiors and wall surfaces stomped—a technique modern tribes still use to prepare ceremonial grounds?

In this digital rendering by Herb Roe, torch-bearing celebrants enter the sacred precinct of a ringed Adena mound once connected to the vast Portsmouth Earthworks complex.

"When the Hopewell saw the mounds, how did they see them? Perhaps the grass was allowed to grow long upon them, but instead, I wonder. Whenever I am at ceremony and preparing the ground, I am called to think upon our efforts in preparing our ground as if I am plucking a stray whisker from the Grandmother or we are combing her hair so that it shines and reflects the love and reverence we have for the Ancient Way that we Shawnees were given, a celebration inherited by the Shawnee that surely was influenced by the Hopewell."

—CHIEF BENJAMIN BARNES (Shawnee Tribe)

The earthworks' geometric precision also invites us to wonder how, or whether, their designers "represented" them, as in drawings, before construction began. The procedures for laying out perfect, interrelated shapes were described in the previous chapter, all of which could have been worked out in advance on deer hide, for example, using charcoal and a cord. An exquisite copper circular cutout displays within its small circumference an intricate precision practically equivalent to that of Newark's Octagon Earthworks. With their still-unknown system of units and divisions, the earthwork designers could well have enlarged their most sophisticated geometric schemes from small-scale representations.

The irregular Tremper Mound, vaguely suggesting an animal, covered the remains of a complex building whose contents included a collection of effigy smoking pipes much like those from Mound City.

PART 3

CONTEXTS

Representatives attending the Ohio History Connection's 2017 Tribal Nations Conference gathered for a reflective moment at Fort Ancient's South Gate.

13.
TRIBAL ENGAGEMENT

"Across the thirteen moons on Turtle's back, across multiples of centuries, the Mother Mounds are calling to their children: 'Come home . . . .' They call, sing, coo, echo, hum. They infiltrate our sleeping and our waking dreams with whispers of thoughts they make as if our very own: 'Come home . . . it's time. Come home to rest your hearts in the layered folds of Mother's skirts.'"

—MONIQUE MOJICA (Guna/Rappahannock)

The post-Hopewell centuries brought cultural changes, movements, and dispersals now long untraceable. Then came the diseases and upheavals induced by European expansion. The last tribes in Ohio, who had been living with and respecting the earthworks perhaps for centuries, were forced out by settlement, war, and ultimately removal. As a result of both federal and state policies, there are no federally recognized tribes based in Ohio today, although some were able to resist and remain in the states along the Trail of Tears toward Indian Country—in Indiana, Illinois, and Missouri, for example. In their new locations (for most, it was Oklahoma), the tribes were then subjected to decades of further acculturation.

Five centuries of political and religious domination shattered Indigenous cultural worlds that were millennia in the making. Tribes in some regions fared better than others, but most suffered a severe loss of their traditions, languages, ceremonies, customs, and self-determination—not to mention their homelands. By the turn of the twentieth century, Indigenous populations in the United States were at their lowest point. When the Society of American Indians was founded in Columbus, Ohio, in 1911, the numbers had dropped from millions to only about 250,000. With no tribes left in Ohio, the inclusion of American Indian perspectives remained absent from the management and interpretation of the earthworks for decades.

But things began to shift in the 1960s. The general cultural and political movements toward justice for previously repressed groups helped expose injustices against America's Indigenous peoples. Insistent activism by Native communities, groups, and their allies demanded legal action and resulted in new laws and policies of respect and affirmation. In 1978, the American Indian Religious Freedom Act established the rights of American Indians to exercise their traditional religions with respect to their associated sacred places, ceremonies, objects, and heritage, and strengthened requirements for tribal values to be considered in historic preservation cases. This recognition often involved the important spiritual connections between Indigenous cultural practices and their sacred landscapes.

The 1990 passage of the Native American Graves Protection and Repatriation Act (NAGPRA) established the rights of American Indian Tribal Nations to determine the disposition of items—including human remains, funerary or sacred objects, and objects of cultural patrimony—when they can demonstrate an affiliation. The law also mandates that tribes must be consulted whenever archaeological work is likely to disturb Native American cultural items or when such items are unexpectedly uncovered on federal or tribal lands. By prioritizing tribal sovereignty, NAGPRA encourages the preservation of archaeological sites, since they may contain burials or other cultural items.

Similar objectives are reflected internationally in the United Nations Declaration on the Rights of Indigenous Peoples (UNDRIP), adopted by the General Assembly in 2007. Its forty-six detailed articles affirm a right of Indigenous self-determination—including the right to protect, maintain, and if necessary to revitalize their artistic, religious, and cultural traditions; their languages and sacred places; and other aspects of cultural heritage and practice. The declaration also covers repatriation of sacred objects, protection of culturally related intellectual property, and the right of Indigenous peoples to maintain and strengthen their own institutions and visions of development.

A CENTURY OF CHANGE

"The first American Indian rights organization, the Society of American Indians, was founded at the Ohio State University in Columbus in 1911. A century later, Ohio State again hosted scholars from around the country for the group's Centennial Symposium. Attendees of both meetings traveled to Newark and visited the earthworks. The 1911 visitors were duly impressed, but the dire conditions of Native life in the US then kept them focused on more pressing questions of survival.

A century later, in 2011, American Indian scholars had a grasp of history that provided insight to both the dire situation of American Indian people at the turn of the twentieth century and the cultural significance of the ancient Ohio earthworks. We had seen the impacts of organizations such as the National Congress of American Indians and legislation such as the right to vote in the 1920s and the American Indian Religious Freedom Act. These rights and policies have been utilized to protect sacred sites and cultural items throughout the country. Many things had changed."

—MARTI CHAATSMITH (Comanche/Choctaw)

"We must acknowledge Native peoples' agency in bringing about this change. Were it not for their struggle to assert their rights in the courts, none of the current consultative and collaborative approaches would have come about. There's a tendency to say 'NAGPRA led to these changes' without acknowledging that Indian activism forced NAGPRA into law."

—BRET RUBY

Indigenous archaeologist Joe Watkins (Choctaw), former chief of Tribal Relations and American Cultures for the National Park Service, delivered remarks at the dedication of a new trail and visitor wayside at the Hopeton Earthworks in 2016.

In Ohio, the lack of attention to Indigenous voices was beginning to change by the late 1990s. Scholars and site interpreters had long recognized that the earthworks are Indigenous sacred sites, but with few exceptions they were not yet seeking out tribal descendants for collaborative work. But the spirit—if not always the letter—of NAGPRA and UNDRIP pointed to renewed participation by American Indian descendants in the sites' interpretation. Since the turn of the millennium, a spirit of openness, respect, trust, and collaboration has gradually been created between Ohio's historic tribes and the agencies who manage and interpret the Hopewell Ceremonial Earthworks.

TOWARD COLLABORATIVE MANAGEMENT

Since 1997, Hopewell Culture National Historical Park has been officially committed to collaborative co-stewardship of the sites with the region's historic tribes. It consults with eleven federally recognized tribal nations: Absentee Shawnee Tribe of Indians of Oklahoma; Delaware Nation, Oklahoma; Delaware Tribe of Indians; Eastern Shawnee Tribe of Oklahoma; Miami Tribe of Oklahoma; Ottawa Tribe of Oklahoma; Peoria Tribe of Indians of Oklahoma; Seneca-Cayuga Nation; Shawnee Tribe; The Osage Nation; and the Wyandotte Nation. Besides regulatory compliance on NAGPRA and other relevant federal laws, through government-to-government consultation, the park seeks tribal input on a much broader set of subjects, including the development of all significant management, interpretive, and visitor experience plans. Since 2023, the park has conducted its archaeological investigations with collaborative leadership from a team of tribal representatives.

Since its founding in 1885, the Ohio History Connection has been responsible for the state's historic places—including the Indigenous sites, objects, and grave contents in its collections. In the 1990s, tribal perspectives began to emerge as a priority for the organization, and by the mid-2000s, staff members were building relationships with the Ohio-affiliated tribes. Exchange visits between Oklahoma and Ohio began soon after. Shared programs about the earthworks, NAGPRA topics, research, and exhibitions followed. In 2015, a director of American Indian relations was hired, with the charge to imbue the entire agency with Indigenous awareness and formalized policies for tribal outreach and consultation—now including an annual tribal nations conference and full collaboration in all management and interpretive planning at all of its Indigenous sites.

The Ohio History Connection and the National Park Service manage their sites independently but coordinate through continuous information sharing. Although there are differences in how each agency works with tribes, for legal and other reasons, the management and interpretation of the Hopewell Ceremonial Earthworks reflect the broad principles and intentions articulated in UNDRIP and in the various pertinent US laws: that Ohio's historic tribes have central roles to play in maintaining, protecting, and developing "the past, present, and future manifestations of their cultures, such as archaeological and historical sites, artifacts, designs, ceremonies." The depth of commitment to these consulting processes grew significantly during the fifteen-year-long World Heritage inscription effort.

RETURNING TO THE SITES

In the early 2000s, the continuing occupation of Newark's Octagon Earthworks by a private country club helped launch the effort toward World Heritage inscription. The arrest of a local woman for praying at the site brought public attention to the problem. A group called Friends of the Mounds advocated for the liberation of the site and began a shift in public opinion—a new awareness that this was an American Indian sacred place. The Friends soon grew into an academic research center at Ohio State University's Newark campus: The Newark Earthworks Center (NEC).

Since its founding in 2005, the NEC has led efforts to connect the removed Ohio tribes with the ancient sites of their homelands and advocated for the sites' preservation and refreshed interpretation. It turned out that knowledge of the earthworks and the ancestors who built them was often lost to the returning tribal members as much as to the regional population in general. The NEC also helped to build the relationships between the displaced tribal nations and the Ohio-based institutions. The center's focus has been on academic conferences and publications, public tours and events (beginning with the 2005 Octagon moonrises), and regional co-development partnerships to create educational materials, exhibits, and research highlighting traditional Indigenous perspectives on the earthworks.

In 2007, Chief Glenna J. Wallace (Eastern Shawnee Tribe of Oklahoma) was a guest of the NEC and attended a tour of the Octagon Earthworks during a scholar's visit. That was when she first learned about the Hopewell

THE SENSE OF LOSS

"There is a stress and tension among many of the American Indians I have brought to the Newark Earthworks over the years. Some of my Native guests have lost track of the sense that such spaces can be sacred. Many others recognize that 'something really important was going on at these places,' but they don't have any idea what it was, which makes them feel acute embarrassment. However, there should be no sense of shame in this. After all, one could ask, what do others know about what their ancestors were doing 2,000 years ago?

Yet, there is a profound sense of loss and grief, and an angst and helplessness, that so much has been lost over time. For me, it is important for all of us to acknowledge that due to the traumatic events of the last few centuries, both before and since our removal from these lands, and simply the passage of so much time, many contemporary American Indians have no knowledge of the original purpose and meaning of the earthworks. But this is irrelevant to their 'ownership' (stewardship) of this ancient heritage.

These sites will always be important cultural patrimony for American Indians and a legacy left to us by our ancestors. Though some of us may know very little about the history or use of these sacred sites, they offer us the opportunity to come together for healing among ourselves and with non-native peoples too."

—JOHN N. LOW
(Pokagon Band of Potawatomi)

Chief Glenna J. Wallace (Eastern Shawnee Tribe of Oklahoma) delivered remarks at Mound City during events celebrating World Heritage Inscription, November 2023.

Ceremonial Earthworks. After seeing the Newark Octagon and its golfers, she converted her astonishment at the architecture—and her anger at its use—into persistent and eloquent advocacy for removing golf from the site and achieving World Heritage inscription. Since then, the Newark Earthworks Center, the Ohio History Connection, and the National Park Service have been regularly engaging tribal participation in earthworks conferences, tours, management, and interpretation.

THE SENSE OF CONNECTION

Contemporary Indigenous people come from strong cultural foundations that have existed for thousands of years. They have demonstrated cultural resilience, as shown in the arts, education, and Indigenous knowledge passed down through the generations. Tribal communities across the Americas retain continuity with their cultural past while embracing innovation and opportunity.

As descendants are returning to the earthwork sites today, deep connections are being recovered and expressed. Many Indigenous ways and ideas have remained entwined with the builders' world, including a sensory engagement with nature and Water–Earth–Sky cosmologies. From today's Indigenous perspectives, the people of the Hopewell culture are ancestors, whose intelligence, creativity, innovation, and industriousness are revealed in the earthworks, along with powerful evocations of still-resonant beliefs. The complex feelings of today's Indigenous visitors generally include a profound sense of spiritual connection.

> *"Once the group arrived at the Great Circle, where access is unrestricted, individuals began peeling off from the tour. They wanted to relate to the Great Circle on their own terms. They wanted to be quiet. Several stood in silent contemplation along the edge of the enormous circle. Others lay on the ground to feel the earth, hear the cicadas in the trees, and listen for earthworks harmonies. This is not unusual behavior when Native people visit earthworks."*
>
> — MARTI CHAATSMITH (Comanche/Choctaw)

> *"As a Native woman residing in Ohio, away from my people and my own ancestral homelands, I know that I can come to the sacred sites in Ohio and feel a sense of belonging. I am blessed to be able to bring my daughter to this sacred place to honor the ancestors and pass on the stories of her ancestors' strength and resilience."*
>
> —APRIL HESTER (Muscogee Nation)

> *"These sites are important as they hold the answers we have been looking for. The knowledge and memory are within the water, soil, rocks, and trees. These sites are waiting for connection to be remembered so that life can continue to exist. Protecting and preserving these living sites is imperative in protecting the living world."*
>
> —SHELLY CORBIN/TAKÓNI KÓKIPEŠNI (Itázipčo/Mnicoujou–Lakota)

INDIGENOUS VALUES

While it may be tempting to focus on the mounds and earthworks as mainly about death and memory, that would be only part of the story of the people who built and lived among them. Core values shared by many contemporary tribes can reveal a more nuanced interpretation. Although varied among different tribal communities, these values define obligations for people to strengthen their connections to each other and to the world around them. Humans have a responsibility to maintain balance through relationships with all beings of the Above, Earth, and Beneath Worlds, and out to the Quartered Horizon. Kinship relationships and acts of reciprocity among humans and nonhuman beings serve as the cornerstone for ensuring this balance. To be a good person is to embody these core values in one's life and actions.

Responsibility involves the obligation to the community: to care for relatives, neighbors, colleagues, and all the things of the world. There is an understanding of kinship—as exemplified in the phrase "we are all related"—to each other as human beings, and to all other beings. Our responsibilities are to the Sky, the waters, the air and the land, animals, plants, geological formations, the stars, the Moon and the Sun.

ORENDA: LIFE FORCE IN ALL THINGS

"Haudenosaunee communities share a concept called Orenda—a life force or power in every person and every entity of Nature, and involved in every operation, interaction, or event. Similar, longstanding ideas among the Algonquian and Siouan language speakers (who call it Manito or Wakanda, respectively) suggest this understanding of the world is rooted deeply in the past, and very likely was shared, in some form, by the earthwork builders. Many of their works of artistry—complex geometrical abstractions of natural subjects, rendered in shimmering materials—evoke an immanent sacred power.

We believe Orenda lies inherent in all things—plants, animals, clouds, rocks, soil, water, people. It influences every operation, interaction, or event, and so affects the well-being of people. Our words in English—magic, mystery, sorcery—fail to grasp its dynamic, measured, enigmatic ways of functioning. Limited in purpose and efficiency, its effects are local and circumstantial, not pervasive and almighty.

Orenda sees all beings as endowed with life, mind, will, desire, and choice. It can only be explained through the observed activities of life and Nature, and it must be honored. It can be transferred, attracted, acquired, increased, suppressed, or absorbed through ritualistic practices. To obtain our needs, we must gain the goodwill of each being through prayer, honor, sacrifice, offering, or a pacifying act—to influence the exercise of Orenda on our behalf, which we believe is controlled by the particular being invoked.

Orenda is the distinctive characteristic of all the life forces, in any manner affecting the prosperity or distress of humans. Our relationship with the world must be maintained by ritual responsibility—to order and structure these life forces for both our engagement with Nature, and our interpersonal relationships."

—JOE STAHLMAN
(Tuscarora/Pennsylvania Dutch)

Attendees at the Ohio History Connection's 2016 Tribal Nations Conference gather on the monumental gateway platform at Newark's Great Circle.

Reciprocity involves the dynamics of giving and receiving, coming and going, dying and renewing. The world and all things exist in cycles of reciprocity, including the seasons, growth and decay, and movements in the Sky. The land is a living thing; it gives its gifts with generosity and wonder. Humans must give back to the land with gratitude and respect, honoring the plant or animal that feeds us, living in mutual support, and maintaining Earth's cycles.

Seen in the context of these widely shared Indigenous values, the Hopewell Ceremonial Earthworks are no longer about death and emptiness but are instead celebrations of life. The tremendous effort to construct even a small burial mound is balanced by the shared understanding of what these places represented to each individual—a love of family and community, a connection to the cycles of time, a respect for the fragility and challenges of life.

As more American Indian people continue to engage with their ancestors' accomplishments, the Hopewell Ceremonial Earthworks will inspire new generations of interpreters, new ideas connecting past and present, and new directions for Indigenous thought and scholarship into the future.

14.
CEREMONIAL ARTISTRY

Much of what we know about the ceremonial life of the earthwork builders comes from the abundant and exquisite artistry that was found in the mounds during archaeological excavations in the nineteenth and early twentieth centuries. Rare, shining, shimmering materials were brought to Ohio at great effort and expense—carried over weeks of walking or canoeing, then worked to perfection by artisans with highly advanced lifelong skills. But, notwithstanding their dazzling materiality and refined beauty, the contexts where they were found show that they were nothing like our modern idea of "art objects."

POWERFUL, SACRED BEINGS

They were made for ritual ceremonies and performances in the great timber temples, laid down on the prepared clay fire basins and sometimes heaped with cremated ancestral remains. Many were broken and burned, or carefully wrapped, or otherwise prepared for burial in ways analogous to the treatment of the deceased. This suggests they were not seen as inanimate objects—not even precious ones—but as other-than-human beings, as entities with agency, personhood, and power, to be beloved or feared.

Items positioned as ceremonial regalia seem to mark the roles and status of valued leaders, decorating the honorific attire that would have conferred the dignity and symbolic differentiation of their various roles in society. Some collections were laid out in elaborate narrative tableaux—careful presentations of a narrative story such as a journey to the afterlife. On their open platforms inside the shrine buildings, these displays may have been left open for years before being buried.

The huge quantities of similar items, brought from many faraway locations and arranged together in highly specific ways, suggest that diverse and distant groups of people brought them to these Ohio sites as pilgrimage offerings. Undoubtedly, many more precious items laid down beneath the mounds were made with perishable materials, but apart from fabric and fur fragments preserved by copper, they are now lost.

This mica hand image by Talon Silverhorn (Eastern Shawnee) resembles the iconic piece from the Hopewell Mound Group, now with the Ohio History Connection. Its elegant proportions evoke a human greeting across the centuries.

FROM EXCAVATION TO CONSULTATION

When the finds from the Hopewell Mound Group were exhibited at the 1893 World's Columbian Exhibition in Chicago, their sheer quantity and artistic brilliance were evident to all. Those pieces, plus many others amassed from excavations at other sites both before and since, were exhibited in museums and became objects of study, illuminating the sophistication of the culture and the meanings and uses of the earthwork sites. But now, under the law, Native descendants have the power of informed consent with regard to how these artifacts are treated, or even whether they are to be seen at all.

In recent decades, respectful consultations with Indigenous communities have led archaeologists and curators to turn away from merely exhibiting the objects—the "cabinet of curiosity" of the nineteenth and early twentieth centuries—and to incorporate Native insights and wider contextual approaches. Those insights include the idea that these artifacts are powerful, sacred beings, intended to accompany revered ancestors on their spiritual journey. Out of respect for that power—of a scope and force now unknowable—many consulting tribal members now say that these pieces must be put away, or reburied, and no longer seen at all.

But their astonishing beauty and sophistication, and their compelling testimony to the brilliance of the culture, make it difficult to agree categorically that they should all disappear back into the ground or into museum storerooms. Tribal representatives do not all agree on this question.

RESPECTING THE OBJECTS' POWER

Seeking a middle ground on this issue, a 2019 exhibit at the Ohio History Connection, designed with extensive tribal consultation and entitled *Indigenous Wonders of Our World*, displays a group of votive offerings (not associated with ancestral remains) in an authentic portrayal of their

THE ESSENTIAL DILEMMA

Archaeologist Bret Ruby recounts the national park's recent consultation on displaying objects with a citizen from the Absentee Shawnee Tribe—a respected traditional gentleman, a speaker of the Shawnee language, and a practitioner of the tribal religion. After his first tour of Mound City, with its artifacts still on display, he was asked what should be done. His reply: "Those things were put in the ground 2,000 years ago for a reason and are not meant to be seen. . . . [They should] never have been disturbed. But I had no idea that an Indian person could make something like that; I just had no idea. And I want to bring my kids to see this."

"Sacred knowledge and sacred objects hold great power; mishandling them can cause great harm. Many American Indian people today believe sickness and even death can result. Recently, Native people have demanded proper respect for their Ancestors' sacred objects and knowledge, and their voices are beginning to be heard. Their success in gaining legal protection for these things has forced the efforts toward reconciliation, and those efforts are now bearing fruit."

—BRET RUBY

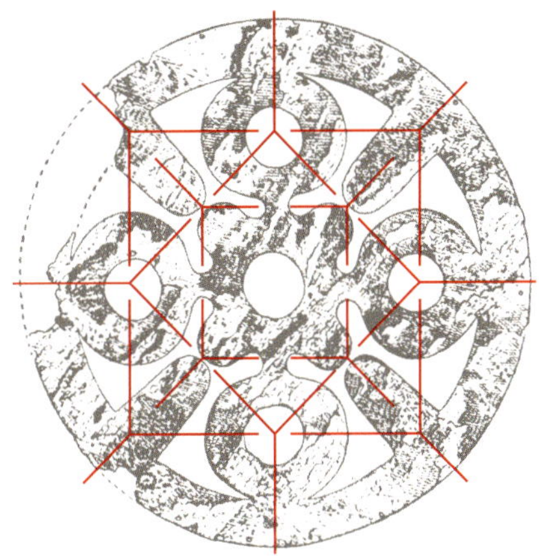

TOP: Talon Silverhorn's digital sculpture of a copper circle is based on one of many found at the Hopewell Mound Group and now with the Ohio History Connection. Its shape and division into four quadrants suggest analogies to the earthworks, or to World Center shrines.

ABOVE: An analysis of a copper circle from the Hopewell Mound Group reveals precision geometry analogous to that of Newark's Octagon, confirming the Hopewell designers' skills for layout, measurement, and visual perfection at both small and huge scales.

original arrangement and context. The exhibit design also offers the visitor a choice—to avoid viewing the excavated objects, or to prepare and approach them with dignity and respect. Another approach, taken at the Chickasaw Cultural Center in Oklahoma, is to avoid original objects or photographs and use only facsimiles, abstractions, or new works of art that can portray their visual qualities.

Respecting this approach, this book does not include photographs of any artifacts. Because photographs are believed to capture the artifacts' power, they are represented here only in abstracted digital media or drawings—or with Shawnee artist Talon Silverhorn's Hopewell-inspired original works of art. As sacred, powerful beings, they are described here with both archaeological and Indigenous knowledge of their materials and workmanship, their use and symbolism, their ceremonial settings, the reverent ways they were prepared for eternal rest, and the sense of connection felt by American Indian tribes today.

> *"I might want people to see these works of artistry, the amazing things we were capable of, but I do not think my wishes outweigh those of the people who buried these pieces. They should never have been disturbed, and they should be put back. But that doesn't mean we cannot create new, similar things for people to see."*
>
> —LOGAN YORK (Miami Tribe of Oklahoma)

MICA AND COPPER

Shiny, delicate, glasslike sheets of silica, called mica, were brought to Ohio from isolated formations in the mountains of western North Carolina, arriving in multilayer chunks called "books" to minimize breakage. Working with mica involves splitting apart the delicate, crystalline sheets to showcase its translucent, pearl-like luster and its silvery-gold patterns and highlights. Artisans cut beautiful shapes from the split sheets using flint bladelets, leaving scrap piles that have helped archaeologists locate their workshops. Preeminent masterpieces in mica from the Hopewell Mound Group include a wonderfully iconic human hand and elegant bird talons. Pieces were also cut into circles; their shimmering surfaces suggest a mirror or an icon of the shining Moon. Some shrine floors were paved with massive spreads of gleaming mica sheets; a grave at the Newark Ellipse reportedly had many bushel-basket loads arrayed over it.

Nearly all the copper used in Hopewell artistry came from the northern and southern shores of Lake Superior, 900 miles away. It was mined with great effort from thin veins in metamorphic rocks, using only fire and stone tools. Working it into the desired shapes—axes, flat sheets for cutouts, or the characteristic doughnut-shaped earspools—required advanced knowledge of metallurgy. The raw copper had to be heated and cooled carefully to prevent its becoming brittle and shattering; if that happened, the material, obtained with such great effort, became useless. Finished pieces were polished to a reflective shine, enhancing their ability to portray an otherworldly power. Their textile, feather, and fur wrappings suggest the caring attention lavished on them as they were kept, perhaps for generations, and eventually laid to rest as if living beings.

A copper mushroom effigy was placed on a platform in the center of Mound City's most ostentatious grave. Carved in wood and then covered with copper foil, it lay on a bed of mica sheets, surrounded by other fabulous copper pieces, in the center of the site's biggest shrine building, all later buried beneath the biggest mound in the very center of the site. This elaborate arrangement suggests a tableau—a carefully arranged scenario to show off the mushroom's power. Of the two known types of Ohio mushrooms that it resembles, one is lethal and the other is a strong hallucinogen; either way, its lavish honors here showed deep respect for its power—that of a living being with its own will and agency.

OBSIDIAN AND FLINT

At least 300 pounds of obsidian were brought to Ohio's Hopewell earthwork sites. The shiny, black volcanic glass came from the Yellowstone Valley (Idaho, Wyoming) 1,500 miles away—the farthest of any of the exotic materials—by trains of walkers with packs, or by canoes up the rivers, probably over several generations. The effort required to procure it gave the material immense value, even before experts chipped it into huge, graceful ceremonial blades. As with flint, the required technique is knapping—precision chipping of a large piece, bit by bit, with a stone tool. The finished blades were up to sixteen inches long—too large, rare, and valuable to use as cutters. A study funded by the Seneca Nation in 2020 found no signs of wear on the blades, although their stems had been tied onto poles or handles so they could be held or carried in a ceremony. The larger pieces are consummate masterpieces, clearly made by an artisan with years of specialized experience. Yet they were broken into pieces and burned before being buried—a ritual transformation analogous to the dismemberment and cremation of the deceased.

Although mined closer to home, flint was also prized, and ceremoniously buried. Before building Mound 2 at the Hopewell Mound Group, the people had brought in nearly eight tons of nearly identical flint discs and arranged them on the prepared floor. There was no associated grave, just a clay basin in the center of the floor. Three more such sets are known from the Hopewell world, one in southern Indiana and two in Illinois; all the discs across all the sites are of similar size, shape, and material. This shared type is not related to any function, or to anything known from typical habitation sites.

A well-known source of the blue-gray flint is the Wyandotte Cave, 300 miles away in southern Indiana. That's a long enough canoe or backpack trip, carrying eight tons of stone, but recent spectroscopy studies show that the Mound 2 flints also came from at least four other places, some much farther away in Tennessee and southern Illinois. This huge collection of similar pieces, brought from so many different places, shows that groups were gathering here to share in rituals and to leave high-value gifts as tokens of their participation. The assembled celebrants almost certainly spoke different languages, but their gifts and offerings spoke of shared artistry traditions and religious practices.

OPPOSITE, TOP: Talon Silverhorn's image of a large obsidian blade is based on one of many found at the Hopewell Mound Group and now with the Ohio History Connection. The asymmetrical, double-curved form was used only on ceremonial blades, never on functional flint ones.

OPPOSITE, BOTTOM: A copper-foil-wrapped effigy resembling a powerful Ohio mushroom was laid down as the centerpiece of Mound City's most richly embellished grave.

RIGHT: On each of several otter pipes, the animal addresses the smoker not only with its delicately rendered face and spirit, but also offering a fish in its mouth. Talon Silverhorn's digital sculpture is based on an example from the Tremper Mound.

EFFIGY SMOKING PIPES

Two great collections of carved stone smoking pipes were laid down in Hopewell mounds—one beneath Mound 8 at Mound City, the other in the Tremper Mound, about forty miles farther south along the Scioto River. The two collections were nearly identical, their pipe bowls carved into a whole menagerie of mostly small animals—snakes, birds, beavers, frogs, turtles, raccoons, and more. Most of the Mound City pipes were carved from a local Ohio pipestone, while the Tremper collection used stone from much farther away in Illinois and Minnesota. Before burial, these exquisitely carved spiritual beings were ritually broken and burned. As with the flints, the number of similar things brought together suggests they were gifts or offerings. And like the obsidian blades, their deliberate breakage suggests they were regarded as living beings, needing death and transformation rituals equivalent to those of their owners.

"These animal depictions were powerful symbols of the spiritual powers and beings that inhabit the Beneath and Above Worlds. They were used in gift exchanges and offerings involving powerful leaders and ancestors, signaling the emergence of a more complex social landscape, in which religious prerogatives were being used to forge alliances and negotiate power relations among individuals and groups, and across generations."

—BRET RUBY

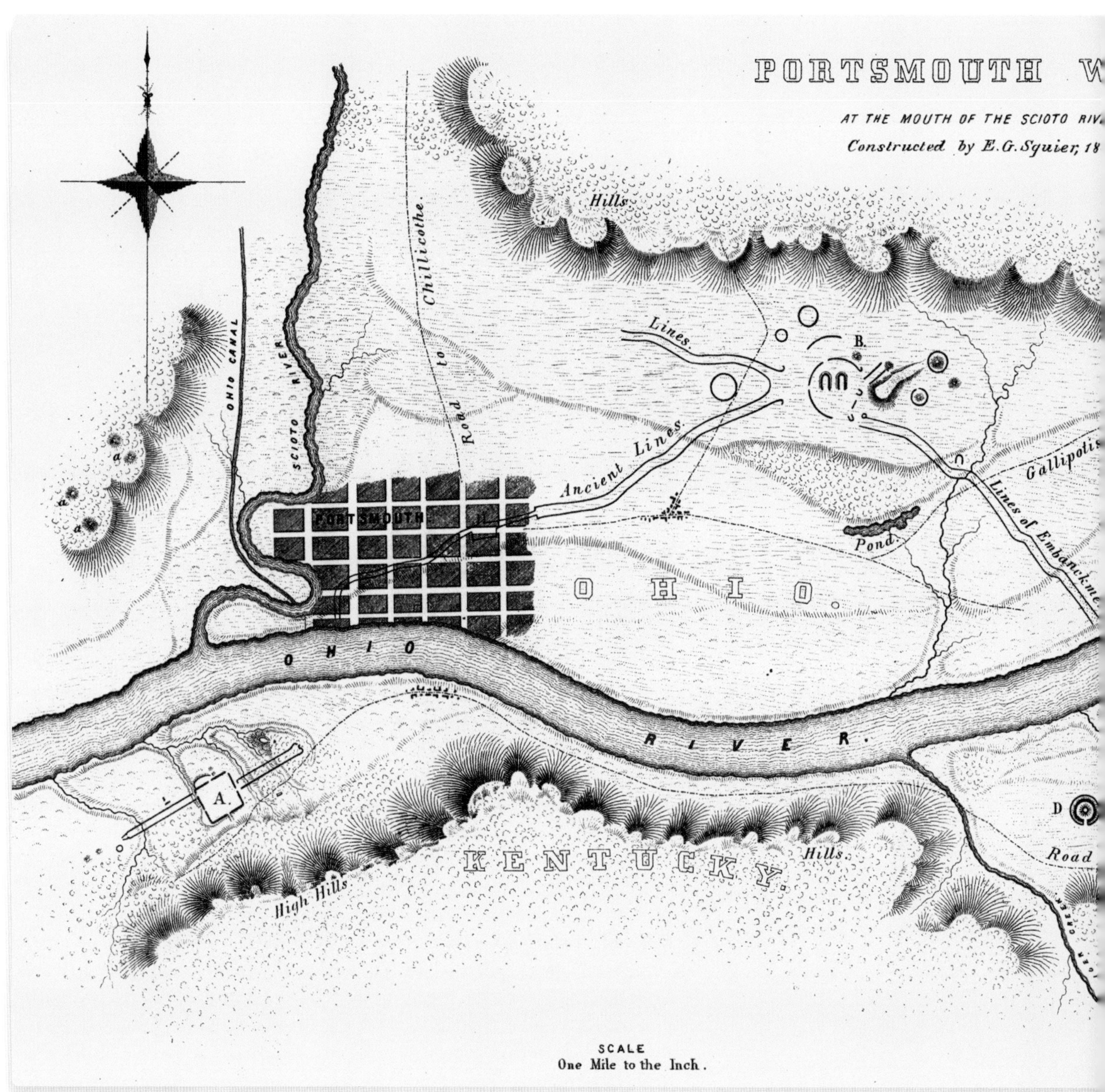
PORTSMOUTH W
AT THE MOUTH OF THE SCIOTO RIV
Constructed by E.G. Squier, 18
Hills
Lines.
B.
OHIO CANAL
SCIOTO RIVER
Road to Chillicothe
Ancient Lines.
PORTSMOUTH
Gallipolis
Lines of Embankme
Pond.
O H I O.
O H I O
R I V E R.
A.
D
K E N T U C K Y.
Hills.
High Hills
Road
SCALE
One Mile to the Inch.

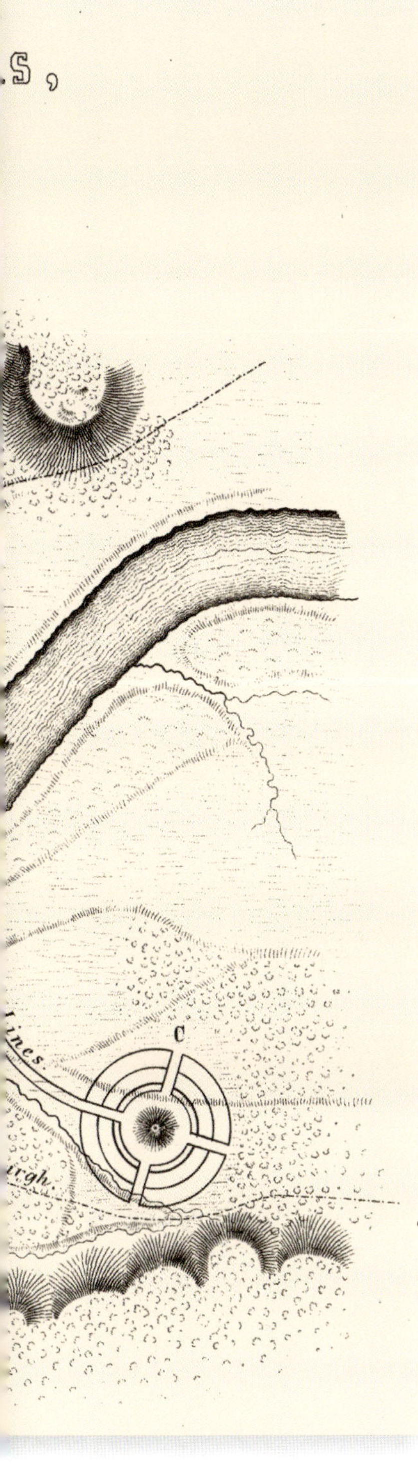

Mounds, earthworks, and parallel walls sprawled across the huge valley where the Scioto River joins the Ohio.

15. OTHER HOPEWELL EARTHWORKS

"Native sacred places are . . . where Native people go to pray, to sing, to dance, for the good day, the precious earth, the blessing waters, the sweet air, and a peaceful life for all living beings. . . . The best advice for the public at these places may be found in the Cheyenne instruction, 'Walk gently through life.' The protocols for Native sacred and historic places are the same as the unwritten rules for guests at a monument, cemetery, royal garden, or grand palace."

—SUZAN SHOWN HARJO (Cheyenne and Hodulgee Muscogee)

The genius and variety of Hopewell architecture extends well beyond the eight earthworks featured in the preceding chapters, even though the sites in this series were selected and justified for World Heritage inscription as the most representative examples. Many more earthworks were spread across southern Ohio, more in the surrounding states, and a few far beyond. Though many are gone now, many others remain, helping to illuminate the breadth of the Hopewell architectural repertoire and the extent of the culture's influence.

Settlement and building activity in the Hopewell heartland of southern Ohio was concentrated in three regional clusters along the major south-flowing tributaries of the Ohio River—the two Miami Rivers in the west (named after the Myaamia Tribe, who lived in the area at the time of contact), the Scioto River (from the Wyandot *skeno-to,* meaning "deer"), and the Muskingum River (from the Shawnee *mshkikwam*—swampy ground).

MIAMI VALLEY REGION

In the Great and Little Miami River watersheds, hilltop works were dominant, notably Miami Fort, Fortified Hill, and the Pollock Works. Just east of what is now Cincinnati, though, along the Little Miami, a concentrated cluster of geometric sites included the Camden, Milford, and Turner Earthworks—all now gone. The Turner site held ritual artifacts on a par with those from Seip,

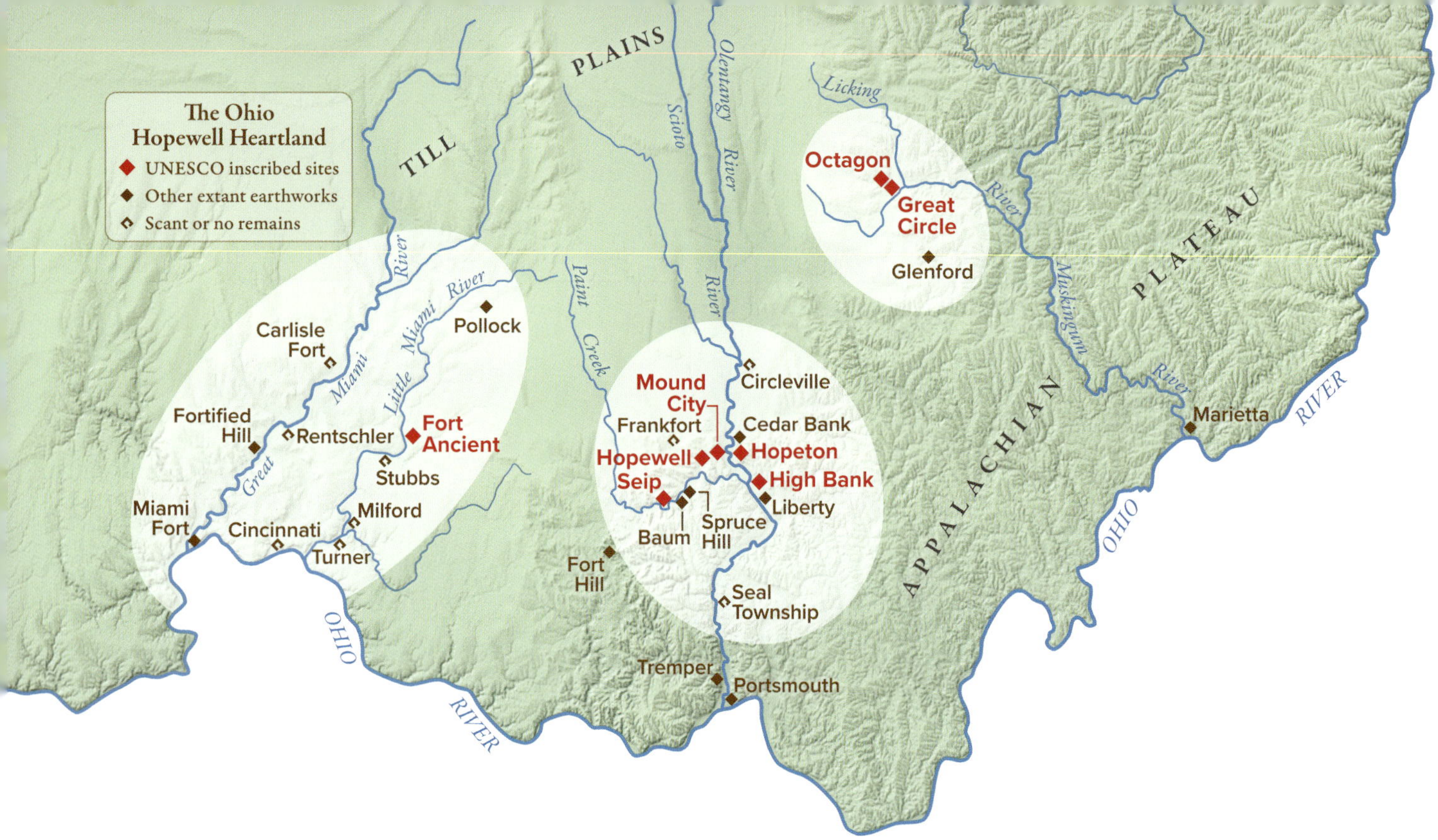

The Ohio Hopewell Heartland
UNESCO inscribed sites
Other extant earthworks
Scant or no remains

TILL PLAINS
APPALACHIAN PLATEAU
Great Miami River
Little Miami River
Paint Creek
Scioto River
Olentangy River
Licking River
Muskingum River
OHIO RIVER

Octagon
Great Circle
Glenford
Carlisle Fort
Pollock
Fortified Hill
Rentschler
Fort Ancient
Stubbs
Miami Fort
Cincinnati
Milford
Turner
Circleville
Mound City
Frankfort
Cedar Bank
Hopeton
Hopewell
Seip
High Bank
Liberty
Baum
Spruce Hill
Fort Hill
Seal Township
Tremper
Portsmouth
Marietta

Mound City, and Hopewell. Milford and Turner each had a distinctive bi-level design, where geometric figures at two different levels were connected by a walled corridor. The terrace where downtown Cincinnati now stands was also covered in geometric embankments, including an ellipse 500 feet across, and several large mounds.

At the Pollock Works, preserved in a Greene County park, a 300-foot-long earthen wall with three gateways gives access to a twelve-acre plateau otherwise ringed by sheer stone cliffs. For many years, beginning in 1981, excavations led by Robert Riordan of Wright State University revealed the details of its complex construction chronology, with several phases of wall building that included the erection, burning, and immediate burying of a massive timber palisade.

Miami Fort is a well-preserved hilltop enclosure in a county park west of Cincinnati. Walls up to seven feet high surround a high, steep-sided mesa about one-third the size of Fort Ancient. Sweeping views overlook the dramatic Great Miami and Ohio River confluence. Several of the earthwork's gateways appear to be associated with springs, and a cascade of constructed ponds hold water along the inside of the enclosure's western edge. At least some of the interior wall surfaces were faced with limestone slabs, while evidence of a burned timber palisade, as at Pollock, was found along the northern edge.

Fortified Hill surrounds a high hilltop overlooking a long stretch of the Great Miami River Valley near the city of Hamilton, Ohio. The 1836 map of

OPPOSITE, TOP: Hopewell settlement and earthwork building activities were mainly concentrated in three clusters within the culture's Ohio heartland.

OPPOSITE, BOTTOM: The Turner Earthworks were one of several geometric sites along the Little Miami River, all now lost among the eastern suburbs of Cincinnati.

RIGHT: Squier and Davis's lithograph of the Pollock Earthworks shows the plateau's western earthwork and its three gateways, with crescents (now lost) standing just outside.

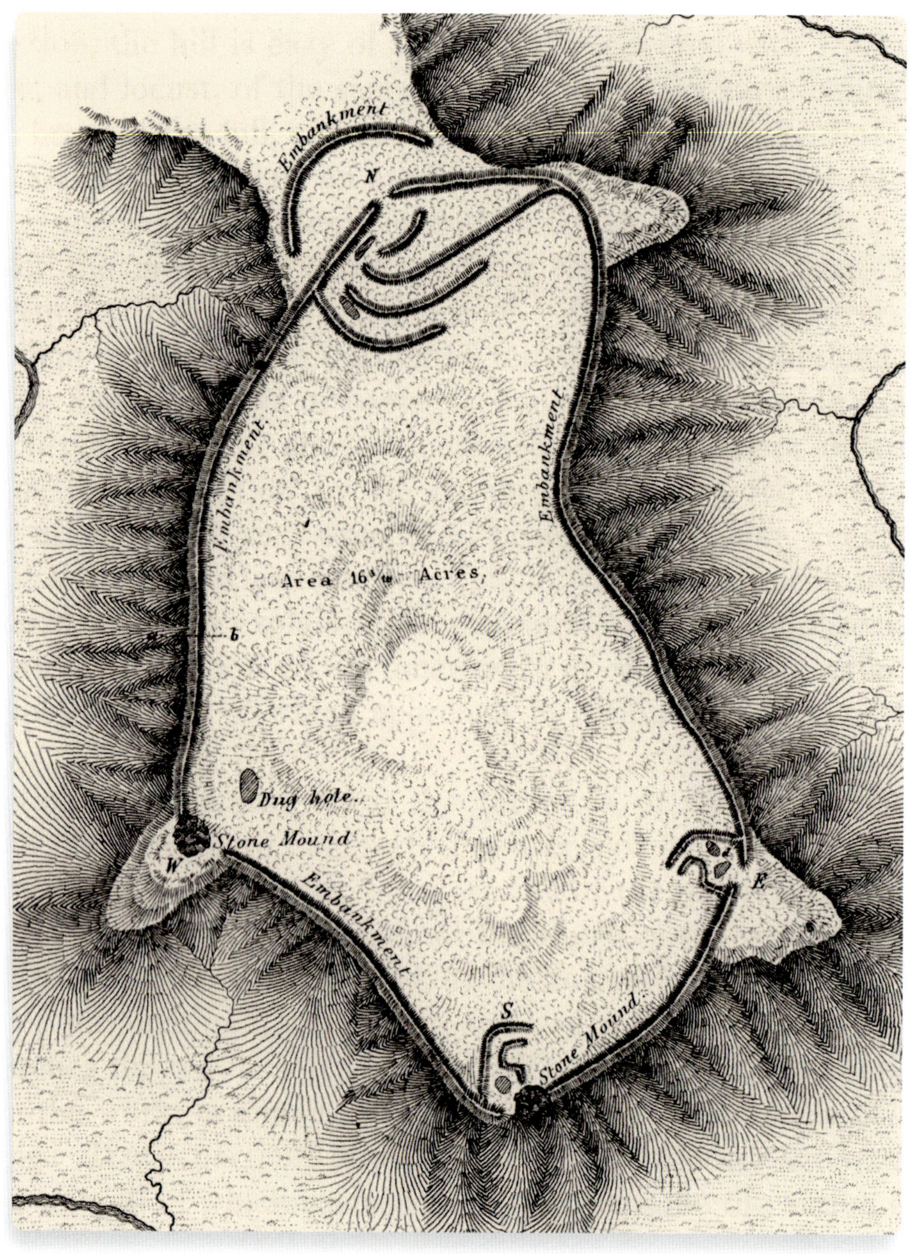

LEFT: James McBride's 1836 map of Fortified Hill shows three of the most unusual and elaborate earth-walled gateway designs known from anywhere in the Hopewell world.

OPPOSITE, TOP: A unique set of well-preserved ancient ponds step down along the inner margins of Miami Fort's western perimeter.

OPPOSITE, BOTTOM: Ramps climb from all four directions to the ten-foot-high rectangular platform of Marietta's Quadranaou Mound.

this eighteen-acre enclosure figured prominently in Squier and Davis's *Ancient Monuments of the Mississippi Valley*. Its most distinctive features are three unusually elaborate—even convoluted—gateways. The two smaller gates to the south and east reflect each other as mirror images—a rare bit of symmetry for a Hopewell hilltop enclosure. The East Gate remains especially well preserved, with a pond that still holds water.

MUSKINGUM WATERSHED REGION

Major earthwork building in the long Muskingum River system was limited to its point of confluence with the Ohio, where the elaborate Marietta Earthworks stood, and to the convergence of its upper tributaries in and near what is now Licking County. The Newark Earthworks were the only

significant geometric complex in this area, although there are several relatively small hilltop works. Also in the vicinity are the Flint Ridge quarries, yielding rainbow-colored stone that has been prized across eastern North America for more than 10,000 years; its proximity may help explain why the finest Hopewell architectural masterpiece was built on the nearest level terrace, eleven miles away at Newark.

Major elements of an extensive earthwork complex survive among the streets of Marietta—in 1788 the first European settlement in the Northwest Territories. This sprawling ensemble included two large, rectangular enclosures surrounding four flat-topped rectangular mounds—otherwise rare in Hopewell architecture (see map on page 30). The town's founders preserved several of the complex's features, giving them quaint Latin names to evoke their obvious yet enigmatic antiquity. Two of the platform mounds

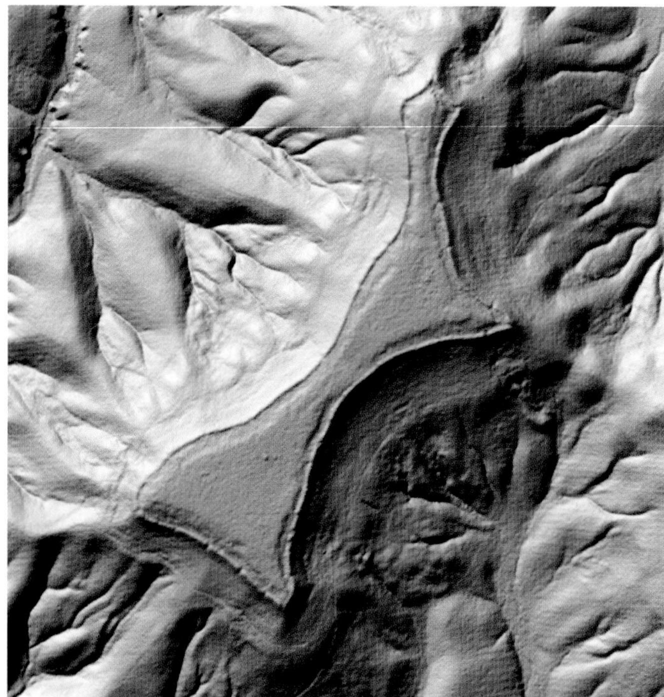

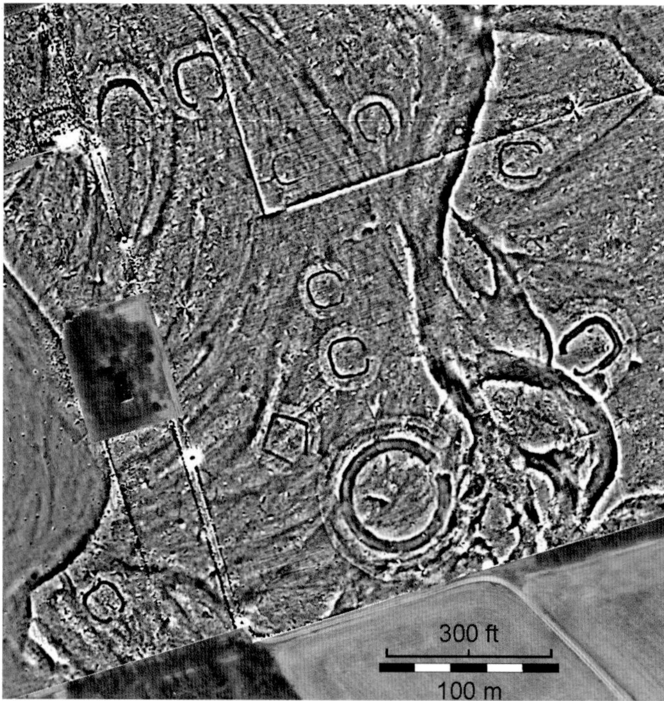

LEFT: A LiDAR image of Fort Hill captures its uniform earthen walls, gateways, and ditches tracing the plateau's perimeter.

RIGHT: A dense concentration of earthwork and posthole patterns appears in magnetic data from the Steel Group of Earthworks just outside Chillicothe.

became the "Quadranaou" and the "Capitolum." The large Adena-era mound, surrounded by its ditch and ring, they named the "Conus." A wide, ancient graded way connected the complex with the Muskingum River; even without its walls today, this "Sacra Via" remains the best surviving example of the monumental ramps that connected many of the Hopewell earthworks to their adjacent rivers.

SCIOTO–PAINT REGION

The lower Scioto valley contained by far the largest number of major geometric earthworks. These included, from north to south, Circleville, named after the now-destroyed work; the whole series of sites in the Chillicothe vicinity; the Seal Township Works about halfway from there to the Ohio confluence; the important Tremper Mound; and finally the elaborate Portsmouth complex, which extended across the Ohio River into Kentucky. West of Chillicothe, the valley of Paint Creek held Seip, Baum, and Spruce Hill, while along its North Fork were the now-lost Frankfort Works, as well as the Hopewell Mound Group.

Located in Highland County, Ohio, Fort Hill is one of the best-preserved examples of a Hopewell-era hilltop enclosure. A wall and ditch enclose a well-defined plateau about half the size of Fort Ancient. The site and its surroundings were never cleared for agriculture, so the stone-faced walls still rise as much as fifteen feet above their adjacent ditches amid the spectacular old-growth forests of a 1,200-acre nature preserve. Limited excavations since the 1950s have shed light on the enclosure's construction process and on Hopewell occupation and ceremonial structures in an adjacent valley.

Artist Herb Roe's digital image reconstructs the central area of the Portsmouth Earthworks, with its two horseshoe-shaped mounds.

A decade of magnetometer surveys have revealed the Steel Works, where Squier and Davis had recorded only two small circles, as the densest known cluster of enclosures in Ohio: thirteen earthworks include a circle, a crescent, a unique "kite" shape, many superellipses, and at least nine timber post circles—all within a thirty-seven-acre area. At nearby Junction Earthworks, a 600-foot open space is surrounded by interior-ditched circles, crescents, superellipses, and a unique "quatrefoil," with individual dimensions ranging from 50 to 165 feet (see magnetometry image on page 101). These concentrated groupings of relatively small yet extremely diverse architectural shapes invite speculation about different functions or communities and even suggest an interest in innovative forms for their own sake.

The Spruce Hill Works follow the rim of a prominent, flat-topped plateau overlooking Paint Creek just west of Chillicothe. Low, broad lines of piled sandstone enclose 140 acres, opening through a distinctive series of reentrant gateways at each end. Large chunks of vitrified soil from the plateau bear the imprints of crisscrossed logs—evidence of what must have been huge timber pyres, with roaring flames that would have been visible for miles up and down the valley. Prismatic bladelets and ceramics in and around the stone wall date its construction to the Hopewell era. Today, Spruce Hill is a unit of the Arc of Appalachia Preserve System.

The Portsmouth Earthworks once spread across the most prominent river confluence in the region, where the Scioto joins the Ohio and where a branch of the ancient Teays River system once took its dramatic turn northward. This sprawling complex of geometric figures included circles, squares, horseshoe shapes, and long, parallel-walled avenues on both banks of the Ohio River. These parallel lines, together with those at several other sites, suggest that such

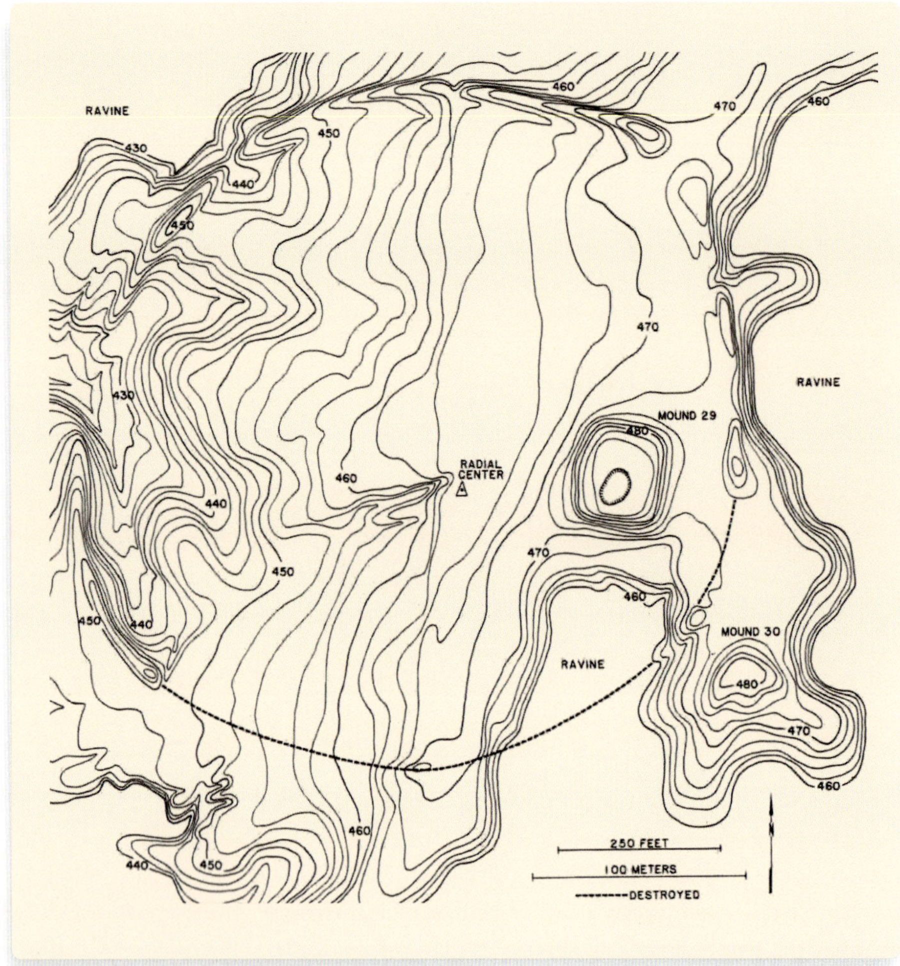

LEFT: An irregular circular enclosure and a very large superelliptical platform mound reflect Hopewell architectural influence at Tennessee's Pinson Mounds.

RIGHT: The interior ditch of the Anderson Mounds' small circular enclosure, called the Great Mound, still retains water.

roadways may have connected more of the earthwork sites than can now be determined.

Five miles above the Scioto–Ohio confluence, on the high western terrace, the irregularly shaped Tremper Mound stands within a 500-foot-wide oval earthwork (see photo on pages 178–179). The mound was built in the late first century BCE, relatively early in the Hopewell era, over the charred remains of a complex, multichambered ceremonial building. The floor of one room was strewn with broken pottery and animal bones, suggesting ceremonial feasts. Many cremated burials and large collections of deposited objects—many of them broken or burned—accompanied several fire basins. Most remarkable here was a set of 136 stone smoking pipes, sixty of which carried exquisite depictions of woodland creatures nearly identical to the ones from Mound City.

BEYOND OHIO

Several smaller Hopewell-influenced enclosure complexes have been recorded in east-central Indiana, of which only the Anderson Mounds are both well-preserved and publicly accessible. The most impressive of four prominent enclosures there is the Great Mound, a circular ditch and gated embankment, in effect a one-third scale replica—or perhaps, given its very early 100s BCE date, a precursor—of Newark's Great Circle. The nearby panduriform-shaped Fiddleback Enclosure covers about two-thirds of an acre. At some distance, an elongated, ditched, superelliptical enclosure orients along an east–west axis.

A huge complex of Hopewell-era mounds and earthworks occupied a high terrace near the confluence of the Wabash and Ohio rivers in extreme southwestern Indiana. Little remains visible today, but the volume of constructed earth at the Mann Site was comparable to the largest of the Ohio sites, and included many mounds, platforms, and enclosures. A loaf-shaped mound rivaled the volume of the Seip-Pricer Mound. The greatest quantity and diversity of exotic goods outside of the Hopewell Mound Group were found here, including pottery styles suggesting connections as far away as northern Florida. Magnetometry has detected a uniquely large concentration of habitation features (ovens, trash pits) across a 100-acre area, in sharp contrast with other Hopewell-influenced sites throughout the mid-continent region.

The Pinson Mounds stand today on Chickasaw tribal lands in southwestern Tennessee, with as many as thirty mounds and a roughly semicircular earthwork comparable in size to Mound City. The entire complex includes habitation areas and related earthworks spreading over nearly 400 acres. Exotic materials and artifacts point to the builders' participation in the wide Hopewell interaction networks. Several of Pinson's mounds are among the largest from the period, and some appear to form equinox and solstice alignments. The site includes some of the best evidence for the use of rectangular, flat-topped mounds as stages for Hopewell-era rituals and ceremonies.

Across the geographic reach of Hopewell interaction, among otherwise diverse cultural groups and otherwise varied landscapes, many other places throughout the eastern half of the continent reflect the Hopewell tradition's ceremonial and artistic practices, earth-building repertoire, and other cultural influences.

ILLINOIS HOPEWELL

Many of the things that have come to define the Hopewell tradition appeared first in the Illinois River Valley as early as 150 BCE, even though the dramatic explosion of architectural, artistic, and ceremonial elaboration developed nearly two centuries later in southern Ohio. The Illinois Valley groups (now called Havana Hopewell) did not build geometric earthworks, though they had a long and vibrant tradition of mound building. Groupings of burial mounds, some arranged in lines or crescents, are spread throughout the region, such as the Ogden-Fettie site, Albany Mounds, and the Toolesboro Mound Group in nearby Iowa.

The honored dead were buried in log-lined crypts with symbols and regalia including platform pipes and zoned stamped ceramics. Exotic copper celts and drilled bear canines indicate their already-widening spheres of influence and interaction. These materials, symbols, and practices are the clear forerunners of the brilliant Hopewell fluorescence in the Ohio Valley. Some scholars suggest that Havana Hopewell culture was also ancestral to the Mississippians—the builders of nearby Cahokia a thousand years later.

Artist Martin Pate illustrates the UNESCO-inscribed Monumental Earthworks of Poverty Point. Concentric segmented arcs frame a large plaza; behind stands the huge, terraced Mound A.

16.

GLOBAL SIGNIFICANCE

The Hopewell Ceremonial Earthworks give testimony to a distinctive cultural tradition, and to the genius of its leaders and architects. Global comparisons help to clarify that distinctiveness and that genius in two contexts: first, among the other monumental earthwork building cultures of Indigenous North America, and second, among examples of comparable works by other nonurban cultures around the world. Those comparisons highlight the rare achievement of Ohio's Indigenous ancestors—that a dispersed, mixed-economy, nonhierarchical society created a series of vast public works with unequalled geometrical and astronomical precision.

OTHER NORTH AMERICAN EARTHWORKS

Indigenous cultures in the greater Mississippi and Ohio valleys have been building earthworks for nearly 6,000 years. The oldest of these monuments predates the Egyptian pyramids, and some southern tribes are still building mounds today. Among all these earth-building cultures, however, both before and after, the precision and scale of the Hopewell achievement are uniquely spectacular.

The oldest North American earthworks are in what is now northern Louisiana. At a place called Watson Brake, an Indigenous earthwork complex arose around 3500 BCE—before Egypt's pyramids or England's Stonehenge. Over several centuries, a hunter-gatherer society built an oval perimeter embankment about 900 feet across, connecting eleven mounds from three to twenty-three feet high. People occupied the site seasonally, then abandoned it by about 2800 BCE. It appears to be completely discontinuous with all later cultural or architectural traditions.

About 1,200 years later, also in northern Louisiana, another monumental center arose—the work of a hunter-fisher-gatherer society whose influence extended across the Mississippi River and down to the Gulf of Mexico. The elaborate earthwork complex at Poverty Point (inscribed on the World Heritage List in 2014) is a singular achievement in earthen construction. Its five sets of roughly parallel, concentric walls surround a plaza about 2,000 feet across. The site's focal point, Mound A, is the second largest mound in North America, and some evidence suggests it could have been built in as few as ninety days—another example of remarkable Indigenous labor mobilization. Most artifacts from this culture were made from local clay and soils, though some materials also suggest a network ranging as far as Ohio (flint), Iowa (galena),

and the southern Appalachians (copper). Poverty Point predates the Hopewell Ceremonial Earthworks by 1,500 years, and despite the presence of Ohio flint, there is no apparent continuity or similarity in earthen architecture across these wide gaps of time and territory.

Cahokia, the largest precontact urban and mound center in North America north of Mexico, thrived during the Mississippian period (900–1350 CE). This city (inscribed on the World Heritage list in 1982) reached its peak between 1000 and 1200—nearly a full millennium after Hopewell. Grand plazas and gridded streets sprawled across more than 4,000 acres and housed at least 20,000 people. The massive Monk's Mound towered 100 feet above the largest plaza, crowned by the lavish temple-palace of the city's powerful hereditary ruler. Just east of Saint Louis in today's Illinois, Cahokia was the greatest of several similar "Temple Towns" in the central Mississippi Valley region whose urban populations were hierarchically organized and dependent on a vast, networked, maize-growing empire. Unlike Hopewell leaders of a thousand years earlier,

ABOVE: In L. K. Townsend's painting of the city of Cahokia, the ruler's palace dominates the city from atop the giant Monk's Mound, which in turn dominated a vast agricultural empire.

RIGHT, TOP: Low afternoon sunlight helps reveal Granville's Alligator Mound. The head, paws, and spiraling tail suggest the Beneath World's Underwater Panther.

RIGHT: Animal-shaped mounds ranging from 70 to 100 feet long line up along the narrow ridgetops of Iowa's Effigy Mounds National Monument, visible here in LiDAR imagery.

these Mississippian chiefs had the authority to compel followers to undertake earthwork and city-building projects.

Also between 900 and 1200 CE, Indigenous groups along the upper Mississippi River, mainly in Iowa and Wisconsin, were living in small settlements and raising both maize and domesticated native plants. They built burial mounds and linear embankments as well as small effigy mounds in the shapes of various animals, including birds, bears, and panthers. Clusters or linear groups of these earthen creatures could stretch up to 1,600 feet and cover up to seven acres. The largest single effigy is the Great Bear Mound, 140 feet long and just over three feet high.

Around 1100 CE, Ohio's Mississippian-influenced Fort Ancient culture was also building effigies—although singular ones rather than clusters. The two major examples appear to represent the powerful creatures of the watery Beneath World—the Alligator Mound near Granville and the world-famous Great Serpent near Peebles. The alligator is probably misnamed; it more likely

The head of the Serpent Mound, receding beyond its three main coils in this image, aligns approximately to the setting sun on the summer solstice.

ABOVE, LEFT: Geometric earthworks hidden beneath the Amazon jungle for more than 2,500 years have come to light since the 1990s, with uncanny similarities to the Hopewell sites.

ABOVE, RIGHT: Ceremonial facilities at Göbekli Tepe in Türkiye are among the earliest known monumental structures in the world, and like the Hopewell sites are the work of a nonurban society.

represents the Underwater Panther reflected in Mississippian iconography of the time. The creature shares its spiraling tail motif with Ohio's much more famous Serpent Mound—indeed, these two mythical creatures were often one and the same.

At more than 1,400 feet long, Ohio's Great Serpent Mound is the largest securely documented effigy mound known from the ancient world. Its most persuasive date, around 1100 CE, would make it another work of the Fort Ancient culture, contemporary with both the Effigy Mounds and Cahokia. The creature's three coils wind between its spiraling tail and enigmatic head, both of which stand above sheer cliffs. Contrasting depictions on nineteenth-century maps have inspired various interpretations of the head shape—as the mouth, the Sun or Moon, an egg, or a frog. Most recently, Mississippian iconographic evidence suggests it may be the womb of First Mother during her mating with the underwater Great Serpent at the creation of the world. Though both impressive and beautiful in its undulating form, Serpent Mound is considerably smaller than the Hopewell-era earthworks, its geometry is imprecise, and claims of astronomical alignments involve considerable margins of error.

Building with earth has been a long, though probably discontinuous, tradition across Indigenous eastern North America for thousands of years. The varieties reflect separations by vast stretches of time, distance, and cultural difference. Among them, the Hopewell Ceremonial Earthworks are a unique manifestation—unlike and largely unrelated to any other Indigenous monument-building culture on the continent. They are far more widespread than those of the earlier Poverty Point culture, far larger than those of the later effigy building cultures, and far more formally sophisticated than either. The Hopewell era's dispersed egalitarian societies are entirely different from the more urban and hierarchical Mississippian cities such as Cahokia (or for that matter, the stone-building southwestern Chaco culture). The combination of a nonurban society with such advanced and widespread earthwork-building expertise is unmatched by any precontact region or period in North America.

ABOVE: Ritual features at the Oyu Stone Circles, one of many Jomon sites in northern Japan, included wooden-post buildings, graves, and storage pits, arranged concentrically outside rings of large river stones.

BELOW: The stone towers of the Chankillo Astronomical Complex crown a ridge high in the Peruvian mountains, calibrating the Sun's rising and setting positions throughout the year.

COMPARABLE GLOBAL SITES

Other sites around the world share some of the attributes of the Hopewell Ceremonial Earthworks: monumental architecture with at least some degree of geometrical and astronomical sophistication and created by nonurban, nonhierarchical societies. Examining some of these other works also helps to put the unique achievement of Ohio's American Indian ancestors into perspective.

In the Amazon regions of western Brazil and northern Bolivia, more than 500 geometric earthworks have been uncovered since the late 1990s. A concentration in Brazil, the Geoglyphs of Acre, dates from 950 to 400 BCE and includes circles, rectangles, squares, and composite figures, often with ditches. Some have parallel-walled roads linking enclosures to each other or to a nearby river. Though they are about half the size, they bear a striking resemblance to Ohio's earthworks in both form and function. Scholars suggest that they too were ceremonial centers, where small, otherwise disparate, nonresident communities gathered for feasts and rituals, cementing relationships around a common set of religious beliefs and practices.

Among the world's earliest known examples of nonurban monumental architecture is Göbekli Tepe in southeastern Türkiye. A series of roughly circular megalithic structures, thirty-five to fifty feet in diameter, date from 9000 BCE. Inside each circle stand twelve decorated, T-shaped limestone pillars up to twelve feet tall, the largest of them decorated with naturalistic bas-reliefs of birds, boars, foxes, snakes, and spiders. No large settlements have been found nearby, so although much more intimately scaled than the Ohio earthworks, Göbekli Tepe shares with them the unusual combination of well-crafted, monumental ceremonial architecture created by a society of egalitarian hunter-gatherers experimenting with agriculture.

Even earlier, beginning nearly 15,000 years ago, the Jomon culture created large-scale ceremonial architecture across the northern Honshu and southern Hokkaido regions of Japan, including shell mounds and stone circles up

Five of Mound City's central mounds are silhouetted by the glow of the late afternoon sun.

to 170 feet across. Their sedentary yet nonagricultural society thrived in the rich ecological diversity offered by abundant forests, waterways, and seacoasts. They maintained long-term settlements and developed a complex spiritual life, expressed in masterful artistry and elaborate burials. Like the Hopewell earthworks—though again much smaller—their circular enclosures held ceremonies for ritual bonding among settlement groups and across generations, and for the assurance of nature's continued abundance.

Sophisticated ancient sky watching, meanwhile, is evident at the Chankillo Astronomical Complex, built between 350 and 150 BCE as a ceremonial and administrative center in the Peruvian highlands. Thirteen mortared-stone towers positioned along a prominent ridge create precise horizon markers for the movements of the sunset and sunrise, when viewed from two observation points directly to the east and west. They precisely mark off units in a complete seasonal cycle—important for a hierarchical economy dependent on intensive maize and potato cultivation.

The world's best-known ancient astronomy site is of course Stonehenge in southern England. Built between 3100 and 1600 BCE, its nested circles and arcs of megalithic pillars align clearly to the summer solstice sunrise and surround the center of a circular ditch and bank half the diameter of Newark's Great Circle. The nearby ring of Avebury encloses the largest ancient stone circle in the world and more nearly resembles the Great Circle in both form and size. Parallel-walled embankments connected the site to nearby rivers; timber post circles stood nearby. These sites all suggest an equivalent cosmology, linking the order of the Earth (geometry) with the order of the Sky (astronomy). Yet although the summer solstice sunrise and southern maximum moonset alignments at Stonehenge are convincing, other claims for the site's astronomical or geometrical properties are less so.

GLOBAL SIGNIFICANCE

Many key attributes of the Hopewell Ceremonial Earthworks are reflected in monuments built by other ancient civilizations around the world. Geometric ordering as a means of marking space, astronomical alignment as a means of marking time, monumentality as a means of framing community rituals—these features may be nearly universal among the world's human cultures.

The earthworks remaining from Ohio's Indigenous ancestors add their own material brilliance to this story. Hopewell-era people gathered from their scattered settlements to design, build, and use some of the most elaborate masterpieces of ancient geometry and earthen architecture anywhere. They recorded and marked the Moon's complex movements more thoroughly than any other ancient culture. Their earthworks, ceremonies, and charismatic leaders drew visitors from hundreds of miles away. They created lavishly ornamented rituals and regalia with meanings and symbols that influenced much of the continent. Themes in their lives and works continue to resonate among their modern American Indian descendants.

For their eloquent testimony to the genius of their builders and the ever-unfolding legacy of their brilliant culture, the Hopewell Ceremonial Earthworks were inscribed in 2023 as a UNESCO World Heritage property—affirming their Outstanding Universal Value to all of humanity.

CONTRIBUTOR BIOGRAPHIES

ABOUT THE AUTHOR

John E. Hancock is professor emeritus of architecture at the University of Cincinnati, where he taught architectural history, theory, and design for four decades. His academic research and international publications have explored the phenomenology of architecture—the nature of interpretation and environmental experience, especially related to premodern places. His former students hold leadership positions in architectural education and practice throughout the world. Since the mid-1990s, he has produced a series of multimedia exhibits and publications on the ancient earthworks of the Ohio Valley. Supported by multiple grants from the National Endowment for the Humanities, these works combine storytelling media from digital animation and multivoiced interviews to augmented reality. He served as a principal author, photographer, and designer of the earthworks' UNESCO nomination dossier, in collaboration with the Ohio History Connection and the US National Park Service.

PRINCIPAL PROJECT TEAM

Marti L. Chaatsmith (Comanche/Choctaw) is the associate director of the Newark Earthworks Center (NEC) at Ohio State University at Newark. She cofounded the NEC and developed the first outreach program to tribal governments in Oklahoma with encouragement from Chief Glenna J. Wallace (Eastern Shawnee Tribe of Oklahoma), resulting in collaborative relationships and programs. She brought key Indigenous themes and voices to the Hopewell Ceremonial Earthworks UNESCO World Heritage nomination. Her research and public outreach efforts focus on Indigenous-centered scholarship emphasizing connections between the people who built the earthworks and Indigenous people today.

Bradley T. Lepper is the senior curator of archaeology for the Ohio History Connection's World Heritage Program. He earned his PhD from Ohio State University. His areas of specialization include the earliest ancestors of America's Indigenous people who first entered this continent sometime before 16,000 years ago, and the American Indian Hopewell culture of 2,000 years ago. As the leading authority on the archaeology and history of the Newark Earthworks and Fort Ancient, he played a pivotal role throughout the Hopewell Ceremonial Earthworks UNESCO World Heritage inscription process. He is the principal author of *Ohio Archaeology: An Illustrated Chronicle of Ohio's Ancient American Indian Cultures*, which received the Society for American Archaeology's Public Audience Book Award in 2007.

Bret J. Ruby retired in 2024 after thirty years as an archaeologist for the National Park Service and the US Army. Most of his career was devoted to research, management, and public outreach at Hopewell Culture National Historical Park in Chillicothe, Ohio. He brought his deep knowledge of its earthwork sites and other archaeological assets to the UNESCO inscription effort. He has a keen interest in the ancient and modern histories of American Indian peoples, with a primary focus on the archaeology of the Hopewell tradition. His key research areas include remote sensing, subsistence and settlement patterns, community organization, craft production, and interregional interaction. He holds a BA in anthropology from Kent State University and a PhD in anthropology from Indiana University.

SELECTED FURTHER READING

GENERAL WORKS AND OVERVIEWS

Atwater, Caleb. "Description of the Antiquities Discovered in the State of Ohio and Other Western States." *Transactions and Collections of the American Antiquarian Society* 1 (1820): 105–267. The first systematic survey of Ohio's major earthwork sites, with extensive descriptions and maps of the sites as they appeared during the earliest years of colonial settlement. Reprint: Commonwealth Book Company, 2022.

Bernardini, Wesley. "Hopewell Geometric Earthworks: A Case Study in the Referential and Experiential Meaning of Monuments." *Journal of Anthropological Archaeology* 23, no. 3 (2004): 331–56. A discussion of Hopewell-era labor mobilization, leadership, and community organization based on earthwork soil volumes, transport, populations, and site spacings. Online at: doi.org/10.1016/j.jaa.2004.06.001.

Byers, A. Martin, and DeeAnne Wymer, editors. *Hopewell Settlement Patterns, Subsistence Systems, & Symbolic Landscapes*. Gainesville: University Press of Florida, 2010. A wide-ranging collection of essays and commentaries (with expansive bibliographies) by many of the leading Hopewell scholars. Bradley T. Lepper's contribution considers the Newark Earthworks in the context of other sites in the broader landscape and their possible uses for procession and pilgrimage. Ray Hively and Robert Horn's "Hopewell Cosmography at Newark and Chillicothe, Ohio" explains possible relationships between the major earthwork clusters and their larger landscape contexts.

Carr, Christopher, and D. Troy Case. *Gathering Hopewell: Society, Ritual, and Ritual Interaction*. New York: Kluwer Academic/Plenum, 2005. A collection of papers aiming to humanize the archaeological record of the Hopewell era by reconstructing social personas, leadership roles, ritual gatherings, rites of passage, spiritual beliefs, and inter-regional interactions. Bret J. Ruby, Christopher Carr, and Douglas K. Charles offer "Community Organizations in the Scioto, Mann, and Havana Hopewellian Regions: A Comparative Perspective," which studies cemeteries, ceremonial centers, and settlements in three core regions of Hopewell expression, with important insights into community organizations, subsistence economies, and ecological relationships.

Charles, Douglas K., and Jane E. Buikstra, editors. *Recreating Hopewell*. Gainesville: University Press of Florida, 2006. Another major collection of essays by leading archaeologists, including Bradley T. Lepper's "The Great Hopewell Road and the Role of the Pilgrimage in the Hopewell Interaction Sphere," explaining the discovery, evidence, extent, and cultural implications of the theorized straight route between ancient Newark and Chillicothe.

Hancock, John E. *Traveler's Guide to Ancient Ohio*. Athens and Cincinnati: University of Cincinnati and Ohio University Press, 2026. An illustrated guide for touring most of the publicly accessible mound and earthwork sites in southern Ohio, including the Hopewell Ceremonial Earthworks, in their current settings among historic towns, nature preserves, and scenic routes, augmented by interdisciplinary and Indigenous perspectives.

———, preparer. "Hopewell Ceremonial Earthworks" (UNESCO World Heritage nomination text), 2023. Summary descriptions, histories, and justifications of the eight UNESCO-inscribed earthwork sites in relation to the criteria of the World Heritage Convention, along with information on site ownership, legal protections, and management; an extensive bibliography is organized by site. Online at: whc.unesco.org/en/list/1689/documents/.

Kennedy, Roger. *Hidden Cities: The Discovery and Loss of Ancient North American Civilization*. New York: Free Press, 1994. A history of the encounters between the founders of the United States and the earthworks, considering their early interpretations, the later progress of research, and the fate of the sites, by the former director of the Smithsonian's National Museum of American History and the National Park Service.

Lepper, Bradley T. *Ohio Archaeology: An Illustrated Chronicle of Ohio's Ancient American Indian Cultures.* Wilmington, OH: Orange Frazer, 2005. An illustrated, general audience survey of archaeological practice and knowledge covering all the periods of Ohio's Indigenous inhabitation, including engaging accounts of the Adena, Hopewell, and Fort Ancient–era earthworks, cultures, and artistry.

Lynott, Mark J. *Hopewell Ceremonial Landscapes of Ohio: More than Mounds and Geometric Earthworks.* Oxford: Oxbow Books, 2014. A thorough survey of the archaeological studies at the principal Hopewell earthwork sites by one of the National Park Service's foremost archaeologists, featuring in-depth descriptions of his detailed studies at the Hopeton Earthworks.

Mills, William C. *Archaeological Atlas of Ohio.* Columbus: Ohio State Archaeological and Historical Society, 1915. Detailed, county-by-county descriptions and maps locating hundreds of mounds and enclosures throughout Ohio known at the time, many of which have now disappeared, compiled by one of the foremost archaeologists in the history of Ohio.

Redmond, Brian G., Bret J. Ruby, and Jarrod Burks, editors. *Encountering Hopewell in the Twenty-First Century: Ohio and Beyond,* vol. 1: *Monuments and Ceremony.* Akron: University of Akron Press, 2019. A collection of essays showcasing new work in Hopewell studies from the turn of the twenty-first century. Topics include remote sensing, archaeoastronomy, Native ontologies, and ritual iconography. Bret Ruby's contribution discusses the Hopewell Mound Group's large post circle in relation to Indigenous traditions. Robert Riordan's essay tells of finding, studying, and interpreting Fort Ancient's Moorehead Circle. Online at: ideaexchange.uakron.edu/encountering_hopewell/.

Redmond, Brian G., Bret J. Ruby, and Jarrod Burks, editors. *Encountering Hopewell in the Twenty-First Century: Ohio and Beyond,* vol. 2: *Settlements, Foodways, and Interaction.* Akron: University of Akron Press, 2020. A collection of essays showcasing the state of the art in Hopewell studies from the turn of the twenty-first century, highlighting settlements, food production, raw material acquisition, and inter-regional interactions. Mark Seeman's concluding essay, "Twenty-First Century Hopewell," summarizes the developing methods, questions, directions, and findings in the study of Hopewell earthworks and society. Online at: ideaexchange.uakron.edu/encountering_hopewell/.

Romain, William. *Mysteries of the Hopewell: Astronomers, Geometers, and Magicians of the Eastern Woodlands.* Akron: University of Akron Press, 2000. A presentation of innovative and sometimes speculative discussions about the astronomical relationships, geometric ordering, and measurement principles used in the earthworks, and their possible uses and meanings for their builders.

Squier, Ephraim, and Edwin Davis. *Ancient Monuments of the Mississippi Valley: Comprising the Results of Extensive Original Surveys & Explorations.* Smithsonian Contributions to Knowledge 1. Washington, DC: Smithsonian Institution, 1848. The indispensable, magisterial first publication of the Smithsonian Institution filled with beautiful lithographs of the Hopewell earthworks and some of their artistry, descriptions of their form and condition at the time, and speculations about their origins and uses. Reprinted with an introduction by David J. Meltzer, Smithsonian Institution Press, 1998.

Thomas, Cyrus. *Report on the Mound Explorations of the Bureau of Ethnology.* Twelfth annual report, 1890–91. Washington, DC: Smithsonian Institution, Bureau of Ethnology, 1894. Four decades after Squier and Davis's *Ancient Monuments,* this extensive report added precision to its earlier findings, described many more mound and earthwork remains from various periods in nearly all eastern states, and settled the question of their Indigenous origins.

INDIGENOUS AND INTERDISCIPLINARY THEMES

Allen, Chadwick. *Earthworks Rising: Mound Building in Native Literature and Arts*. Minneapolis: University of Minnesota Press, 2022. A contemporary study connecting Indigenous earthen architecture to precolonial settlements through arts analysis and demonstrating their sustained meanings and future interpretive capacities by centering Native voices.

Barnes, Benjamin, and Stephen Warren. *Replanting Cultures: Community-Engaged Scholarship in Indian Country*. New York: SUNY Press, 2022. A presentation of models for respectful, collaborative research between Indigenous tribal nations and academic institutions, scholars, and museums.

Barnes, Benjamin J., and Bradley T. Lepper. "Drums along the Scioto: Interpreting Hopewell Material Culture through the Lens of Contemporary American Indian Ceremonial Practices." *Archaeologies* 14, no. 1 (2018): 62–84. An essay detailing the authors' joint, collaborative research reinterpreting five round stones from the Seip Earthworks in light of contemporary Native American knowledge.

Blaeser, Kimberly. *Copper Yearning: Poems by Kimberly Blaeser*. Duluth, MN: Holy Cow! Press, 2020. A collection of vivid, evocative poetry about earthworks, various watery domains, and their meanings to Indigenous audiences, opening to the worlds of nature, history, justice, mythic truth, and the uncanny.

Bowes, John P. *Land Too Good for Indians: Northern Indian Removal*. Norman: University of Oklahoma Press, 2016. An account of the removal of Wyandotte, Seneca-Cayugas, Delaware, Potawatomi, Odawa, and Ojibwa peoples from the old northwest (essentially the modern states of Ohio, Illinois, Michigan, and Indiana), including Indigenous perspectives.

Chaatsmith, Marti. "Singing at a Center of the Indian World: The SAI and Ohio Earthworks." Society of American Indians and Its Legacies, a joint special issue of *American Indian Quarterly* 37, no. 3 and *Studies in American Indian Literatures* 25, no. 2 (Summer 2013): 181–98. From the Society of American Indians' Centennial Symposium in 2011, this article discusses the group's visit to the Newark Earthworks and the changes that had taken place during the century since the organization was founded. Online at: doi.org/10.1353/aiq.2013.0038.

Deloria Jr., Vine. *God is Red: A Native View of Religion* (Thirtieth Anniversary Edition). Lakewood, CO: Fulcrum, 2003. A comparison of Native religious views with the dominant world religions, raising profound questions about our humanity and our ultimate fate and reminding us "that we are a part of nature, not a transcendent species with no responsibilities to the natural world."

Echo-Hawk, Roger C. "Ancient History in the New World: Integrating Oral Traditions and the Archaeological Record in Deep Time." *American Antiquity* 65 no. 2 (2000): 267–90. An approach to implementing interpretive partnerships of Indigenous oral histories with archaeological or historical data, as both forms of knowledge provide complementary perspectives on a shared past.

Ellingson, Erica, and Fabio Silva. "The Major Lunar Standstill Season is Here!" *Journal of Skyscape Archaeology* 9, no. 2 (2024): 281–88. An accessible explanation of the astronomical relationships among the movements of the Sun, Moon, and Earth, and how they produce the long and complex patterns of the observable lunar cycle. Online at: doi.org/10.1558/jsa.28181.

Hall, Robert L. *An Archaeology of the Soul: North American Indian Belief and Ritual*. Urbana: University of Illinois Press, 1997. A scholar of Mohican descent offers powerful insights into the richness and complexity of Native American spiritual belief across the Midwest and Plains, with roots going back three thousand years, examined through history, archaeology, anthropology, linguistics, and mythology.

Jones, Lindsay, and Richard D. Shiels. *The Newark Earthworks: Enduring Monuments, Contested Meanings*. Charlottesville: University of Virginia Press, 2016. A diverse collection of essays covering the growing knowledge and expanding interdisciplinary interests around the Newark Earthworks, from archaeological, astronomical, architectural, Indigenous, and international perspectives.

Kimmerer, Robin Wall. *Braiding Sweetgrass: Indigenous Wisdom, Scientific Knowledge, and the Teachings of Plants.* Minneapolis: Milkweed Editions, 2015. Connects Anishinaabe traditions to sustainable ecology, especially in the Eastern Woodlands, presenting Indigenous knowledge as an alternative or complementary approach to Western scientific methods.

Marshall, James. "An Atlas of American Indian Geometry." *Ohio Archaeologist* 37, no. 2 (1987): 36–49. A detailed conjectural analysis of predominant dimensions found in Hopewell architecture and the author's derivation of a consistent system of units relating the sides to the diagonals of squares.

Stockwell, Mary. *The Other Trail of Tears: The Removal of the Ohio Indians.* Yardley, PA: Westholme, 2016. A popular history of the factors, complexities, and tragedies of tribal removal from Ohio following the War of 1812, the death of Tecumseh, the failure of his confederacy's resistance, and the accelerated rate of changes in the region.

Townsend, Richard F., and Robert V. Sharp, editors. *Hero, Hawk, and Open Hand: American Indian Art of the Ancient Midwest and South.* Chicago and New Haven: Art Institute of Chicago and Yale University Press, 2004. A beautifully illustrated presentation of works of artistry from the ancient American Midwest and Southeast, presented in their cultural contexts and in light of themes and rituals continuing today among Indigenous communities. Mark Seeman's "Hopewell Art in Hopewell Places" discusses the elaborate regalia of the earthwork builders as evidence of the society's social structure and the acquisition of various types of leadership. George E. Lankford's contribution reads the ethnographic literature of postcontact tribes to interpret Native pottery and engraved shell masterpieces from the Mississippian period as expressions of the Native American cosmos. F. Kent Reilly III's "People of Earth, People of Sky: Visualizing the Sacred in Native American Art of the Mississippian Period" provides an accessible account of pre-contact Native cosmology from an archaeological and ethnographic perspective. Bradley T. Lepper's essay presents an overview and orientation to the Newark sites with emphasis on their geometrical and astronomical properties.

Volker, John J. "The Geometry of the Newark Earthworks." Published online 2025. An analysis of the shared dimensions, areas, and perimeters of ancient Newark's principal figures, with consideration of possible layout methods using empirical geometry. Online at: ohioarchaeology.org/file_download/inline/c4c66d52-46f0-4f0a-a428-e90eb4b170b1.

Wali, Alaka, and Tom Skwerski. *The Future is Indigenous: Stories from the New Native North America Hall at the Field Museum.* Oxford: British Archaeological Reports, 2024. Multi-voiced accounts of Indigenous collaboration in creating the Field Museum's 2018 exhibit, with transformative perspectives on museum curation, and new practices honoring Native communities, worldviews, and contemporary concerns.

Weiser, M. Elizabeth, Timothy R. W. Jordan, and Richard D. Shiels. *The Fertile Earth and the Ordered Cosmos: Reflections on the Newark Earthworks and World Heritage.* Columbus: Ohio State University Press, 2023. A varied collection of short articles about the significance and experience of the Newark sites and the other Hopewell Ceremonial Earthworks, mainly by participants in the UNESCO World Heritage nomination process.

INDEX

IMAGE CREDITS

t = top, *b* = bottom, *m* = middle, *r* = right, *l* = left

All photographs not listed below are by John E. Hancock.

2–3: Photo by Timothy E. Black; **5*m***, **5*b***: Photo by Steven W. Plattner; **6**: © AECOM 2010, photo by David Lloyd; **8**: Photo by Steven W. Plattner; **12**: Photo by Timothy E. Black; **14*l***, **19*t***: From Ephraim Squier and Edwin Davis, *Ancient Monuments of the Mississippi Valley: Comprising the Results of Extensive Original Surveys & Explorations*. Smithsonian Contributions to Knowledge 1. Washington, DC: Smithsonian Institution, 1848; **19*b***: US Department of Agriculture; **22–23**: Photo by Matthew Traucht; **26**, **27*t***, **27*l***: Cartography by Mike Boruta; **27*r***: From Squier and Davis, *Ancient Monuments*; **29*b***: Artwork by Talon Silverhorn; **30**: From Squier and Davis, *Ancient Monuments*; **35*l***: From Charles C. Willoughby, 1892; **35*r***, **37**, **38**: Artworks by Talon Silverhorn; **40**: From Charles C. Willoughby and Earnest A. Hooton, *The Turner Group of Earthworks*. Cambridge, MA: Peabody Museum Press, 1922; **41**: Artwork by Talon Silverhorn; **46**: From Squier and Davis, *Ancient Monuments*; **48**: Courtesy American Antiquarian Society; **50**: Courtesy Ohio History Connection; **52**: From Squier and Davis, *Ancient Monuments*; **54**: National Park Service; **56–57**: Photo by Steven W. Plattner; **58**: Photo by Bradley T. Lepper; **60**: Courtesy American Antiquarian Society; **63**: Artwork by Talon Silverhorn; **64*b***: Courtesy of the author; **65**: From Squier and Davis, *Ancient Monuments*; **66**: Courtesy Ohio History Connection; **68*l***: Cartography by Mike Boruta; **68*r***: After Ray Hively and Robert Horn, from Lindsay Jones and Richard D. Shiels, "The Newark Earthworks: Enduring Monuments, Contested Meanings. Charlottesville: University of Virginia Press, 2016; **70–71**: Photo by Timothy E. Black; **72*t***, **72*b***: Courtesy Ohio History Connection; **75**: Courtesy of the author; **78*l***: Cartography by Mike Boruta; **79**: Courtesy of the author; **80–81**: Photo by Timothy E. Black; **83*t***: Courtesy of the author; **84*t***: Courtesy American Antiquarian Society; **84*b***, **86**: Courtesy Ohio History Connection; **89**: Photo by Marek Ropella, Pixabay; **90**: Adapted from Squier and Davis, *Ancient Monuments*; **92*l***: Cartography by Mike Boruta; **92*r***: National Park Service image by Andrew Weiland; **93*l***: National Park Service photo by Mark J. Lynott; **93*r***: Courtesy of the author; **94–95**: Photo by Bret J. Ruby; **97*l***: National Park Service and *Deutsches Archäologisches Institut*; **97*r***: From Squier and Davis, *Ancient Monuments*; **98**: National Park Service photo by Tom Engberg; **99**: National Park Service photo by Susan Knisley; **100**: National Anthropological Archives, Smithsonian Institution; **101**: Heartland Earthworks Conservancy image by Jarrod Burks; **104**: Cartography by Mike Boruta; **105**: After James Brown and Jarrod Burks; **106*l***: Adapted from Squier and Davis, *Ancient Monuments*; **106*r***: After James Brown; **108**: From Squier and Davis, *Ancient Monuments*; **109*b***: Courtesy of the author; **112**, **114**: Courtesy Ohio History Connection; **117*l***, **117*r***: Artworks by Talon Silverhorn; **120**: Cartography by Mike Boruta; **121*l***: Image by William Romain and Jarrod Burks; **121*r***: Ohio Valley Archaeology image by Jarrod Burks; **122*l***: Image after Hively and Horn; **122*r***: Courtesy of the author; **124**: From William Henry Holmes, 1892; **126**, **128**, **130**: Courtesy of the author; **133**: Cartography by Mike Boruta; **135**: National Park Service and *Deutsches Archäologisches Institut*; **136*t***: Courtesy of the author; **136*b***: From Warren King Moorehead, *Primitive Man in Ohio*. New York, NY: G. P. Putnam's Sons, 1892; 137: Courtesy of the author;**138*t***: National Park Service; **138*b***: National Park Service and *Deutsches Archäologisches Institut*; **141*t***: From Squier and Davis, *Ancient Monuments*; **141*b***: From Warren K. Moorehead, *Neg. No. 913 Hopewell Group, Mound 25*, 1891. https://hopewell.unl.edu/; **142**: National Anthropological Archives, Smithsonian Institution; **144**: From Squier and Davis, *Ancient Monuments*; **145**: Artwork by Talon Silverhorn; **148*t***: From Squier and Davis, *Ancient Monuments*; **148*b***: Courtesy of the author; **149**: Cartography by Mike Boruta; **150**: Image after N'omi Greber; **151**: Artwork by Talon Silverhorn; **153*l***: National Park Service and *Deutsches Archäologisches Institut*; **153*r***: Image after Hively and Horn; **154–55**: Courtesy Ohio History Connection; **156**: Image after N'omi Greber and Jarrod Burks; **157**: From Squier and Davis, *Ancient Monuments*; **158**: National Park Service and *Deutsches Archäologisches Institut*; **159*r***: Photo by Bret J. Ruby; **161**, **164*l***: Courtesy of the author; **164*r***: Image by Jarrod Burks, courtesy Ohio Valley Archaeology;**165**: Cartography by Mike Boruta; **170**: Photo by Matthew Traucht; **171*l***: Courtesy of the author; **171*r***: Photo by Robert V. Riordan; **173**: Courtesy Ohio History Connection; **177**: Digital rendering by Herb Roe; **178–79**: Photo by Steven W. Plattner; **180**: Courtesy Ohio History Connection; **183**: National Park Service photo by Tom Engberg; **185**, **187**: Courtesy Ohio History Connection; **188**, **191*t***, **192*t***, **192*b***, **193**: Artworks by Talon Silverhorn; **191*b***: Courtesy of the author; **194**: From Squier and Davis, *Ancient Monuments;* **196*t***: Cartography by Mike Boruta; **196*b***: Courtesy of the author; **197**, **198**: From Squier and Davis, *Ancient Monuments*; **200*l***: Image by Jarrod Burks; **200*r***: Heartland Earthworks Conservancy image by Jarrod Burks; **201**: Image by Herb Roe, courtesy the Scioto Historical Project; **202*l***: From Robert C. Mainfort Jr., "Pinson Mounds: A Middle Woodland Ceremonial Center," Tennessee Department of Environment and Conservation, Division of Archaeology, Research Series, No. 7, 1986; **204**: Painting by Martin Pate, courtesy of the artist; **206**: Painting by L. K. Townsend, courtesy Cahokia Mounds State Historic Site; **207*t***: Photo by Steven W. Plattner; **207*b***: National Park Service; **210*l***: Photo by Sanna Saunoloma, Wikimedia Commons; **210*r***: Photo by Teoman Cimit, Wikimedia Commons; **211*t***: Photo by Z Tanuki, Wikimedia Commons; **211*b***: Photo by Escuela de Nivin, Wikimedia Commons; **212**: Photo by Matthew Traucht.

QUOTE CREDITS

8: John N. Low, "Hopewell Ceremonial Earthworks" (UNESCO World Heritage Nomination 1689, 2023), 2, adapted from John N. Low, *Imprints: The Pokagon Band of Potawatomi & the City of Chicago* (East Lansing: Michigan State University Press, 2016), 2. **13**: Donald L. Fixico, "Hopewell Ceremonial Earthworks," 7. **25**: David McCullough, praise for Roger G. Kennedy, *Hidden Cities: The Discovery and Loss of Ancient North American Civilization* (New York, Free Press; Toronto: Maxwell Macmillan Canada, 1994), front cover. **28**: Joe Stahlman, email message to author, November 2024. **31**: America Meredith, "Hopewell Ceremonial Earthworks," 121. **40**: Marti Chaatsmith, discussion with the author, September 2024. **45**: H. B. Cushman, *History of the Choctaw, Chickasaw, and Natchez Indians* (Greenville, TX: Headlight Printing House, 1899), 312. **47**: Warren King Moorehead, *Fort Ancient: The Great Prehistoric Earthwork of Warren County, Ohio* (Andover, MA: Phillips Academy, 1908), 31. **59**: Chief Glenna J. Wallace, video interview by the author, October 2011. **63**: Brad Lepper, discussion with the author, September 2021. **73**: Ray Hively, video interview by the author, July 2000. **74*t***: Hìtakonanu'laxk, *The Grandfathers Speak: Native American Folk Tales of the Lenapé People* (New York: Interlink Books, 1994), 47. **74*m***: Jeff Gill, video interview by the author, February 2011. 74–75: Richard Shiels, video interview by the author, February 2011. **75*m***: Christine Ballengee-Morris, video interview by the author, February 2011. **75*b***: Linda S. Poolaw, video interview by the author, December 2000. **77**: Stacey Halfmoon, discussion with Marti Chaatsmith, September 2017. **87**: Brad Lepper, adapted from "You Don't Need to Be in the Air to Appreciate the Newark Earthworks," *Newark Advocate* (Newark, OH), September 4, 2022. **88**: Joe Stahlman, email message to author, November 2024. **91**: Benjamin Barnes, *Indigenous Wonders of our World—The Hopewell Ceremonial Earthworks* [exhibition], Ohio History Connection, Columbus, OH. **96*m***: Brad Lepper, discussion with the author, September 2024. **96*b***: John N. Low, email message to author, September 2024. **103**: Kimberly Blaeser, "Hopewell Ceremonial Earthworks," 257, adapted from Kimberly Blaeser, "Tribal Mound, Earth Sutra," in *Copper Yearning: Poems by Kimberly Blaeser* (Duluth, MN: Holy Cow! Press, 2020), n.p. **108**: Joe Stahlman, email message to author, November 2024. 116: Vine Deloria Jr. and Daniel R. Wildcat, *Power and Place: Indian Education in America* (Golden, CO: Fulcrum Publishing, 2001), 25–26. **117**: Marti Chaatsmith, "Hopewell Ceremonial Earthworks," 172. **119**: Glenna J. Wallace, video interview by the author, October 2011. **131**: Vine Deloria Jr., *God Is Red* (New York: Dell Publishing, 1973), 81. **139**: Bret J. Ruby, *Encountering Hopewell in the Twenty-First Century, Ohio and Beyond*, vol. 1, *Monuments and Ceremony*, ed. Brian G. Redmond and Jarrod Burks (Akron: University of Akron Press, 2019), n.p. **140**: Marti Chaatsmith, "Hopewell Ceremonial Earthworks," 96. **144**: Joe Stahlman, email message to author, November 2024. **147**: Margaret Wickens Pearce, "The Cartographic Legacy of the Newark Earthworks," in *The Newark Earthworks: Enduring Monuments, Contested Meanings*, ed. Lindsay Jones and Richard D. Shiels (Charlottesville: University of Virginia Press, 2016), n.p. **151**: Brad Lepper, adapted from "Teaming Up on the Mystery of the Hopewell Pebbles," *Columbus Dispatch* (Columbus, OH), April 22, 2018. **160**: William Romain, *Mysteries of the Hopewell: Astronomers, Geometers, and Magicians of the Eastern Woodlands* (Akron: University of Akron Press, 2000), 49. **163**: Barnett Newman, "Ohio, 1949," Barnett Newman and Mollie McNickle, *Barnett Newman: Selected Writings and Interviews*, ed. Philip O'Neill and Mollie McNickle (Berkeley: University of California Press, 1992), 174. **168**: Vine Deloria Jr., *God Is Red: A Native View of Religion*, 2nd ed., *The Classic Work Updated* (Golden, CO: Fulcrum Publishing, 1994), 66–67. **176**: Chadwick Allen, "Serpentine Figures, Sinuous Relations: Thematic Geometry in Allison Hedge Coke's *Blood Run*," *American Literature* 82, no. 4 (December 2010): 816. **177**: Benjamin Barnes, email message to Brad Lepper, May 2021. **181**: Monique Mojica, "In Plain Sight: Inscripted Earth and Invisible Realities," *New Canadian Realisms: New Essays on Canadian Theatre*, vol. 2, ed. Roberta Barker and Kim Solga (Toronto: Playwrights Canada Press, 2012), 218. **182*l***: Marti Chaatsmith, "Singing at a Center of the Indian World: The SAI and Ohio Earthworks," in "The Society of American Indians and Its Legacies: A Special Combined Issue of SAIL and AIQ (Summer 2013)," *American Indian Quarterly* 37, no. 3 and *Studies in American Indian Literatures* 25, no. 2 (Summer 2013): n.p. **182*r***: Bret Ruby, email message to author, September 2024. **184**: John N. Low, email message to author, September 2024. **185*t***: Marti Chaatsmith, "Singing at a Center of the Indian World," n.p. **185*m***: April Hester, discussion with Marti Chaatsmith, September 2019. 185*b*: Shelly Corbin/Takóni Kókipešni, discussion with Marti Chaatsmith, September 2019. **186**: Joe Stahlman, email message to author, November 2024. **190**: Bret Ruby, email message to author, December 2024. **191**: Logan York, email message to author, December 2024. **193**: Bret Ruby, email message to author, December 2024. **195**: Suzan Shown Harjo, "Sacred Places and Visitor Protocols," *American Indian Places: A Historical Guidebook*, ed. Frances H. Kennedy (Boston: Houghton Mifflin, 2008), 81.